# Racialised Barriers

*Racialised Barriers* is an explicit and systematic comparison of key distinct differences and striking similarities between the experience of Black people in the USA and England in the 1980s. It highlights the continuing significance of the racialised barriers, boundaries and identities in patterns of racialised inequality that prevail in each nation. Stephen Small argues that racialised hostility is woven into the social fabric of the US and England in ways that ensure its continuation well into the next century. However, he rejects the idea that the best way to combat hostility is for Black people as a whole to join in a class allegiance with white leaders, or to uncritically accept the agendas of so-called Black leaders. Instead he argues for an approach that builds on shared racialised identities, and Black organisations.

This book will be of immense interest to academic analysts of 'race' and 'racism' in industrialised societies, and in particular will be of interest to students of sociology, international relations and ethnicity studies.

**Stephen Small** lectures in Sociology at the University of Leicester.

# Critical Studies in Racism and Migration

## Edited by Robert Miles

*University of Glasgow*

# Racialised Barriers

## The Black Experience in the United States and England in the 1980s

Stephen Small

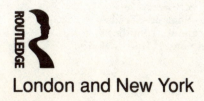

ROUTLEDGE

London and New York

First published 1994
by Routledge
11 New Fetter Lane, London EC4P 4EE

Simultaneously published in the USA and Canada
by Routledge
29 West 35th Street, New York, NY 10001

© 1994 Stephen Small

Typeset in Baskerville by
Ponting–Green Publishing Services, Chesham, Bucks
Printed and bound in Great Britain by
Mackays of Chatham PLC, Chatham, Kent

*British Library Cataloguing in Publication Data*
A catalogue record for this book is available from the
British Library.

ISBN 0–415–07725–7 (hbk)
ISBN 0–415–07726–5 (pbk)

*Library of Congress Cataloging in Publication Data.*
Small. Stephen
    Racialised barriers: the Black experience in the United
States and England in the 1980's / Stephen Small.
        p. cm. – (Critical studies in racism and migration)
    Includes bibliographical references and index.
    ISBN 0–415–07725–7: $50.00 – ISBN 0–415–07726–5
    (pbk.): $15.95
    1. United States–Race relations. 2. England–Race
relations.    3. Afro-Americans–Civil rights.
4. Blacks–Civil rights–England.    5. Afro-Americans–
Social conditions–1975–   6. Blacks–England–Social
conditions.    7. Afro-Americans–Economic conditions.
8. Blacks–England–Economic conditions. I. Title. II. Series.
E185.615.S574        1994
305.896'073–dc20                                        94–5584
                                                            CIP

# Contents

# Preface and acknowledgements

Over the last fifteen years I have studied, researched and lectured in various educational and research institutions across the United States and England. I have also been an active participant in a range of Black organisations, as well as organisations whose membership was open to non-Blacks. Initially I made occasional comparisons of the experiences of Black people in each country; as time passed the comparisons became much more explicit and systematic as I strove to unravel what appeared to be both distinct differences and striking similarities. This book is born of these experiences. In writing it I set myself a limited number of goals and I expect that some people will be disappointed; such is the nature of the written enterprise. Nevertheless, I hope that this contribution to the continuing analysis of racialised relations in the modern world will stimulate discussion and debate.

A primary goal of the book is to further the systematic comparison of the experiences of Black people in the United States and England. I have focused on several key aspects of this experience during the 1980s and hope that it will challenge some of the myths and superficial impressions that many people, Black and non-Black, policymaker and practitioner, academic and activist, hold about the other nation. A second goal is to highlight the continuing, if increasingly complex, significance of racialised barriers, boundaries and identities in the patterns of racialised inequality that prevail in each country. I have not tried to resolve the perennial (if sometimes futile) debate on the relative importance of 'race' and class, in the experiences of Black people, though I hope what I have written demonstrates that it would be foolish to attempt to do so without reference to the complex inter-relationships between the two. If I have spent more time focusing on racialised rather than class factors that is because I believe that such factors have become more and more marginalised as patterns of racialised hostility in the 1980s became more covert.

As with all projects, this book has benefited from the support of colleagues and friends. Thanks to the members of the Institute for the Study of Social Change (ISSC) at the University of California, Berkeley: particularly Troy Duster, David Minkus, and graduate students associated with ISSC. They listened to versions of chapters from the book and offered insightful comments and supportive criticisms. I also benefited from comments made by participants during a presentation of an early draft of Chapter 3 in 1991 at the Birkbeck College Seminar on Public Policy (University of London) jointly organised by Clive Harris, John Solomos and Michael Keith; and from comments made on an early draft of Chapter 4 at the Conference on 'Afro-Caribbeans in Britain' in 1992, organised by Abebe Zegeye of the Centre for Modern African Studies, University of Warwick.

Thanks to Kamaldeep Deol who worked for one year as my research assistant and particularly contributed to Chapters 2, 3 and 4; to Maud Blair of the Open University whose detailed comments on an early draft of Chapter 4 led to significant improvements; to Julia O'Connell-Davidson of the University of Leicester, who provided detailed written comments on the entire manuscript; and to David Wellman, at ISSC, who provided me with helpful written comments on Chapter 3. Special thanks to the series editor, Robert Miles, who has offered strong support and encouragement at all times. His suggestions made the book a better project. Thanks also to the anonymous reviewers of both the original draft proposal for the book, and the final draft of the manuscript. If I could identify them I would thank them personally.

# Chapter 1

# Introduction

**SETTING THE SCENE**

When most Americans think of England numerous clear, if divergent, images often come to mind. Some think of a society steeped in centuries of tradition, with castles and cathedrals, architecture and other artefacts of so-called high culture. Some think of democracy and the Houses of Parliament, the grace and splendour of the Royal Family, or the archaic and bizarre rituals of the aristocracy. For others a different set of images comes to mind – the rock music of Pink Floyd, the inane humour of Benny Hill, or the profound and irreverent comedy of Monty Python and Black Adder. But Americans in general know a lot less about the Black experience and they have few images of Black people. Like Ralph Ellison's *Invisible Man*, Blacks in England seldom catch attention, except in the most obvious and stereotypical scenes. In sport they may know of multiple world-title-holder decathlete Daley Thompson, of the world-title-holder for the 100 metres sprint, Linford Christie, or the British heavyweight boxer, Frank Bruno; in music, the soul and funk of Imagination, the soft sounds of sultry Sade, the mid-tempo beat of Loose Ends, and the unsurpassed jazz of Courtney Pine; in reggae, the phenomenal success of Steel Pulse, of Aswad and of UB40. Americans are used to thinking of the United States as a society plagued by racialised antagonism as African-Americans and others live a precarious existence in their quest for the American Dream. They have seldom had reason to visualise England in that way, except for a short time during 1981, and again in 1985, when widespread rioting (so-called 'race riots') rocked these popular perceptions. But this soon passed. The image of England still prevails in the minds of many Americans as one of civil calm.

If people in England asked residents of the United States about 'racialised relations' in England they would be surprised to learn that England is often seen as a nation of racialised calm.[1] This impression is usually held whether you ask the general public, policymakers or academics (Glazer and Young, 1983). Americans maintain that, unlike the United States, England has never had plantation slavery or Jim Crow segregation, or the three-fifths clause of the Constitution declaring Africans three-fifths human, has less racialised antagonism and few 'race riots', no Ku Klux Klan, or ghettos, and no 'Black on Black' crime or drug involvement (Pitts, 1989). They are more likely to talk about the widespread evidence of racialised integration throughout England: on the television, in the streets and houses, in the schools and in many other areas of social life including sport, music and discothèques (Voice, 1990).[2] This, they say, has no parallel in the United States and many have concluded that England is ahead of the United States and that the best way forward in the United States is to follow the examples set there.

In addition, the goals of many institutions in combating racialised conflict in the United States are shaped by impressions of racialised harmony in England, or by goals which England is believed to have achieved some time ago.[3] For example, much of the racialised conflict which exists in the United States has been attributed to the physical and social segregation of Blacks and whites, and policies promoting integration are seen as a way to alleviate such tensions (Farley and Allen, 1989: 157). Many American universities see the increasing numbers of minority students as a means to achieve racialised integration not only on the campus but in the broader economic, social and political spheres (Farrell and Jones, 1988; ISSC, 1991). The same is true for the growth of a multi-racialised workforce. Historically, Blacks and whites went to England to learn lessons and gain experience about 'racialised relations'. There were struggles in the United States which were shaped by impressions of England, for example, abolitionists and the anti-lynching campaigns, when a solidarity movement developed (Davis, 1984: 192). We know that some Black people fled to England when they escaped slavery, and others like Frederick Douglass, Phyllis Wheatley and Booker T. Washington visited England, attracted by its appearance of racialised harmony (Blackett, 1983).

The same Americans might well be surprised to learn that many people in England, especially Black people, believe that Black people in the United States live a better life. Again, this is usually true whether you ask the general public, policymakers involved in efforts to promote racialised equality, or academics.[4] There are several reasons for this. First, policies introduced by national and local government to achieve racialised equality have drawn extensively upon the United States. Substantial parts of the legislative and institutional framework of 'race relations' in England have been begged, borrowed or stolen from the United States, and England has not hesitated to send cohorts of theoreticians and policymakers across, or to invite their counterparts to England, to achieve their goals (Bindman, 1980; Glazer and Young, 1983; Banton, 1984). In the 1990s we are seeing increasing efforts to learn from the American experience of a multi-cultural workforce. All of this is because many in England – Black and white, policymaker and public – see the policies and practices of the United States as the way forward for achieving 'good race relations'.[5] Of course, the idea of 'good race relations' resonates in different ways with different audiences; while local authorities such as the Greater London Council (in the early 1980s), as well as many Black groups, look for racialised equality, much of this borrowing has been for purposes of containment and control – whether lessons from police chiefs on how to get more Blacks into forces, or for purposes of immigration legislation.

Second, Black people in England have looked to the United States for ideas and inspiration in their struggles against racialised hostility.[6] They have drawn upon black politics, institutions and culture in the literature, philosophies and music from African-Americans. From the philosophies of Marcus Garvey and W.E.B. Dubois, Angela Davis and Kwame Ture (formerly Stokely Carmichael), to the strategies of Malcolm X, Martin Luther King and the Black Panthers; and from the tactics employed at the Mexico Olympics, to the music of James Brown, Aretha Franklin, and rap, American Black culture pervades Black Britain. African-American culture reiterates itself, and is transformed, in the lifestyles of Blacks in England. Black people in England want Black institutions (universities, businesses, churches) and a Black 'middle class'. The establishment of Black mentor schemes, the pursuit of Black universities and businesses and the development of 'Britain's biggest black networking organisation', Rapport, all testify to the continued impact (*Voice*, 22 January, 1991: 23).

In addition, Blacks in England have used their perceptions of

Black success in the United States as a yardstick, implicit or explicit, against which to evaluate their own progress. This has both positive and negative effects; the former because it has provided insights, ideas, strategies and encouragement; the latter because Black success in the United States is used to beat Black people in England about the head, and Black accomplishments in England always end up looking pathetic compared to those of their brothers and sisters in the USA. Whether in business and the professions, in politics, music, or sport, Blacks in England look worse off. For example, in an otherwise positive report about a conference on Blacks in Education to celebrate Black History Month the Viewpoint section of the *Voice* related:

> We should learn from the example of the Americans who are far in advance of the Black community in Britain when it comes to making sure that our perspective is a part of what is taught in school.
>
> (*Voice*, 26 November, 1991: 6)

This puts particular pressures on Black leaders in Britain who are asked 'Why have we got no Angela Davis, Malcolm X or Louis Farrakhan?'; or 'Why has there been no Civil Rights Movement here?' It is one thing to inspire and motivate, another to insult and molest.

In support of their arguments that Blacks in England should emulate African-Americans such groups have pointed to the proliferation of Black businesses and Black universities; to Black representation in many other walks of life including politics (L. Douglas Wilder, Sharon Pratt Kelly, David Dinkins), the business world, the military (Colin Powell), the legal profession, academia and medicine, as well as in sport, entertainment and music (*Voice*, 22 January, 1991: 5; *Voice*, 26 March, 1991: 11; *Voice*, 11 June, 1991: 15). It has been argued that the presence of Black people in top positions such as these is unparalleled in England, and provides the necessary role models and mentors to stimulate further the success of Black young people. Much of this, they add, has resulted from the strenuous initiatives taken to curtail racialised discrimination and promote equal opportunity, in particular affirmative action, as well as from the sustained activities of Black people in the Civil Rights Movement and Black Nationalism (Bindman, 1980). Like their counterpart commentators in the USA they too suggest that the United States is 'miles ahead' of their country and the way to promote better 'race relations' in England is to follow their example.[7]

Scholarship, study and research about 'racialised relations' in the United States has impacted on study of such problems in England. In the academic study of 'racialised relations' many of the paradigms, theories, concepts and methods developed and employed in the United States have become entrenched in the approaches of scholars in England. For example, the early empirical studies of Black people in England drew extensively on the works of Americans (Little, 1948; Richmond, 1954; Banton, 1955). As others have pointed out, British writers continue to borrow uncritically from across the Atlantic (Rex, 1970; Banton, 1983; Miles, 1989b). There is a voluminous literature on 'race relations' within the context of national boundaries for both nations, but little attempt at systematic international comparison. In addition, references are made in the popular literature and media. In fact it is almost impossible to pick up a book on 'race relations' in England without seeing frequent references to the United States (Hall *et al.*, 1978; Banton, 1983; Jacobs, 1986). There are comparatively fewer references to England in American books, with some exceptions (Schaefer, 1990). Information about the Black experience in each country abounds in the literature and popular media. When we examine this, though the comparisons are not as vividly portrayed or starkly contrasted, there remain many errors and misinterpretations, superficial comparisons, distortions and over-simplifications (Rose, *et al.*, 1969; Jacobs, 1986; Shaw *et al.*, 1987; Killian, 1987b; Kilson, 1987). Many comparisons suffer from limitations of scope and depth, as well as conceptual and theoretical inadequacies. They add few theoretical advances, little to our political education or to the exchange of ideas in ways that can contribute towards combating racialised hostility. In any case, the vast majority of people, particularly non-specialists, continue to read the single-nation literature which is plagued by problems (Jacobs, 1986).

There also remain significant gaps in the literature about these issues. An extensive literature on class, social mobility, industrial relations, politics and education fails to address matters of racialised hostility (Edwards, 1983; Kerckhoff, *et al.*, 1985; Trow, 1988).[8] Work on immigration is increasing (Institute for Research in History, 1983; Brubaker, 1989). Where comparisons consider 'racialised relations' they are often problematic because they distort the contexts of the Black experience, or use inappropriate or misleading concepts (Jacobs, 1986). This has to be rectified. Perceptions such as those just described are all the more surprising when we recognise in both countries that there is considerable information contradicting these perspectives. For example, many pieces appear which, while highlighting certain positive aspects of the Black experience in the United States, also highlight the continuing segregation and conflict (*Voice*, 22 January, 1991: 16). Apparently the significance of such information is passed over or minimised, with few exceptions.[9]

## UNRAVELLING THE THREADS

These kinds of comparisons remain true at a time when most eyes in England are turning towards the ethnic relations and conflict in Europe for insights and alliances. Conferences on community politics and policies and on academic matters have been convened, organisations established, and networks set up as people respond to the new reality of 'Fortress Europe'.[10] One reason for this has to be that Europe promises access to resources via the European Social Fund. While there are many benefits to be had from that quarter we have yet to assess fully the impact and limitations of the USA on study, policy and political action in England. While attention must be paid to Europe and to the impact which its structures will have on Blacks in England, we cannot afford summarily to dismiss the influence of the United States. There is much that needs to be addressed, and no nation in Europe can offer such benefits (Small, 1993). How are we to account for these misconceptions? Comparisons like the ones above are selective, partial and limited. They often contain many accurate elements but do not tell the full story, or unravel the complexities. Because most observers are not in a position to obtain detailed information, or to construct a better context of comparison, misconceptions persist. In addition, various groups focus selectively on certain aspects because they seek direction, guidelines, models to emulate, or motivation and reassurance that their struggles are not in vain. These include national and local governments, Black groups, policymakers. Consequently, the impression continues to remain for many people of each nation that the grass is greener on the other side.

The overall picture is complex. The structural and institutional frameworks, and the cultural and ideological contexts of the Black experience in each country, reveal undeniable differences: for example, in the size, pattern of settlement, extent of social integration and length of residence of the Black population, and in its representation in the political realm. But there are also a number of striking similarities (including multiple 'racisms', systematic exclusionary practices, the continued impact of racialised discrimination and the relative disadvantage experienced by Blacks *vis-à-vis* non-Blacks in all economic and social realms).[11] Though their manifestations and expressions have changed over the centuries, and economic obstacles have always been present, there is clear evidence of the continued persistence of racialised barriers, boundaries and identities of both an individual and institutional nature.

Trying to unravel the intricacies of these patterns and to decipher the apparent paradoxes and contradictions that they disclose reveals two key problems. First, there is a failure to establish an appropriate context of comparison which specifies the variables to be compared and the criteria by which they must be assessed and evaluated.[12] Second, there is the problem of the continued misconception of 'race relations', based on spurious assumptions, misleading implications and ramifications and the specification of contradictory and conflicting goals.[13]

While the images held of one another are real, they are too narrow a portrayal of the variety and vitality of Black life, or the range and diversity of our contribution to society and the human experience. Such images do not fully convey the struggles and strivings which have so long been a part of our endeavour to survive and succeed. Nor do they relate the dramas and disasters which have befallen Black people, the activities and sufferings of the thousands upon thousands that were the foundation for the successes of the few, or our tenacious refusal to give in as a people before all the obstacles levelled against us (Akbar, 1984; Christian, 1988; Sivanandan, 1990).

## HISTORICAL DIVERGENCE AND CONVERGENCE

A more informed comparison of the two nations presents a strikingly different portrayal – pictures somewhat at variance with these perceptions. Groups in each nation may think that Black people are better off in the other nation, but many of the assumptions of such evaluations are spurious. Slavery did take root on the shores of England, but conditions were inimical to its development, and while there was no constitutional endorsement of slavery it was condoned by England's most senior judicial authorities (Lester and Bindman, 1972; Shyllon, 1977). There are several instances of institutional discrimination being sanctioned in law, particularly regarding sailors and the military (Harris, 1991; Rich, 1986). There has always been de facto segregation in occupations and education as well as clear evidence of ghettos and housing inequality (Rex, 1988, Smith, 1989); Anti-Black riots are evidenced in England, as is white supremacist persecution and violence against Black people (Walker 1977). Black on Black crime is increasing, as is hard drug involvement. Though the relative proportions of all these activities seem small compared with the USA this is of little consolation to Black people there, and the impact is none the less pernicious.

In the United States, the economic and educational achievements of Black businesses and universities, and their numbers and strengths, are less impressive when compared with the size and length of residence of the Black population, though many have striven steadfastly against a tide of opposition and inadequate funding. Though some prominent Black politicians make the headlines, this does not convey the continued dramatic under-representation of Blacks in office and voting nor the very different political colours of Black people. Prominent Blacks might be seen as role models by some – but role models on their own cannot change structures of inequality. Many see top Blacks not as mentors to be emulated but as sell-outs to be avoided. Professor William King writes of Colin Powell:

> Whites and middle-class blacks are proud of him. But it is very difficult for the young brother on the corner to see Powell as a hero. To them Powell is a 'light-skinned bro' done good . . . for himself.
>
> (*Voice*, 26 March, 1991: 11)

The Black population was sorely divided over the appointment of Clarence Thomas to the Supreme Court, with evidence of strong disagreement between Black men and women (*Black Scholar*, 1992). The achievements of affirmative action have been limited (Small, 1991a). A striking positive aspect remains that of the spirit of striving which characterised the Civil Rights Movement and Black Power, not only among the leaders but among the thousands of unknown foot soldiers. In fact we can observe both major differences and major similarities in the history and present circumstances of Black people in each nation. We have to confront the complexities of both if we are to achieve a better comparison.

The United States is a former colonial plantation society welded into a nation state, characterised by several hundred years of immigration, both forced and voluntary. The American obsession with the melting pot has its origins in conquest, slavery and the exploitation of foreign labour: from the Indians uprooted and banished to reservations; the Mexicans conquered and subjugated by expansionism; the Africans abducted and forced into perpetual servitude; and the Asians coaxed and cajoled into exploitative indentureships (Blauner, 1972; Takaki, 1982; Omi and Winant, 1986). The political parties in the United States have emerged out of the ethnic organisations through which European immigrants protected their interests, but in the context of the forced exclusion of African-Americans from this process (Lieberson, 1980; Steinberg, 1981). Jim Crow segregation, legal and extra-legal, was pervasive and profound in its effects until the 1960s. Recent decades have seen remarkable legislative change in promoting equal opportunity, much of it occurring only after sustained opposition to inequality mounted by African-Americans and other minority groups (Glazer, 1975; Morris, 1984; Bloom, 1987). The American concern with minorities is on a much greater scale and they have had much longer to deal with how they may be successfully allowed to participate fully in society.

The size, pattern of settlement and length of residence of the Black population in the United States compares starkly with England. Blacks add up to 11 per cent of the population (people of colour to around 20 per cent), are overwhelmingly urban, with many cities possessing majority Black residents, and have been in the USA for centuries (Blackwell, 1985; Farley and Allen, 1987; Lieberson and Waters, 1988). The majority of Blacks in the United States are indigenous – over 97 per cent of them (Farley and Allen, 1989: 370). There is much greater socio-economic stratification within the Black population, a significant 'middle-class' and considerable political representation, especially at local level (Wilson, 1987; Landry, 1987; Smith *et al.*, 1987; Pohlmann 1990). In that country, repatriation is not discussed as a viable option for solving 'race relations' problems. Americans are characterised as manifesting marked explicitness on issues of 'race', but decided implicitness on issues of class (Vanneman, 1980; Glazer and Young, 1983). Needless to say, the economic and political fortunes of the two countries have varied almost diametrically, the British Empire giving way to the United States Empire (Marwick, 1980; Krieger, 1986).

Despite being a country of net immigration for a long time, England's dealing with minorities at home, especially Black people, has been limited. Through its economic and political expansion and exploitation of numerous foreign lands, England established relationships with many diverse cultural minorities (Williams, 1944; Walvin, 1971; Rich, 1986). But it remained essentially a homogeneous country forcing its immigrant settlers to accept and adopt its own cultural values (Walvin, 1973; Shyllon, 1977). Britain's political system is based upon class bargaining and the emergence of a welfare state, in the absence of minorities (Glazer and Young, 1983). It is only in recent decades that Britain has had to come to terms with the settlement of large numbers of Black people. Initially English policy was to turn all minorities into English men and English women, believing in the superiority of English values, ideals and institutions (Rose *et al.*, 1969). But this policy was short-lived, for it was challenged vigorously and forcefully (Moore, 1975; Sivanandan, 1982). The settlement of Black people has been received with much hostility and resentment, especially as England's economic fortunes have declined, and its people have had to suffer a challenge to their established standards of living. The climate of racialised and ethnic relations in the 1980s was marked by a concern with how to contain the fury and rebelliousness of the indigenous young Black population, and how to lift them from the bottom rungs of the socio-economic order (Scarman, 1981; Cashmore and Troyna, 1982; Small, 1983a; Benyon and Solomos, 1987).

In England in the 1980s almost the majority of Blacks were immigrants, and the overwhelming majority of the indigenous Black population was young (Brown, 1983; Brown, 1984; Bhat *et al.*, 1988; Smith, 1989). England also lacked significant socio-economic stratification within the Black population, though there was evidence of a middle class emerging, with limited political power (Brown, 1984; Jones, 1993). Because of the relatively recent arrival of the Black population and because much of the hostility towards them was articulated through the terminology of 'immigrants', the notion that a viable solution to the 'race relations' problems in the country could be achieved through repatriation holds popular appeal, and is advocated by a number of politicians (Miles and Phizacklea, 1984; Layton-Henry and Rich, 1986).

In the light of such differences a number of people have argued, and others might conclude, that comparisons make little sense.[14] But this approach overlooks the remarkable resemblances in the experience of racialised barriers, boundaries and identities, of people of African descent in each country. Despite the fact that the United States has practised segregation at home, and England abroad, there are several important reasons for thinking that they manifest essential similarities. A focus on this set of issues reveals some perplexing parallels and suggests another set of concerns. Three sets of issues in particular serve as the point of departure for this comparison – the process of 'racialisation', the continuing impact of multiple 'racisms', and the sustained resistance and resilience demonstrated by Black people. The role of the state must also be considered if we are to understand the way in which these trends have unfolded.

The process of 'racialisation' is embedded and endures in each nation, and is central to contemporary political realities. In the economic and political expansion of each nation the use of con-quest, slavery and the exploitation of the labour power of people of colour has played a preeminent role (Williams, 1944). Despite the perception of the United States (and of many in Great Britain until recently) England did experience slavery (Walvin, 1973; Shyllon, 1977; Fryer, 1984).[15] The United States and England were leading players in the 'racialisation' of Africans and their descendants during slavery, and more recently, at home and abroad (Jordan, 1968; Shyllon, 1977; Miles, 1989). This process was extended during colonial expansion and exploitation, and con-tinued to be manipulated in the 1980s for political advantage at national/federal level and local/state level regarding immigration, elected office and the distribution of resources. A wide array of racialised images and divisions have been generated and dissemin-ated by a range of institutions, including the media.

Both countries have struggled with the ideals that they espouse and their failure to extend these ideals to Black people. White exclusionary practices have operated, and systematic racialised discrimination has forced the concentration of Blacks in the most disadvantaged sections of society (Myrdal, 1944; Daniel, 1968; Smith, 1977; Lieberson, 1980; Steinberg, 1981; Brown and Gay, 1985). Both countries have many people who hold ethnocentric views as to who should qualify as full members of the country and community, socially and politically. These views have often become enshrined in institutional form, particularly in immigration legislation (Foot, 1965; Moore and Wallace, 1975; Bean *et al.*, 1989). Access to each country has consistently been predicated on the notion that each is a 'white man's country' (Berlin, 1974; Miles and Phizacklea, 1984).[16] That is, ethnocentrism, 'racism', notions of insiders/outsiders and of 'the other', have all served to indicate who is to be included in and excluded from full rights to citizenship. So despite lofty ideals of freedom, equality, democracy and fairness, both countries have systematically excluded a significant proportion of their population from the benefits of such ideals and there has been a consistent gap between law and practice. Thus one might also conclude that the American dilemma is, and has for a long time been, the British dilemma (Myrdal, 1944).

Multiple 'racisms' – and multiple rationalisations for inexorable racialised hostility – have been articulated and rearticulated, embraced and employed, not only by various parts of the state, but also by other actors such as the working class and intellectuals. Many argue that the old crude 'racism' has been replaced by a new subtle 'racism', as the means used to express racialised hostility has changed from the overt to the covert, and 'racism' has become, in the words of Sivanandan, 'less visible but no less virulent' (Hall, 1978; Barker, 1981; Centre for Contempory Cultural Studies, 1982; Reeves, 1983; Omi and Winant, 1986; Sivanandan, 1988: 8). More invidious types of racialised hostility are pervasive and efficacious (Brown and Gay, 1985; Commission for Racial Equality, 1989; Gifford, 1989). Some forms of racialised hostility reveal a will-o'-the-wisp character utilising codewords, *double entendres* and shared images. Others are palpable and painful – they penetrate with force and brutality into the lives of their victims (Miles and Phizacklea, 1984; Omi and Winant, 1986; Walker, 1977). Despite a preoccupation with 'new racisms' there is certainly evidence that the harsh and simplistic racialised theories of the past retain a strong hold on the minds and imaginations of many in the majority population. The evidence reveals that despite legislation, direct racialised discrimination continues unabated. Ideologies which are predicated on the concept of distinctive racialised groups possessing mental and physical abilities, are still embraced by many, as will be demonstrated in Chapter 3.

Identifying and combating racialised hostility was made more difficult in the 1980s due to the fact that each country shared a focus on the use of anti-discrimination laws in the field of policy as the mechanism for defusing social conflict and breaking down patterns of disadvantage and discrimination (Lustgarten, 1980; Glazer and Young, 1983; Wilson, 1987; Jenkins and Solomos, 1987). The principal political parties and most leading political actors formally disavowed any affiliation with racialised ideologies while embracing policies that maintained racialised inequality and were predicated on notions that few would deny were 'racist' (Miles, 1989: 66). In the United States this included Reagan's dismissal of 'welfare queens' and his encouragement of whites to sue against affirmative action, and Bush's manipulation of Willie Horton (White, 1988). In England, it is reflected in immigration legislation and the manipulation of refugees (Wrench and Solomos, 1993). They smile in your face and stab you in the back.

An undeniable aspect of the Black experience in each country has been the remarkable resistance to racialised exploitation and oppression – physical, ideological, cultural – and the incredible resilience demonstrated by Black people. They have undoubtedly been victims, but they have refused to adopt a victim mentality. Black people have always and in all places refused to submit to the imposition of racialised barriers and have utilised diverse tactics for asserting their humanity and affirming their dignity (Moore, 1975; Walvin, 1973; Fryer, 1984; Bloom, 1987; Bonnett and Watson, 1990). Black people have reached deep into their culture, religion, heritage and personal experiences to employ various tactics and strategies – individual and collective, ideological, cultural and physical – to resist the imposition of inequality, and to carve out space to create their own lives and priorities (Mama, 1989; Marable, 1984; Marable, 1992). Their opposition has led to the development of separate – and often separatist – institutions, many Black people in each country believing this the best way to defend, strengthen and expand a viable way of living (Blauner, 1972; Shyllon, 1977; Law and Henfrey, 1981; Morris, 1984). These institutions, and the ideologies underlying them, have a much longer history and are more widespread in the United States than in England, though they have always had a presence in the latter nation and seemed to enjoy a resurgence in the 1980s (Ramdin, 1987; Sivanandan, 1982).

A predominant aspect of African-American resistance has been the tendency to look abroad for inspiration and insights, fortification and fulfilment, for perspectives and frameworks, to offer support elsewhere and to give meaning to their lives. During these times key advances were made: in the Back-to-Africa movements of Paul Cuffee, Martin R. Delany and Bishop McNeal Turner (Redkey,

1969); the trips to Europe of Alexander Crummell, Frederick Douglass or Sarah Parker Remond (Blackett, 1983); the early involvement with the Pan-African Movement by W.E.B. Dubois in England (Fryer, 1984); the Universal Negro Improvement Association of Marcus Garvey; and the trips by Malcolm X, Martin Luther King and Jesse Jackson (Ramdin, 1987). In 1989, Jesse Jackson visited five African nations seeking greater contact, communication and cooperation among Africans in the diaspora. As the pillar of the British Empire, England has always been a port of call. Angela Davis, June Jordan, and Maya Angelou visit England frequently. Even Minister Louis Farrakhan tried to spread the message there but was denied entry. A notable fact about the Black experience in England is that Black people there have always looked beyond their shores for insight and inspiration, for comfort, support and ideas. The United States has consistently figured in that vision – from Olaudah Equiano and Ignatius Sancho, to C.L.R. James, George Padmore and Claudia Jones (Ramdin, 1987). This influence endured in the 1980s through the travels of Bernie Grant, Paul Boateng and Diane Abbott.

The state has been central to these processes, giving rise to 'racialisation' and multiple 'racisms', and containing and constraining resistance. It played a role in rearticulating racialised ideology and in managing racialised and economic crises, often engaging in conflicting and contradictory methods (Sivanandan, 1976; Miles and Phizacklea, 1984; Omi and Winant, 1986). No president was elected to office in the 1960s without playing the 'race card'; during the same period no government was elected to office in England without taking 'a strong stand on immigration', that is on 'keeping the Blacks out' (Miles and Phizacklea, 1984). During the 1980s the 11 per cent of the population of the USA which was African-American, and the less than 2 per cent of the population of the UK which was African-Caribbean, continued to be manipulated for purposes of election to office, and for economic reasons (Ball and Solomos, 1990; Edsall and Edsall, 1991a).

To summarise, each country has been influenced by the other in ways which are not always readily apparent to analysts and policy practitioners; if scholars and specialists get it wrong, it is not surprising that the non-specialists make mistakes. When inspected closely and systematically, each country offers the other an opportunity to examine the efforts and obstacles to overcoming racialised hostility and achieving racialised parity. Alongside the gains and progress remain a multitude of challenges – Black people have made many strides towards racialised parity, but still have a long way to go. The impact which each nation has had on the other must be thoroughly examined and critically evaluated and the assumptions upon which such comparisons exist must be assessed and contested.

## RACIALISED BARRIERS, BOUNDARIES AND IDENTITIES

This wide array of forces and activities is reflected in the establishment, growth and transformation of racialised barriers, boundaries and identities. Racialised barriers and boundaries were erected to secure political and economic goals; the former blocked Black access to resources and power, while facilitating non-Black access; the latter demarcated the acceptable terrain (political, economic, social) which could be traversed by Black people, while keeping all terrains open to non-Blacks. And racialised identities were the ideological terrain that shaped the changing interpretations of these activities. In creating racialised identities for themselves Anglo-Europeans have also given rise to a racialised identity for people of African origin, though for the latter it is one which has for the most part grown in opposition to injustice, exploitation and oppression. It is, however, an identity which is not without its problems.

Whether the emphasis is on the continuities or discontinuities is all a matter of perspective. My goal is to outline the benefits that derive from a comparative analysis and my point of departure is captured in the metaphor of the 'Colour Line'. This concept was introduced by Dubois at the start of the twentieth century to characterise racialised inequality and injustice between Europeans and people of colour across the world:

> The problem of the twentieth century is the problem of the color line, – the relation of the darker to the lighter races of men in Asia and Africa, in America and the islands of the sea.
>
> (Dubois, 1961: 23)

In this book the 'Colour Line' refers to the disadvantaged position occupied by minorities of African descent, *vis-à-vis* the non-Black majority, on the basis of just about every essential economic, political and social indicator.[17] Black people in both countries are under-represented among the ranks of the wealthy and affluent, in the upper levels of the business world and the professions, and in the key political parties and elected office. They are over-represented in the ranks of the unemployed and the poor, those without higher educational qualifications, those who do not vote, those suffering ill-health and the incarcerated (Brown, 1984; Farley and Allen, 1989; Bhat *et al.*, 1988; O'Hare *et al.*, 1991).

This 'Colour Line' has both material dimensions – as reflected in the distribution of property, power and privilege – and mental dimensions – as reflected in attitudes and ideologies which account for racialised inequality, and in states of psychological well-being. Racialised inequality at all levels is pervasive and profound. Blacks and non-Blacks offer very divergent views of why inequality exists and subscribe to divergent ideologies of racialised abilities. The overarching collective response has always been resistance and resilience, and the overarching priority has always been to end the 'Colour Line' and attain racialised parity.[18]

## THE BENEFITS OF COMPARISON

When regarded closely, the circumstances confronting Black people in each country are complex. Clearly, we remain at a disadvantage if we do not undertake comparisons, yet several problems emerge if the comparisons are not carried out with care. The overall goal of any comparative analysis of 'racialised relations' must be to develop conceptually clear, empirically grounded and theoretically driven studies that illustrate and analyse continuities and discontinuities across historical and cultural contexts. A 'contextualised' comparison highlights the need to step back and contemplate our research and political strategies. In particular, comparison compels us to consider issues we otherwise take for granted in our work and thus requires us to reflect upon the framework, focus and facts which we deem appropriate.[19]

A comparison of the United States and England enables us to consider theories, policies and political activities in contexts of racialised interaction and conflict. Each country displays a long history of studying racialised and ethnic relations, a huge literature exists and many scholars are working in this area; this is the foundation upon which comparisons can be based. Comparative analysis is of benefit to scholars engaged in studies of single nations as well as those interested in comparisons for their own sake. First, comparison makes it indispensable for us to consider the paradigms, models, theories and concepts we utilise when we explore patterns of racialised and ethnic group relations. As noted earlier, for those carrying out analysis in England, the body of knowledge about these issues has been greatly influenced by the work of social scientists from the United States (see note 14); while scholars in the United States frequently fail to inform their own analyses with considerations from abroad. The effects of such borrowing need to be evaluated. Comparative analysis dictates that we consider whether or not to move in the direction of general models or theories of 'racialised relations'. This reflects the perennial debate among social scientists on the usefulness of universal versus medium-range theories. Should the goal of analysis be the generation of culture-free or culture-specific theories and concepts?

Some argue that a primary task of racialised and ethnic analysis should be to internationalise the concepts in an attempt to identify what are the culture-specific assumptions and to make theoretical structures more nearly culture-free (Banton, 1983). But others have argued that the proper goal is not culture-free but culture-specific concepts (Hall, 1978; Gilroy, 1987a). These theorists emphasise the socio-historical nature of 'race' and ethnicity, the multiplicity of economic and cultural factors involved in its construction and recommend that our goal should be to undertake concrete studies of different contexts and cultures to refine our analysis. Consideration of these issues will enable us to compare the usefulness of our theories and paradigms, as applied to particular contexts, and how far they can be utilised in other situations. This will lead us beyond simple affirmation, to the exploration and explanation of the relative impact of economic and cultural factors, including the role of economic crises and class factors, of demographic variables, of the state, of consciousness and action within minority groups, and relations between minority groups in a range of historical and contemporary settings.

Second, comparison dictates that we examine the process of racialised group formation, transformation and disintegration, and of racialised barriers, boundaries and identities. In comparisons we see most lucidly the social construction of 'race', and thus 'race' (and class) cease to be objective realities innocently reflecting natural divisions of humankind. Rather, they become social inventions, constructions amenable to our critical activity, and subject to modification, manipulation and negotiation (Lieberson and Waters, 1986; Rex and Mason, 1986; Miles, 1989a; Waters, 1990). 'Race' is 'pre-eminently a socio-historical concept' and consideration of how it is mediated through economic, political and social institutions in two advanced industrial societies will facilitate an analysis of the relative impact of structural and cultural/ideological factors in the context of asymmetrical power relationships (Omi and Winant, 1986: 60). We have no choice but to define the specifics of the concepts being used, and to take into account the variations. Such an enterprise inevitably (often immediately) leads to a consideration of ethnic differences within the Black population – for example, between African-Caribbeans and African-Americans in the United States, and between African-Caribbeans and others called 'Black' in England, as well as the group traditionally called 'mixed-race' (Farley and Allen, 1989; Wilson, A., 1987; Waters, 1990).

Third, comparison facilitates an analysis of the intricate interplay of racialised discrimination and class (or socio-economic) disadvantages. This is one of the major areas of scholarly inquiry in contemporary analysis of racialised and ethnic relations in both countries (Rex and Tomlinson, 1979; Steinberg, 1981; Wilson, W., 1987; Boston, 1988). The common underlying theme here has to do with the relative importance of variables that are explicitly racialised (ideologies, laws, structures, organisations, prejudices) and those that seem free from racialised significance (economic needs, employment, class relations, the state) in accounting for the experiences of minorities (see Chapter 3). That racialised hostility and discrimination played a central role in the 1980s and continues to do so in the 1990s is beyond dispute. This is evidenced clearly in the works of several authors (Miles and Phizacklea, 1984; Omi and Winant, 1986). They show how in both countries the state has played a key role in rearticulating racialised ideology so that racialised hostility can still be manifested without any mention of 'race'. There is also clear evidence of the continued impact of direct and indirect racialised discrimination (Brown and Gay, 1985; Gifford *et al.*, 1989; Hacker, 1992; Bell, 1992). As I have argued elsewhere, it would be foolish to assess the full impact of such hostility without considering economic and class factors (Small, 1991b).

I believe that analysis of the process of 'racialisation' offers the best way forward here, especially given the incessantly changing nature of racialised hostility and the multiple manifestations of 'racisms'. This concept has been defined, elaborated and applied empirically in a number of contexts, and it remains a potent tool for analysis (Banton, 1977; Miles, 1982; Omi and Winant, 1986; Satzewich, 1988; Satzewich, 1989; Miles, 1989a). It can be considered as part of a broader process of differentiation or 'signification', especially of 'the other!' (Miles, 1989a). It is described further in the following section.

Finally, comparison enables us to demystify the notion of 'race relations,' and leads to consideration of racialised parity and racialised integration, both theoretically and as targets for policies. This obliges us to consider the various meanings of equality, particularly of opportunity and outcome. The notion of 'race relations' is mystifying theoretically because it suggests 'race relations' are a distinctive field of social relations between 'races' and thus reifies the notion of 'race'; a position that has been subjected to considerable criticism (Banton, 1977; Fenton, 1980; Gilroy, 1987a; Miles, 1989a).[20] In practical terms it is mystifying because the multiple variables involved in assessing whether trends in 'race relations' are progressing or regressing comprise a complex matrix, are not co-terminous and do not collectively lend themselves to simple evaluation. They usually include racialised equality – in economic or other objective terms – and racialised harmony – in terms of non-antagonistic social interaction. This means that any overall assessment of progress is bound to be equivocal at best. Consequently we need to move to a concept with greater clarification.

Beyond the benefits for theorists are those for policy analysts. Comparison generates concrete policies which can be examined and evaluated – especially regarding the obstacles to implementation – and it challenges us to think more carefully about the criteria by which we judge what is viable, desirable, achievable or otherwise. We can examine what has been tried and tested, the philosophical assumptions underlying policies, and the methods of implementation. Despite the fact that the situation in the United States is different from the impression held by many in England, there are many advances from which we can learn, especially in terms of policies and initiatives. Needless to say, these benefits are also indispensable to others involved in the analysis of, and contribution to, more fundamental social change. As Katznelson has pointed out 'one need not be a Leninist to recognize that action without prior information, careful thought, and theoretical direction is likely to be diffuse and ineffective at best' (Katznelson, 1973: xi). One way of achieving this is by transcending the 'dominant "value-free", objective, technically-oriented, largely behavioural research orientations' to arrive at a 'critical posture' which helps 'clarify and widen the space of political choice' (ibid.: 207). The theoretical assumptions one makes about the role of the state in managing, controlling or improving 'race relations' – that is to say, whether one sees the state as protector or predator – must be explicit and precise (Gilroy, 1987a; Sivanandan, 1988; Miles, 1989b).

Overall, comparisons of this kind will facilitate a greater understanding of the role of the state in the management of 'racialised relations', the role of multiple 'racisms' and of other forces and ideologies in maintaining racialised disadvantage. This is central theoretically, politically and in terms of policy. For example, in the work of Black organisations campaigning to combat racialised hostility, is the state seen as an ally or adversary, a protector or predator? This impinges directly on organisational strategies at a day-to-day level, as regards the way forward in each nation.[21] And you can bet it will not simply be those promoting social justice that will take cognisance of these benefits; no doubt the 'special relationship' between the United States and England so often voiced by presidents and prime ministers will foster special arrangements for the exchange of security, military surveillance and documentation to manage migration. In light of the fact that a former CIA chief has stated that the European Community represents a threat to American national security, it is clear that Trevi and Schengen will go transatlantic (*The Guardian*, 6 September, 1991).[22]

Black people are to be found among the ranks of academics and theoreticians, policymakers and political activists so they will benefit individually from all these realms. There are, too, collective benefits for groups and organisations which mobilise their activities around racialised identities – such as the National Association for the Advancement of Coloured People and the Urban League in the United States, the Society of Black Lawyers and the National Black Caucus in England. A comparative analysis like the one offered here can enable such groups to escape from the blinkered vision of a single society, as Blacks in both countries historically have always done, and have benefited from so doing.

In England in particular a tremendous opportunity exists for Black people to benefit from such comparisons. Despite continuing obstacles to success in the United States, Black people there have still established agendas, developed strategies and tactics, and achieved goals from which Blacks in England can learn. African-Caribbeans can learn from the diverse ways in which 'problems' have been defined and from the formulation of policies to respond to them; from the initiatives launched, the obstacles encountered and the tactics developed to circumvent them; from the strategies developed for gaining access to power and decision-making positions, the alliances formed and reshaped; and from the practical day-to-day lessons of those who have spent years striving to gain entrance to, as well as working in establishment institutions. African-Americans in the United States have a wealth of experience to offer at this level which can be captured by anyone willing to study their situation.[23] Black organisations and other institutions in the United States can also benefit from considering some of the assumptions upon which many of their policies are based. In all this we can benefit from the spirit of striving and the determination to succeed which characterises so much of the African-American experience there.

## THE GOALS OF THIS STUDY

Any useful analysis of the Black experience in these two nations must be selective and must have clear goals and a specific focus. In this book, the following goals are pursued:

> to provide contextualised comparative analyses of several key aspects of the Black experience in each nation.
> to provide an overview of the demographic profiles and the economic, political and social circumstances of Black people in each nation, especially *vis-à-vis* the non-Black majority.
> to establish a framework within which we might address how far each country has come towards achieving equality, and how far each has yet to go.
> to offer a framework within which we can critically review successes and limitations of policies and practices.
> to systematically apply the racialisation problematic.
> to outline some of the elements of a new language of analysis for examination of 'racialised relations'.[24]

Chapter 2 provides a detailed contemporary profile of the Black population in the 1980s including demography and economic, political and social profiles. Stratification within the Black population is extensive in the United States, and increasing in England. The chapter describes such patterns and considers the nature of the 'middle class' and the 'underclass'. It also examines the particular circumstances of women. The relative size of the Black population, the proportion that is immigrant and indigenous, and patterns of settlement are indispensable factors in any framework of comparison. The 'success' of African-Americans cannot be understood outside the context of their several hundred years of enforced presence in the United States, the fact that 97 per cent are indigenous and the massive size of the population (30-plus million, or 12 per cent in 1990). In contrast, the relatively recent arrival of the vast majority of African-Caribbeans and the tiny numbers involved (just over half a million in 1991) provides their context. The chapter describes attitudes towards racialised inequality, and suggests that despite extensive discrimination and disadvantage, there are exceptions to the general rule, and clear evidence of resistance.

Chapter 3 considers the complex linkages in the unfolding of multiple 'racisms' in each nation. There has been increasing attention to transformations in the nature of 'racism' and a suggestion that a 'new racism' has emerged. In the formal political realm there is evidence of a move from a 'racism' which is crude, blatant and predicated on biological notions to a variety of 'racisms' which are disguised and subliminal, but none the less effective. In this chapter I suggest that few analysts explore other areas of social life than the formal political realm. Outside the political realm historically established forms of 'racism' continue to be embraced as their advocates continue their relentless dehumanising threats and their violence and atrocities, claiming lives and disrupting communities. Here 'racism' remains visible and vicious, its consequences brutal, barbaric and bloody. New rationalisations for new 'racisms' go hand-in-hand with old rationalisations for old 'racisms'. In a climate in which official denunciation of 'racism' goes hand-in-hand with policies based on racialised notions of citizenship and ability, and where political electioneering around policies that manipulate racialised boundaries and identities are at the very heart of state practice, a greater appreciation of the changes in racialised discourse to suit contemporary circumstances is necessary.[25]

Chapter 4 considers the increasing stratification within the Black population and the growth of a Black 'middle class'. In the United States this group has increased tremendously and many of its members enjoy almost parity with their white counterparts (Edsall and Edsall, 1991a). Alongside this middle class there has developed an entrenched 'underclass' of Black people, unemployed, never employed, in poverty and without educational qualifications or work experience. The divide between the groups dominates academic and policy discussions of African-Americans (Wilson, 1978, 1987; Hacker, 1992). But many important issues are overlooked, some key problems ignored and complexities sidestepped as the array of political affiliations embraced by the 'middle class', and the range of activities in which they participate are submerged and forced to fit a common umbrella. In England small numbers of Blacks can now be found in occupations described as 'middle class'. The growth of this group is often supported by Black people there as a source of uplift and/or liberation for other Blacks (Cashmore, 1991, 1992). Earlier this century some African-American theorists, like W.E.B. Dubois and E. Franklin-Frazier, offered prognoses of the Black 'middle class' (Frazier, 1957; Dubois, 1961). I draw upon these theoretical debates as a foundation for interpreting patterns in the 1980s, especially the political affiliations and activities. I ask whether this 'middle class' acts as a 'Talented Tenth,' or a 'Black Bourgeoisie'? And whether they have been a blessing or curse for other Black people?

In Chapter 5 I consider images, attitudes and policies designed to achieve racialised progress. What notions of racialised progress are common in Black and white populations? What policies have been implemented and with what results? I examine how attitudes and policies are organised around the goal of reducing racialised conflict, promoting racialised harmony and integration, and achieving racialised equality. Though the language in each nation is different there is a common stock of assumptions which reveal contradictions. I seek to demystify the notion of 'race relations' by examining exactly what is meant by 'good race relations'. The three goals – or institutional interests – of racialised integration, harmony and parity are considered, as are the contradictions implicit in strategies to attain them. It is suggested that the conflicting methods required to achieve different goals leave us clambering for limited achievements.

Chapter 6 summarises the main findings, links them to the general theme of the book – the changing nature of racialised barriers, boundaries and identities – and considers some of the implications. I suggest that racialised identities are central to any efforts to overcome racialised inequality.

These issues are examined in the light of trends emerging in the 1990s' economic and political world order – a context of dizzying global transformations at all levels. From the Gulf War and Middle East turmoil to the disintegration of the Soviet Union, and from the consolidation of the Single European Market and the unification of Germany to the new developments in South Africa and the new strengths of Pacific Rim countries, the economic and political ramifications are immense. This approach enables me to examine several patterns emerging in England which are long-established in the United States(for example, the growth and role of a Black 'middle class'), as well as patterns emerging in the United States which are long established in England (or which are the basis of desired policy, for example, social integration, especially at universities).

## METHODOLOGY

There are many benefits to comparative international analysis and there is an extensive literature on the strategies and methodologies of comparative analysis (Skocpol and Somers, 1980; Bovenkerk *et al.*, 1990). But while certain comparisons abound others are scarce and there are many pitfalls to be avoided as Yinger has noted:

> There is a lot to be learned by seeing similarities embedded in systems that differ greatly. The whale that swims, the lion that runs and the bat that flys have much in common. . . . The question is, how large are the differences we are omitting from the analysis; and how much are we led to exaggerate the similarities?. . . Are we comparing lions and tigers or bats and whales?
> (Yinger, 1986: 23, 34)

The pitfalls include failure to provide a useful context of comparison, inapplicable or inappropriate use of concepts and theories, exaggeration and caricature. We can avoid many of the shortcomings of existing comparisons if we carry out contextualised analysis and are not mystified by the notion of 'race relations'. We must also identify and clarify the criteria by which we would assess improvements in 'race relations'. In this book my approach has been to identify several key issues and to develop a theoretical and conceptual framework within which they can be described and evaluated. This sets the foundation for further empirically grounded comparisons of more narrowly defined topics.[26] The two main elements of the approach utilised here are the concepts of 'contextualisation' and the 'racialisation' problematic.

## Contextualisation

In any comparison of the Black experience in the United States and England we have a right to expect some description of who is the subject of attention, an overview of the contemporary profiles and some consideration of the possible historical influences on contemporary processes. Otherwise the context within which an assessment can be made is absent. The idea of 'contextualisation' is introduced here to provide a framework for comparison, to direct our attention to some of the more important factors which continue to shape Black opportunities and to help develop a set of criteria for assessing progress towards racialised parity. It is an attempt to answer the question 'If I want to understand, explain and compare how patterns of "racialised relation" unfold in different contexts what factors must be taken into account?' The main goal is to help us avoid caricature or exaggeration. Its use facilitates an identification of some important dimensions of the Black experience and helps us unravel their intricate inter-relationships. Taken collectively the various elements of a contextualised analysis enable us to describe the material (property, power and privilege) and mental (attitudes, ideology and psychology) dimensions of the 'Colour Line'.

Some analysts have used similar notions, but none have yet applied it to the international comparative analysis of 'racialised relations'. For example, Wilson employed a similar framework in his macro-historical analysis of African-Americans (Wilson, 1978). He rejected a uniform reliance on 'race' or class and argued that different historical contexts of American 'race relations' reflected a unique configuration of economic and political structures. These configurations structured the particular pattern of 'race relations' that unfolded (Ibid.: 2–3). In sum, he argued that:

> different systems of production and/or different arrangements of the polity have imposed different constraints on the way in which racial groups have interacted in the United States, constraints that have structured the relations between racial groups and that have produced dissimilar contexts not only for the manifestation of racial antagonisms but also for racial group access to rewards and privileges.
>
> (Wilson, 1978: 3)

For Wilson it is futile to attempt an analysis of 'race relations'

outside its appropriate context because the context sets the parameters for what might be achieved. He identified three periods
– the pre-industrial, early industrial and modern industrial – described the particular arrangements of each and how 'race relations'
were structured within them. He identified five aspects of each
context and considered each element in its historical context.[27]

In this book, contextualisation means: delineation of the
social parameters of the context which is being analysed, and a
specification of the criteria by which the phenomenon under
consideration will be evaluated.

The specific aspects to be included in each contextualised
analysis will vary from case to case. I identify the following aspects
for this book: the economic and political structures of each nation;
the demographic profile of the Black population and its length of
residence; a comparison of its economic, political and social profile
with that of the counterpart white population. A contextualised
comparison also requires conceptual clarification. A full answer to
the question 'how far have Blacks come towards achieving racialised
equality?' and 'how far do they still have to go to achieve racialised
equality?' would require greater historical analysis than is provided
here but a general answer can be provided.

The United States and England share a similar economic and
political system dominated by a free market economy, wage labour
and state regulation, in which bourgeois democracy prevails
(Krieger, 1986). They also reveal similar patterns of economic and
political inequality, with wealth and political power concentrated
in the hands of a few (Hoover, 1987; Gamble, 1988). Many of the
differences often noted in popular accounts – differences in the
labour market and social mobility, the high proportion of funds
spent on health and welfare in England, preoccupation with the
language of 'class' – do play a central role but their relevance in
specific instances is not the priority in this book. The greater focus
that I give to racialised barriers, boundaries and identities in
interpreting patterns of racialised inequality is not meant to suggest
that economic and class inequalities are irrelevant. However, my
primary concern is more to explicate similarities in these racialised
patterns, than to provide an analysis of the interplay of racialised
ideologies, practices and structures with class and economic forces.

One cannot begin to compare and explain the disadvantaged
position of Blacks in each country without recognising, as described
above, that during the 1980s Blacks made up only around 1.5 per

cent of the population in England, but around 11 per cent–12 per cent in the United States (Smith, 1989; Farley and Allen, 1989). There are three times as many Blacks in the state of California alone, as there are in England. Furthermore, while Blacks make up over 40 per cent of the population of several major cities in the USA (including Washington DC, Oakland, California, and Detroit, Michigan) they are less than 10 per cent of the population of any city in England. Or that the vast majority of Blacks in the United States are indigenous, while just under 50 per cent are indigenous in England (Smith, 1989; Farley and Allen, 1989). In addition, if one is to assess equality of opportunity (as well as equality of condition) then we must compare the experiences of the Black population with those of the white majority. This kind of analysis has been carried out within national boundaries but seems to fall by the wayside in international comparisons (Brown, 1984; Wright, 1988; Farley and Allen, 1989).

Furthermore, many of the comparisons listed above suffer because they employ concepts which have different empirical referents in the two contexts. These concepts are not universal or transferable and to treat them as such is to make an error. For example, Bikhu Parekh compared the size of the 'Black' population in the United States and Britain, but the definition of 'Black' that he used included all 'ethnic minorities' in England, but only people of African origin in the United States (Parekh 1987). Thus he gets figures for the 'Black' population of less than 4 per cent in Britain and around 11 per cent in the United States. If he had compared only people of African origin in each country he would have arrived at a figure of 1.5 per cent for Britain. If he had included all people of colour in the United States the figure would have been around 20 per cent (Parekh, 1987; xi–xii). This type of confusion also surrounds concepts such as 'Asian', 'bussing', 'race riots', 'ghetto', and 'integration' (Omi and Winant, 1986; Killian, 1987a. See also Jacobs, 1986).

As part of our effort to contextualise our analysis and to evaluate progress it is also necessary to demystify the notion of 'race relations'; in particular, to clarify whether the goals and priorities expressed by different groups are embraced in policies and political action. Many of the problems that arise in assessing progress in 'race relations' derive from our failure to clarify the criteria by which we will evaluate progress. This is all the more necessary given the multiple variables which might be drawn upon, especially since such variables are not co-terminous. Are policies designed to achieve: racialised integration (in numerical terms); racialised harmony (measured in terms of non-antagonistic interaction); or racialised parity (measured in terms of access to and distribution of resources)? Efforts can be made to achieve all three, and they can exist alongside one another, though that does not have to be the case. Each requires a different set of priorities, and different methods. Efforts to achieve one may well give rise to problems in achieving the others.

For example, there can be considerable racialised harmony alongside substantial racialised inequality (and discrimination). Furthermore, efforts to promote harmony are often injurious to parity, as whites who want to discriminate (for whatever reasons) are unlikely to be disposed towards racialised harmony if they are prevented from doing so; thus, racialised harmony might be achieved only by turning a blind eye to discrimination – an option unlikely to be acceptable to most Black people. An historical example elucidates the point. In 1969 Rose and associates carried out a survey of 'racial attitudes' and concluded that the 'majority of people are tolerantly inclined' (Rose *et al.*, 1969: 675). This was taken as a sign of harmonious 'race relations'. At about the same time, Political and Economic Planning carried out a survey of 'racial discrimination' which indicated that it existed 'from the massive to the substantial' (Daniel, 1968: 209). Is this 'good race relations?' I am not suggesting that the two are always mutually exclusive, but we must recognise the implicit unresolved problems, not least of which is that by this definition 'racial harmony' prevailed on most slave plantations, as others have pointed out (Genovese, 1968).

In Liverpool exists the highest pattern of racialised inter-dating in the country, and the pattern of settlement is often hailed as harmonious – by members of parliament, the city council and city leaders (see examples in Liverpool Black Caucus, 1986). Yet alongside this fact is a Black population that is disproportionately unemployed, without educational qualifications, more likely to be confined to poverty, segregated, and often under attack (Gifford *et al.*, 1989). There are numerous obstacles to ending racialised discrimination, and promoting 'good race relations', as a plethora of articles on 'anti-racism' have demonstrated (Gilroy, 1987b; Miles, 1988); as there are to achieving 'racial parity'. This demonstrates that an image of racialised harmony can co-exist alongside extensive inequality. Furthermore, we can conceptualise a situation of antagonistic integration, or one of racialised separation with parity (for example, some sections of the Black 'middle class' in the United States have parity but are far from integrated residentially (Wilson, W., 1987).

## Racialisation

Although much progress has been made in the analysis of 'racialised relations' a number of problems remain. The language employed is imprecise and entails a series of assumptions which are false and misleading. Such language often conflates biological and social differences, and confuses issues of 'racism' with issues of 'racialised identity'. These approaches almost invariably define Black people as a problem. This leads to confusion and mystification analytically, politically and in policy areas. The concept of 'racialisation' is introduced here to challenge this. It offers several strengths over previous approaches to apprehending and interpreting the relative interplay of racialised inequality and the role of racialised barriers, boundaries and identities, as compared with other factors such as ethnicity, nationality and religion, or indeed, economic, class and political variables.

The term 'race relations' denotes a conventionally accepted area of focus, though the paradigms utilised for analysis of these phenomena are divergent. In this book I reject the notion of 'race relations' both theoretically and in practical terms as one which mystifies the phenomena we study.[28] One problem with many social scientific analyses of 'race' is that while they often acknowledge that 'race' is a social construct that is flexible and fluid they then go on to talk about 'race' as if it were a naturally occurring phenomena, treating it as real and adding credibility to its status as an explanatory factor in social relationships.[29] This practice is of course widespread in the various legislative measures in the United States and England, is pervasive in the parlance of practitioners and among the general public (Miles and Phizacklea, 1984; Edsall and Edsall, 1991b).

The definitions of 'race' and of 'race relations' employed in most popular and many academic and policy discourses are a mish-mash of all that is bad from the past. They combine and confuse scientific, pseudo-scientific, popular definitions and misconceptions about 'race' and we cannot afford to use them in order to understand 'racialised relations'. Many analysts thus fall victim to the language, concepts and assumptions which they decry. This may be part and parcel of our endeavour, as Barzun maintains:

> It is one of the penalties of toying with the race-notion that even a strong mind trying to repudiate it will find himself making assumptions and passing judgements on the basis of the theory he declaims.

> (Barzun 1938, cited in Miles, 1989a: front page)

Similarly the field of 'race relations' is discussed as if it were a distinctive field of study, with a unique set of social relations governed by a specific set of rules. In fact in any context described as 'race relations' attitudes and notions about 'race' are only one aspect of the social relationships involved – and may not even be the most central aspect.[30] These relations are inextricably entangled with issues of economics, employment, politics and demography, as well as nationality, language and religion.

To comprehend better the processes at work we need to move from an analysis of 'race', 'race relations' and Black people, to one of 'racisms', 'racialised relations' and white people. More specifically, we should make an analysis of these intricate relationships. The problem with a focus on 'race' and 'race relations' is that it assumes that 'races' exist and seeks to understand relations between them, presuming what needs to be proven. By contrast, a focus on 'racisms' and 'racialised relations' questions the existence of 'races', looks at how groups not previously defined as 'races' have come to be defined in this way, and assesses the various factors involved in such processes (Banton, 1977; Miles, 1982; Green and Carter, 1988). The problem with a focus on Black people alone is that it conceives the Black population as a 'cause' of racialised antagonism, rather than it being a consequence of white attitudes and actions. One of the most invidious outcomes of all this is that Black people continue to be the main focus of the magnifying glass in attempts to understand 'race relations': it is as if the problems inhere in 'race' or skin colour (Lawrence, 1982). But in fact, the problem is not 'race' but 'racisms', not relations between 'races' but relations which have been racialised, not the physical attributes of Blacks or their presumed inferiority, but the motivations of non-Blacks, and the obstacles they impose. The theoretical and practical ramifications are thus considerably changed.

For example, the riots in Liverpool in 1919 and 1948 were blamed on Black sailors for 'taking' white jobs (and women), instead of on the discrimination of employers and trade unions, and the 'racism' of white men (Dimmock, 1975; May and Cohen, 1974). In the 1930s the problems experienced by 'Black people of mixed origins' were seen as a result of their biological inferiority and social maladjustment, instead of the consequences of stereo- types and discrimination (Fletcher, 1930; Fryer, 1984). Black people were seen as incapable of deciding and implementing measures to achieve their uplift, while whites were deemed the best guardians of Black futures (Rich, 1984; Wilson, 1989). I argue that, rather than perceiving the problem to be the 'special needs and preferential treatment' of Black people, it is better to see it resulting from the special need to prevent white discrimination (Richmond, 1966; Solomos, 1988). Instead of viewing a pattern of inter-dating as evidence of racialised harmony it is better to note that it is confined to a small section of the non-Black population whose participation is regarded with disdain, even disgust, by others and the attitudes and perspectives of Black women are not taken into account (Gifford *et al.*, 1989). The dominant role of white people and their economic, political and cultural priorities figure prominently in this type of analysis.

Similar problems arise over the concepts of 'racial disadvan- tage' and 'racial discrimination'. The latter is seen as 'just another handicap from which blacks suffered' – comparable to the experi- ences of non-Blacks who are disadvantaged – and one amenable to simple legal measures, rather than as a significant cause of disad- vantage, and one that is intractable (Solomos, 1988: 153; see also Rex and Tomlinson, 1979; Ben-Tovim, 1989). The differences between these two concepts were elaborated some time ago and others have offered persuasive critiques (McIntosh and Smith, 1974; Smith, 1977; Solomos, 1988: 153, 235). A prime example of this approach is reflected in the proposal to the Third European Anti-poverty Programme in Liverpool in which a multitude of problems are identified (all located within the Black population, and many pathological). A multitude of proposals are made, again all aimed at magnanimously uplifting the poor Black victims (Third Community Action Programme, 1989). At no time is racialised discrimination or hostility identified as an item for action (it is mentioned in passing); it is simply reduced to another form of disadvantage which the Black population must struggle to over- come. It is perplexing that such agencies still see racialised inequality as simply a matter of Black people lacking the necessary credentials to progress. It becomes clear then that the motivations of those who would conflate the two – as the government has done for decades, and as other agencies continue to do so – must be questioned.

Attempts to resolve the contradictions and inconsistencies thrown up by the assumptions embedded in the language of 'race relations' by substituting the term with 'ethnic relations' confuse more than they clarify because they collapse and conflate patterns of ethnic and racialised boundaries and identities into the same matrix (Williams, 1990). They fail to bring out the differences between the two and prevent us from disentangling and seriously tackling the real differences which they manifest. There are critical differences in the experiences of African-Americans and ethnic immigrants to the USA (Steinberg, 1981; Lieberson, 1980). Similarly there are great differences between migrants and settlers from the Caribbean and the Asian Sub-continent as compared with those from Ireland, Italy or Cyprus (Daniel, 1968).

A further problem is that issues of 'racism' or 'racialised ideologies are confused with issues of 'race consciousness' or racialised identities. Sometimes the language of 'race relations' is rejected as being an example of 'race thinking' (Green and Carter, 1988). The argument offered is that 'race' is a spurious biological concept which claims to account for social relations between people defined as 'Black' and 'white'. It is suggested that rather than approach these issues unproblematically (as if assuming that 'Blacks' and 'whites' exist as real groups) it is better to question why it is commonly believed that 'race relations' is a distinctive area of social relations (Miles, 1982). One answer offered is that 'Blacks' and 'whites' were historically constructed during European colonisation of the Americas (a result of 'racism'), and that such categories continue to serve the interests of powerful European élites, as well as, to a lesser degree, all other Europeans. But I suggest that while 'race' as a biological concept is spurious, racialised identities as social phenomena have become entrenched, and are embraced by various groups for different goals. This has to be confronted by questioning the goals of these groups. I thus suggest that we reject racialised ideologies, while retaining acknowledgement of the usefulness of racialised identities as a means to moving forward. This argument is developed throughout the book.

One way of negotiating some of these problems is provided by adopting the 'racialisation' problematic. By addressing the question: 'if "race" is not biology then what is it?' one can unravel the relative influence of multiple factors (economics, politics, demography, culture, ideology and myth) in patterns of 'racialised relations'. The 'racialisation' problematic has been called a problematic, a process, a concept, a theory, a framework and a paradigm (Banton, 1977; Miles, 1982; Reeves, 1983; Omi and Winant, 1986; Green and Carter, 1988; Satzewich, 1989; Smith, 1989). The most consistent advocate has been Robert Miles (1982, 1989a, 1989b; Miles and Phizacklea, 1984). Its use by authors of divergent theoretical orientations emphasises that it is a framework not tied to any particular theory (Banton, 1977; Reeves, 1983; Jackson, 1987; Smith, 1989). While there are differences between the writers that employ it, it is what they agree upon that links them in a common enterprise.

I draw a distinction between the 'racialisation' problematic and the process of 'racialisation' (Small, 1989; Small, 1990a). The former refers to a theoretical model (a framework of analysis within which competing theories can be evaluated against empirical data); the latter to a process of attribution which has been unfolding historically, and continues to unfold. If it is conceptualised as a framework then the relative influence of the state, migration and economic relations are indispensable, as several authors have demonstrated (Miles, 1982; Miles and Phizacklea, 1984; Miles, 1988). The 'racialisation' problematic thus represents a paradigm within which competing theories can be advanced for an understanding and explanation of the creation and variations in racialised barriers, boundaries and identities in various socio-historical contexts. I have articulated these views in greater detail elsewhere and have employed the concept in an analysis of Liverpool (Small, 1989a; Small, 1991b).

Consequently, in this book I analyse what is conventionally called 'race relations' within the 'racialisation' problematic. This enables me to problematise the field and entails a new conceptualisation of 'racism' and 'race' which changes the framework, focus and facts of the phenomena conventionally studied in this field and enjoins us to a new set of questions. This redirects our primary concern from 'race', 'race relations' and Black people to 'racisms', 'racialised relations' and whites; by demystifying 'good race relations' (taking account of the distinction between racialised integration, racialised harmony and racialised parity); and by disentangling racialised disadvantage from racialised discrimination. This transfers attention from the notion that Black people are a 'race' to the historical process whereby Europeans racialised Africans (Banton, 1977; Omi and Winant, 1986; Green and Carter, 1988). In this way I render primary, contentious and problematic notions which are often treated as secondary, non-contentious and unproblematic.

When we examine the process of 'racialisation' we find that our beliefs about 'races' and 'race relations' have more to do with the attitudes, actions, motivations and interests of powerful groups in society; and less to do with the characteristics, attitudes and actions of those who are defined as belonging to inferior 'races'. Examples of this can be found when we examine attitudes towards sexuality and sporting ability (see Chapter 3). But we must also acknowledge that definitions, ideas and images once begun can vary and endure in ways that are complex. The beliefs of those around you directly affect your behaviour and a self-fulfilling prophecy can be set in motion. Definitions can also be manipulated. 'Race' was used to oppress, and is now being used to uplift. There are no 'races', but there are racialised group affiliations embraced by many. Not only is it unlikely that such affiliations will disappear in the short term, there is much evidence to indicate they are being increasingly embraced to facilitate liberation. This is why consideration of racialised identities is central to any analysis of racialised barriers and boundaries.

One criticism of this approach is that it is simply semantic. I argue otherwise and believe there is a fundamental difference between those who explicitly subscribe to the problematic and those who do not. This approach changes not just the language but also the framework and focus of the analysis, leads to a fundamentally different definition of 'the problem' and to different types of policy and political proposals. For those who employ the 'racialisation' problematic the rigorous assessment of the nature and meaning of 'race' and of the differential power relations amongst those who seek to ensure their definitions prevail is immediate and mandatory, while for those who do not it is optional. One cannot discuss 'racialised relations' without being forced to raise what is meant by the term; but for those who talk of 'race relations' – in courses, units, articles and books – this may well be avoided, neglected or postponed. Once it is raised in this way, the likelihood that it will be sustained throughout research, writing and teaching seems to me to be greater.

One last point: working within the 'racialisation' problematic is not about developing some kind of algebraic formula which can be applied to each context to give us an answer to racialised interaction. I do not believe that this can be achieved but I do believe that we can compile an inventory of variables which, while not definitive, will highlight the features invariably present in racialised contexts.

## DEFINITIONS AND TERMINOLOGY

In this book a number of new phrases are introduced and consistently employed. They are introduced to render concepts problematic in a way that is consistent with analysis within the 'racialisation' problematic. I believe that the few problems we might encounter, because the phrases are clumsy and lengthy, are far outweighed by the analytical usefulness they provide, and the challenges they offer. They are briefly defined and outlined here and will be developed in greater detail throughout the book.

The term 'Black' is used to mean all peoples of African descent. It does not include others conventionally called 'Black' in England or other 'people of colour' in the United States because inclusion of these groups would have added considerably more complexity to an already complex topic. The term 'Black' is used as synonymous with 'African-American' (in the United States) and 'African-Caribbean' (in England). Some of the sources of data refer to 'Afro-Caribbeans' or to 'West Indians/Guyanese'. Again these are taken as synonymous with African-Caribbean. In general, Africans are included in the general rubric 'Black' as they face most of the problems that Black people face. Black people of mixed European and African origins are treated in the same way. Africans not of Caribbean origin in each nation tend to display a different economic profile from those of African-Americans and African-Caribbeans and this might make for increasingly divergent experiences. For example, Africans in England are more likely to gain higher education and be employed in professional jobs than are African-Caribbeans (Haskey, 1989; Skellington *et al.*, 1992). The complexities which arise as a result of the experiences of Africans, and of Black people of mixed origins, cannot be taken up in this book in any detail but some mention is made where appropriate. Sometimes where data are not available for Black people alone, data for 'ethnic minorities' are provided to give some indication of differences *vis-à-vis* the white majority. This is not entirely satisfactory, given the differences in circumstances between Blacks and other racialised groups (such as Hispanics in the United States, and Asians in England) but this practice is kept to a minimum.

The term 'racialised' is used in a variety of ways, and some of this has been explained above. In general it is used to suggest that social structures, social ideologies and attitudes have historically become imbued with 'racial' meaning, that such meanings are contingent and contested, and that they are shaped by a multitude of other variables, economic, political, religious. It emphasises the continuing need to see the intricate relationship between 'racial' meanings and other (economic, political, religious) meanings. This process is far from fixed today – in fact it must remain variable by its very nature (dependent as it is on a host of economic, political, cultural and ideological variables). As the 1990s progress, racialised boundaries are likely to become more intricate, complex and contested as a result of increasing patterns of economic and political stratification within the Black population, increasing patterns of racialised intermarriage across historically maintained boundaries, and a changing international situation (Small, 1993).

The term 'racialised group' is used in place of 'race'. This emphasises the social (and thus changing) nature of racialised boundaries. It emphasises its contingent nature and the historical variations in racialised group boundaries. Racialised barriers and racialised boundaries refer to the pervasive incidence of discrimination and demarcation predicated on assumptions of 'race'. The terms 'racialised group affiliations' and 'racialised identities' are used in recognition of the social identities often embraced by groups which we call 'Black' and 'white'. The nearest equivalent in the redundant language of 'race relations' would be 'race consciousness'. Again, such identities are not fixed, are influenced by a host of other factors (such as class, gender, religion) but remain a primary organising feature of social relations in both nations today. They will become more complex, contradictory and conflicting for the very reasons outlined with regard to racialised group boundaries.

I have suggested that in discussions of 'good race relations' three main indicators are usually employed: racialised integration, harmony and parity. It is important to distinguish each and have a clear understanding of what each means. I have provided an elaboration and critique of these concepts elsewhere (Small, 1991a). Racialised integration usually refers to the physical and social integration of

Blacks and whites in housing, education, employment and other social spheres. It is not precisely defined. Few people think that each street, school or workplace should be 50 per cent Black and 50 per cent non-Black, but there is a clear notion that there should be 'significant' numbers of Blacks and whites freely living, working and going to school alongside one another.

Racialised harmony usually refers to non-antagonistic relations between Blacks and whites, and is taken to exist when there is an absence of racialised attacks, and/or high levels of racialised dating and marriage. Racialised harmony is a major goal of 'anti-racist' and equal opportunities initiatives.

In contrast, racialised parity – usually called 'racial equality' – means equal access to, and/or enjoyment of, the property, power and privilege experienced by the white population.[31] Many analyses suggest such equality is possible within the broad contours of the existing social structure.

None of this language is meant to be preemptive. It is advanced as a way to come to terms with the complex and contradictory language, ideologies and identities which are embraced by institutional and individual agencies and actors.

One final note: although the comparison is of two nations, the primary geographical focus of the book is England, not Britain, given the overwhelming concentration of 'Blacks' in England.

## CONCLUSION

The point of departure for this book then is the shared experience of racialised barriers, boundaries and identities, the persistence of the 'Colour Line' and the sustained opposition mounted by Black people against exploitation, hostility and humiliation in each country. The sad but simple fact is that Black people remain entrenched at the bottom in both societies by any of the accepted social indicators – wealth, income, poverty, employment or health. Despite overwhelming odds and entrenched disparities in resources, Black people have fought at every opportunity against injustice and repression. This is testimony to our resistance and resilience. Our hearts remain committed to struggle. All of this emphasises that both countries have much in common.

My goal is to describe, document and explain continuities and discontinuities in the Black experience in the United States and England by providing a comparative contextualised analysis; and to outline, elaborate and apply the racialisation problematic to this comparison. Aspects and lessons from the experience of each country will be elaborated so as to inform continuing analysis of the other country, especially where this is done comparatively.

I explore several key areas of the Black presence in the United States and England, and I examine the circumstances and experiences of Black people in each nation. I look at the size, pattern of settlement and experiences of the Black population, and at some of the substantial obstacles that were imposed during the 1980s. I examine the positions that different sections of the Black population occupy and at how they have tried to fulfil their aspirations. In doing so I discuss 'racisms' and class hostility, class stratification in the Black population, ideas and notions of equality and the many aspects of resistance. In this book I document many examples of the magnitude of the ordeals confronting Black people, and of their fortitude. In these reflections we shall find much testimony to perseverance and resilience.

Readers from each nation will be surprised at how far the facts conflict with the popular conceptions that prevail. They will also be intrigued by the similarities between the two countries. Though they exhibit important contrasts in their histories, and in their political and social organisation, the United States and England reveal amazing similarities in the experiences of their minority populations of African origin: from the slave trade and forced migration; slavery as a social institution, legal discrimination and hostility; from exclusion and injustice; to recriminations, resentment and reform. Both nations have struggled to extend the rights bestowed on the majority to their minority populations and both have faced constant and unrelenting demands for justice.

Even greater will be the surprise at how much African-Americans see a reflection of themselves in Blacks in England. Without always being aware of it, Blacks in the United States have exercised a remarkable influence on the culture, lifestyles and political ideologies of Blacks in England. In its politics, struggles and resistance, in its music, art and other popular culture, and in a host of other ways, Black America is reiterated and relived through the lives of Black Britons. Black people today will learn greatly by reflecting on the experiences of their African sisters and brothers on other continents. Not only will it liberate their minds from the blinkered perspectives, limited assumptions and narrow visions of a single society, but it will open their eyes to a whole new world of vision.

As Marcus Garvey and Malcolm X said, and as Minister Louis Farrakhan reiterated, Blacks in the United States may be a minority, but people of colour across the world are a majority. In a shrinking world whatever our nationality, ethnicity, or racialised group affiliation, we cannot afford to remain 'culturally retarded'. Reflection will help us to understand, interpret and act upon our situation.

Given the increasing complexity of structures and ideologies of racialised inequality in the 1990s (in ways that will be elaborated below) there is great urgency for theoretical and conceptual clarity. We need to examine and learn from other contexts and to understand the continued impact international forces exert on our own local situations. The benefits of systematically describing, and critically evaluating, the ramifications of the similarities and differences in the Black experience, and of the successes and limitations, will be elaborated in this book. I describe some of these patterns by highlighting the 'Colour Line' as the consistently shared experience of Black people on both sides of the Atlantic. I provide a detailed economic, political and social profile of the circumstances in which Black people found themselves in the 1980s. I then focus on several key areas – the multiple 'racisms' that bombard Black people, the implications of increasing Black stratification and the conflicting notions underlying attempts to achieve racialised equality. Each nation offers the other a chance for detailed comparison and for benefits to academics, policy analysts and others interested in social and political change.[32]

# Chapter 2

# Black people in the United States and England: a profile of the 1980s

## INTRODUCTION

In this chapter I give a contextualised account of the main circumstances in which Black people found themselves in each nation in the 1980s, so as to provide an overview of the extent of racialised inequality that will serve as the basis for a systematic comparison.[1] An analysis of the details and nuances of these patterns follows in subsequent chapters. I consider briefly the continuing institutionalised obstacles to success, and identify areas in which Black people as a group excel, as well as those in which Blacks have made some significant advances in light of the obstacles.[2] There is a need to confront the facts of racialised inequality and discrimination, especially taking account of what remains similar as well as the variations and nuances within the Black population as it becomes more stratified in a variety of ways.[3] The need for contextualisation is even greater in international comparisons. Concepts, terminology, measurements and data all differ and thus make comparisons more difficult. Few books that carry out comparisons provide commensurate and easily accessible social, economic and political profiles that can serve as the basis for comparison.[4] This calls for clear definitions and for accurate data so that readers in each nation can begin to understand some of the implications of the patterns in the other nation. Only by confronting such facts can we begin to analyse the factors that continue to sustain such patterns and assess the ways in which they might be challenged and overcome.

There are a number of changes in the circumstances of Black people which make the 1980s different from any other period. Among such changes in the United States are the large numbers of Blacks who have gained educational qualifications, the significant upper section of the Black population socio-economically, the increasing willingness to express conservative attitudes, and the even greater willingness of the press and media to highlight them. These factors, in conjunction with the changing political and economic circumstances of the United States on the world scene, make for an increasingly complex picture. In England the transformation of the Black population from an immigrant to an indigenous one, and the increasing, if slow, pattern of stratification and diversity in political views creates new complexities, as does the advent of the European Community.

Most studies of inequality present Blacks as almost overwhelmingly victimised (Farley and Allen, 1989; Hacker, 1992; Daniel, 1968; Brown, 1984; but see Bhat *et al.*, 1988 for an exception). The same is true in the general media where images of Black poverty, educational failure, unemployment, teenage childbirth and crime, dominate coverage. Clearly, as will be seen, these images have a basis in fact – a tragic and often terrifying basis as Black people find themselves at a disadvantage in almost every major social, economic and political category. But this is not the whole story and there are exceptions to these patterns – some major and notable ones – and acknowledgement of them is important for analytical purposes.

For example, while large numbers of African-Americans in the 1980s were in poverty (around 33 per cent), with similar proportions in England (twice as many African-Caribbean households were dependent on child benefits as compared with white households), nevertheless a growing number were to be found in professional occupations in the United States (where one in seven African-American families had an income of $50,000 or more, and 15 per cent of Black men were to be found in professional occupations), as were small numbers in England (Cashmore, 1991). While more than twice as many Black men in the United States suffered unemployment (11 per cent compared to less than 5 per cent for white men), as did an identical proportion in England (25 per cent as compared with 12 per cent), nevertheless most Black men in the United States were employed, (a significant minority, 7 per cent, were self-employed), as were most Black men in England (Brown, 1984). While large numbers of Blacks in both the United States and England continued to be failed by the educational system (Black young people in each nation were less likely to gain educational qualifications or go on to higher education), nevertheless significant numbers in the United States did well (11 per cent of Blacks in the United States got a degree in the 1980s), as did smaller numbers in England (Skellington *et al.*, 1992).

While Black teenagers in the United States were more likely than any other racialised group to give birth to children, often outside wedlock (African-American babies are four times more likely to be born to an unmarried mother), as were similar proportions in England (Haskey, 1989), nevertheless a substantial proportion of Black babies were born to married couples in the United States (3.8 million children live in two-parent families, O'Hare *et al.*, 1991: 20), as are large numbers in England (*Social Trends*, 1992). Finally, while families headed by women accounted for around 43 per cent of African-American families in the United States, as did a similar proportion in England (42 per cent), nevertheless around 50 per cent of African-American families were married-couple families and six in ten African-Caribbean families were married-couple families (and over 20 per cent of all African-Caribbean families were married couples with children) (Haskey, 1989).[5]

In addition, the evidence on resistance and resilience belies the picture, images and connotations suggested by a simple presentation of the facts of inequality. Black people have not passively accepted the racialised hostility which bombards them; communities and cultures of resistance have been forged to oppose and overturn such hostility. So while a study of the facts of inequality alone might suggest total decimation, this is not so; Black people may be victims but they have not been overwhelmed and they do not have a victim mentality. What this means is that while we must confront the dismal facts of inequality we must also look at the other side of the picture; we must look at the variations and nuances, some of them major; and we must look at the spirit of striving which such resistance reveals. We must examine them because they are facts too, and very relevant facts at that. A detailed contextualised picture of Black people in the United States and England in the 1980s shows that although we arrived via different routes, and although there still remain major differences in our experiences, and in the institutional obstacles which confront us, nevertheless, as a racialised group we find ourselves in similar circumstances. Racialised inequality is a fundamental fact of life; the situation for the majority of Black people is desperate and worsening. Black people continue to face common racialised barriers obstructing their aspirations, and racialised boundaries demarcating their activities. These are characterised by major inequalities and inequities, major obstacles of an institutional and individual nature imposed by non-Blacks.

Among the existing analyses of the circumstances and life chances of Black people, analysts on the left and those on the right, radical and reactionary, Afrocentric and Eurocentric, and those in the centre, all agree on one thing; by just about every major indicator that exists – economic and educational, wealth and health, employment and housing, poverty and penury – Blacks as a group are at a disadvantage compared to whites. This is true for all Blacks compared to all whites, it is true for Black men compared to white men, and it is true for Black women compared to white women. The general picture holds true when we compare the entire United States with the whole of England (or indeed Britain). There are differences by regions and by cities, but none of these differences change the general picture. The major differences that exist between these studies are only in the new words employed, the passion evoked, or the indifference with which they are described. When it comes to the facts of the 'Colour Line', major disagreements exist only over tiny fractions, statistical computations, margins of accuracy, and other such niceties of detail. It is sad and tragic, demoralising and damning, tear-generating and anguish causing – if it does not cause despair then it can only cause despondency.

But a further dimension to this is the racialised identities and affinities to which racialised hostility has given rise. The facts and processes of racialised barriers and boundaries do not go unchallenged. Racialised groups are mobilised with a spirit of striving against inequality and injustice. So there are also exceptions to the overall pattern and clear evidence of a refusal to give up in the face of obstacles, and of common racialised identities which form a basis for collective resistance. Despite the persistent denial of opportunities, these processes are continually confronted by a determination and refusal to give up. These challenge the overall picture of desolation, and leave us with suggestions for the way forward. Two factors must be born in mind in interpreting these profiles. First, there are many examples of individuals and communities that have fought against racialised imperatives, that have gone beyond survival to success. Their success should be an inspiration to us. Second, in general this tale is also the source of our future – the struggles and strivings, the resistance and resilience, the spirit and soul which has sustained Black people through conquest and colonisation, international and internal. We can conclude that we must take spirit and inspiration from the fact that we are still here, determined, obstinate, obdurate, and that we refuse to give up.

Among the debris are some signs of hope, some glimmer of potential remains. This chapter is not simply about telling the tale of woes which currently befalls Black people in each nation – though that is the necessary context within which the analysis in subsequent chapters must be carried out. Rather it is also about the staying power of Black people, the spirit of striving. If it were not for Black women's resilience, we would not still be here fighting:

> Even centuries of slavery, oppression and sexual abuse, of attacks on our culture and on our right to be, have not succeeded in breaking Black women's spirit of resistance. Instead of distancing us from the African heritage which has sustained us, the thousands of miles we have travelled and the oceans we have crossed have simply strengthened our collective sense of self-worth. It is this firm and durable tradition of drawing strength and purpose from the culture in which our experience is grounded that is Black women's most precious legacy to the next generation.
>
> (Bryan *et al.*, 1985: 239)

And this resistance has not always, or even most often, been spontaneous without analysis, or theory. Quite the contrary:

> People of color have always theorized – but in forms quite different from the Western form of abstract logic. . . . How else have we managed to survive with such spiritedness the assault on our bodies, social institutions, countries, our very humanity?
>
> (Christian, 1988: 68)

It may be simplistic to say, with Martin Luther King, that we must judge a (wo)man not by whether (s)he is at the top or not, but by how far (s)he has climbed. We can take inspiration from the fact that despite hostile and inflexible barriers and hostility, Black people have so often survived and succeeded.

## BLACK PEOPLE IN THE UNITED STATES

Who do we mean when we say 'Black' in the context of the United States? As stated in Chapter 1, 'Black' is used in general in this book to refer to people of African origin. In the United States, in Federal government and other official data, 'Black' usually refers to non-Hispanic Blacks, that is, African-Americans, African-Caribbeans from islands colonised by the English and the French, and Africans (Farley and Allen, 1989; O'Hare *et al.*, 1991). Where the definitions used in collecting the data vary, these variations are indicated in the text.

**Demographic profiles**

Black people have always been a minority in the United States as a whole, though their particular pattern of settlement (both forced during slavery, and less forced since then) has been highly uneven and has led to large concentrations at the state and city level (Franklin, 1956). The data for the 1980s reflect the strong impact of a variety of historical forces which have pressed Black people into particular patterns.

At the start of the 1980s, the Black population totalled 26 million, constituting 11.7 per cent of a national population of 226,504,825 (Blackwell, 1985: 16). By the end of the decade:

> The 1990 Census counted 29,986,060 African-Americans, nearly 3.5 million more than in 1980. . . Blacks represented 12.1 per cent of the estimated 248.7 million Americans, up from 11.7 per cent in 1980. This percentage was the largest since 1880, when Blacks accounted for 13.1 per cent of the population.
>
> (O'Hare *et al.*, 1991: 4)

This means that during the 1980s the African-American population grew by 13 per cent, a rate more than double that for the white population (6 per cent), but far below the increase for Asians or Hispanics.[6] The growth rate is accounted for mainly by the higher birth rate of African-Americans, though 'between 1981 and 1989, 144,000 persons immigrated to the United States from Africa and 414,000 entered from Haiti, Jamaica, Trinidad and Tobago, and other predominately Black Caribbean islands' amounting to around 9.6 per cent of the 5.8 million legal immigrants to the United States during the 1980s (O'Hare *et al.*, 1991: 6). These numbers look set to grow in the 1990s and beyond: 'According to Census Bureau projects, the proportion of blacks in the population should continue to increase into the next century and may exceed 15 per cent by 2040' (ibid.: 4).

It has been calculated that by the late 1980s there were 300,000–500,000 Black/white 'biracial offspring' in the USA (Gibbs, 1989: 323). Njeri reported that in the 1980s there was an estimated one million 'mixed-race' children in America (a figure which includes the children of all 'people of colour' rather than just African-Americans (Njeri, 1988: 2). In the 1980 census there were 815,000 foreign-born Blacks, adding up to three per cent of the total Black population (Farley and Allen, 1989: 370). This number includes Hispanics that were foreign born and defined themselves as Black in the racialised identity question of the Census.[7]

African-Americans have a younger age structure than the US population generally – their median age of 27.7 years is 5 years younger than the median for the American population as a whole. In 1980, 40 per cent of the Black population, compared with 32 per cent of the population as a whole was below the age of 20 (Blackwell, 1985: 22). Because they are more likely to be in the childbearing age group this means the population will grow significantly in the next decade, even taking account of mortality.

At the start of the 1980s there were 6.1 million Black families (Farley and Allen, 1989: 167); by the end of the 1980s there were 10 million families. O'Hare *et al.* report that:

> The vast majority of the 10 million African-American households are family households (that is, the household members are related by birth, marriage, or adoption), (but) only about half the families were headed by a married couple in 1990, down from 68 per cent in 1970 and 56 per cent in 1980. A much higher percentage (83 per cent) of white families are headed by married couples, although this percentage also has slipped over the past two decades.
>
> (O'Hare *et al.*, 1991: 16)

They also relate that 'the average black household contained 2.9 persons in 1990, compared with 2.6 persons for all whites' (O'Hare *et al.*, 1991: 16). Most analysts agree that the proportion of families headed by women has dramatically increased, that it is likely to continue, and that it poses major problems for the Black community. For example:

> The share of African-American families maintained by women virtually doubled in the course of 25 years, from 22 percent in 1960 to 43 percent in 1988.
>
> (Amott and Matthaei, 1991: 183. See also O'Hare *et al.*, 1991)

This is significant because of the fact that 'just over half (55 percent) of black children lived in a single-parent household in 1990, 51 per cent with their mother. In contrast, 19 per cent of white children lived in single-parent households in 1989' and: 'More than a fourth (27 per cent) of all African-American children live with mothers who have never married' (O'Hare *et al.*, 1991: 19). This is crucial because female-headed families generally have fewer economic resources than married-couple families with nearly two-thirds poor and living in central cities, while over one quarter live in public housing (ibid.: 19). African-American babies are nearly four times more likely to be born to a single mother, and three times more likely to be born to a young teenage mother (ibid.: 11). For example, 'In 1988, 64 per cent of black babies were born out-of-wedlock, compared with 18 per cent of white babies' (ibid.: 11). This disproportionately high rate of teenage childbearing exacerbates social problems: 'Health problems, high infant mortality, educational deficiencies, long-term welfare dependency, and poverty are among the consequences risked by teens who have babies' (ibid.: 12). Teenage mothers are much less likely to be married, and, in a system which discriminates against women in education, training and employment, leaves them facing greater obstacles in their efforts to earn an income.

This contrasts starkly with the realities for the African-Americans that form two-parent families, so that:

> The 3.8 million black children living in two-parent families appear privileged in comparison. Their parents are more educated, earn nearly four times as much money, and are more than twice as likely to own their own home. These stark differences highlight the two separate worlds inhabited by poor and middle class black children, and suggest that the African-American population will become more polarized as these children mature.
>
> (O'Hare *et al.*, 1991: 20)

A debate about issues of female-headed families continues because such analysts are often accused of being Eurocentric (see O'Hare *et al.*, 1991). This debate concerns whether the current family structures which prevail in the Black community, especially the lower likelihood of marriage:

> Resulted directly from the disruptive effects of slavery; whether it is only indirectly associated with slavery through the continuing

economic marginalization of blacks; or whether black culture and social structure, emanating from African roots, lead to different marriage and family patterns.

(O'Hare *et al.*, 1991: 18)

There are implications for policy and political action, especially for strategies to challenge racialised disadvantage. But while this is academic for some (i.e. the analysts) it is life and death, survival versus success, for others (that is, the families). This is because, despite the problems facing nuclear families, the fact remains that in a society holding tenaciously to that ideal, and providing resources to maintain such an ideal, those who deviate from it find themselves at a greater disadvantage. The likelihood of being poor, unemployed and with less education is higher for precisely this reason. In other words, there is nothing inherently wrong with female-headed families, except that in a society where nuclear families are idealised, one is at a disadvantage.

Transgressing the racialised boundary of sexual relations may occasionally occur on a casual basis in the United States, but it infrequently translates into marriage. Overwhelmingly, Blacks still marry other Blacks: 'In 1987, only 3 per cent of married blacks had a non-black spouse. . . . When African-Americans do marry a non-black, it is usually the wife who is white, Asian, or of another race' (O'Hare *et al.*, 1991: 19). This is the lowest rate for any racialised group in the United States. For example, 'about 16 per cent of married Asians and Hispanics had a non-Asian or non-Hispanic spouse' (ibid.: 19).

## Residential patterns

The 1980 census revealed the continuing pattern of high rates of residential segregation which have characterised American society since its inception. The pattern of settlement of African-Americans is heavily urban, and within urban areas strictly segregated from whites. The majority of both Blacks and whites live in metropolitan areas, but they tend to live in different communities. For example, 'One-half of whites, compared with just over one-quarter of blacks, lived in suburban areas in 1990. . . . In 1970, just 16 per cent of blacks lived in suburban areas; in 1980, 23 per cent lived in the suburbs' (O'Hare *et al.*, 1991: 8). This is true, regardless of income. African-Americans are the most residentially isolated US minority group (ibid.: 9). In 1980, '58 per cent of Blacks lived in central cities, where they made up almost one-quarter of the population. In contrast, more than half of whites lived in the suburbs, compared to only 23 per cent of Blacks' (Amott and Matthaei, 1991: 180).

This pattern continued throughout the 1980s at both state and city level. For example, 'In 1990, 16 states had African-American populations of over 1 million, led by New York, California, Texas, and Florida – the 4 most populous states. . . . In contrast, 19 states are home to less than 100,000 blacks, most of them rural states in the West, the Great Plains, or New England' (O'Hare et al., 1991: 8). Thirty-one cities have African-American populations of 100,000 or greater, and twelve have at least 250,000 blacks. Among the 26 largest cities in the nation, the black population in 1980 had reached 40 per cent or more in 6 of them. The largest concentration of Blacks was in the following cities: New York, 1, 784,124; Chicago, 1, 197,000; Detroit, 758,939; Philadelphia, 638,878; Los Angeles, 505,208; and Washington DC, 448,229 (Blackwell, 1985: 18–19). By 1990, 'the percentage of blacks living in metropolitan areas stood at 84 per cent, compared with 76 per cent for whites' (O'Hare et al., 1991: 8).

One notable feature of residential change in the 1980s has been the decline of the Black 'middle class' in the inner cities. It has been argued that this was primarily the result of prosperous Blacks seeking residence in the suburbs, and employment elsewhere (Wilson, W., 1987). However, it is also now clearly true that a significant element in the shrinking of the Black 'middle-class' population in the inner cities has been caused by their downward economic mobility, as more and more Blacks have lost their 'middle class' jobs in the midst of the economic decline of their neighbourhoods (Amott and Matthaei, 1991: 183).

## Racialised wealth and poverty

One of the most distinctive features of African-Americans' economic fortunes in the 1980s has been growing economic polarisation, the widening split between rich and poor. This divergence in fortunes has attracted considerable attention with much talk of a rich 'middle class' and a poor 'underclass' (Wilson, 1978; Landry, 1987; O'Hare et al., 1991). O'Hare points out that few people define precisely what they mean by the terms 'middle class' and 'underclass' and suggests it is better to consider data on differences in wealth, income and earnings when assessing stratification within the Black population. Generally the picture that emerges is one that shows a significant section of Black people (especially younger and educated Blacks) with incomes and occupations matching their white counterparts, and a growing section of Blacks in poverty. Some of the rich Blacks are very rich. But it is important to note, however, that the rich whites are much richer than their Black counterparts, and that Blacks in poverty tend to be worse off, and to remain worse off for longer, than their white counterparts.

When it comes to wealth, there is a much bigger disparity between whites and African-Americans than most other measures of socioeconomic status: 'Blacks account for only 4 per cent of households with assets of $50,000 or more' and 'the median wealth of whites is higher than that of blacks at every income level' (O'Hare *et al.*, 1991: 30). Furthermore, while 'black income is roughly 60 per cent that of whites, the median net worth (total assets less liabilities) of black households in 1988 was only about one-tenth that of whites' (ibid.: 30). There are some African-Americans with sizeable incomes, yet they do not begin to match their counterparts in the white population. For example, 'Even among those (African-Americans) in the highest income quintile, blacks have less than half the wealth of whites. Only 16 per cent of black households had assets of $50,000 or more in 1988, compared with 47 per cent of white households' (ibid.: 30).

Data for 1989 reveal that 'the median annual income for black families was $20,200, a 6 per cent improvement over 1980 after adjusting for inflation, but slightly below the comparable figure for 1969' and 'Black family income was 61 per cent that of whites in 1969, but only 56 per cent as high in 1989' (O'Hare *et al.*, 1991: 27). Again, in 1989, '26 per cent of black families had incomes below $10,000, 32 per cent earned between $10,000 and $25,000, and 42 per cent received $25,000 or more per year' (ibid.: 27). Among whites, however, only '8 per cent of families had incomes under $10,000, while 69 per cent were in the $25,000 or over category' (ibid.: 28). And in the same year 'black female-headed families had only a third the annual income of black married-couple families, $11,600 compared with $30,700' (ibid.: 27).

Although their success has been overshadowed by the plight of poor Blacks, a growing number of Blacks have become affluent since 1980. Thus:

In families headed by younger blacks, especially those with a college degree, average income is almost as high for blacks as it is for whites. Among married-couple families where the head of household is 25 to 44 years old and a college graduate, the median income of blacks ($54,400) is 93 percent that of whites ($58,800).

(O'Hare *et al.*, 1991: 28)

Similarly, 'In 1989, nearly one in seven black families had an income of $50,000 or more' (O'Hare *et al.*, 1991: 29). This compares with almost one in three white families with incomes of $50,000 or more, a figure which was up from one in six white families in 1967 (ibid: 29). Affluent African-Americans 'tend to be well-educated (32 per cent are college graduates), home owners (77 per cent own their own home), in the prime-earning ages (66 per cent are age 35 to 55), married (79 per cent are married), and suburbanites. Also like affluent whites, most black families reach the $50,000 a year income level by combining earnings from two or more family members' (ibid: 29). But rich Blacks are not frequently super-rich: 'Less than 2 per cent of black adults have personal incomes in excess of $50,000 a year' (ibid.: 29).

At the opposite end of the economic spectrum Black people are more likely to be found in poverty, in the worst conditions of poverty, and to have greater difficulty escaping from poverty. O'Hare reports that 'The rate of poverty among blacks has been roughly three times the rate for whites over the past two decades' (O'Hare *et al.*, 1991: 31).[8] For example:

By the late-1980s, the share of Blacks who lived in poverty had increased; in 1988, nearly one-third of all Blacks lived in poverty. The share of Blacks who were very poor – living on less than half of poverty-line income – increased by 69 per cent between 1978 and 1987. Blacks are far less likely to escape poverty than whites: a Black person's chances of being persistently poor in the late-1980s were eight times higher than those of a white person.

(Amott and Matthaei, 1991: 190)

Poverty has become even more concentrated. 'Between 1980 and 1990, the number of blacks living in high-poverty areas (defined as census tracts with at least 20 per cent of the residents in poverty) jumped by 19 per cent, while the black population as a whole grew by 13 per cent' (O'Hare *et al.*, 1991: 9).

In addition 'Poor blacks are poorer than poor whites. . . and are also more likely to be poor for long periods' (O'Hare *et al.*, 1991, p. 31). 'In 1989, the average poor black family had an income $5,100 below the poverty line, while the average poor white family had an income only $4,000 below it' and '28 per cent of whites who were poor in 1985 moved out of poverty within a year, while only 17 per cent of poor blacks escaped poverty during that year' (O'Hare *et al.*, 1991: 31–2). A major contributing factor has been that many cities in the 1980s faced budget crises, and with African-Americans overwhelmingly an urban population these budget crises resulted in devastating losses of crucial human services and well-being. Since the public sector employs a disproportionate share of Blacks, lay offs in the state and local governments hit Blacks especially hard.

### Patterns of employment

Patterns of employment for African-Americans during the 1980s have not been good. For example, 'Between 1981 and 1985, 5 per cent of Black men and 6 per cent of Black women lost their jobs as a result of plant closings alone' (Amott and Matthaei, 1991: 180). 'The percentage of black men in the labor force began to drop after 1970, with the decline accelerating after 1980. In 1990, 70 per cent of black men age 16 and older were in the labor force, compared with 77 per cent of white men'. In 1990, 58 per cent of both African-Amercian and white women aged 16 and older were in the labor force (O'Hare *et al.*, 1991: 23).

Fifteen per cent of Black men and 30 per cent of white men worked in an executive, administrative, managerial or professional speciality in 1980 (Farley and Allen, 1989: 276). For women the proportion was 19 per cent for Blacks and 26 per cent for whites (ibid. 1987: 276). This pattern continued throughout the decade so that 'In 1990, white men were twice as likely as black men to hold a job in administration, management, or a profession. Conversely, black men were more likely to work as semi-skilled laborers and twice as likely as white men to hold service jobs' (O'Hare *et al.*, 1991: 24). The situation facing Black woman was comparable:

In 1990, 19 per cent of black women were in managerial and professional occupations, and 39 per cent were in technical or administrative. While these percentages are well below those of white women in higher paying jobs, the gaps are narrower than they are for men.

(O'Hare *et al.*, 1991: 25)

Black women in managerial and professional jobs are more likely to be found in the public sector than the private sector. For example, 'Sixty per cent of Black managerial and professional women in the 15 cities with the highest Black populations worked for national, state, or local government, compared with only 31 per cent of white women managers and professionals' (Amott and Matthaei, 1991: 187).

Black-owned businesses have grown in number dramatically since 1972, but with minimal impact on the economic status of the Black community. They grew in number from 187,600 in 1972 to 424,200 in 1987 (a 126 per cent increase). But most of these new businesses were very small firms. Only 17 per cent of Black-owned firms in 1987 had any paid employees, and less than 1 per cent had more than 100 employees. Average receipts for a Black-owned firm totalled $46,600 per year. Indeed, Blacks remain heavily under-represented among business owners. And African-Americans own only about 3 per cent of the nation's firms, a number whose total receipts are only about 1 per cent of business receipts (O'Hare *et al.*, 1991: 26).

The unemployment rate was 11.8 per cent for Black men, in 1990, compared with 4.8 per cent for white men. Teenage African-American women faced the highest unemployment rate – 47 per cent – of any racialised group (Amott and Matthaei, 1991: 180). Blacks also remain unemployed for longer periods than did whites, accounting for approximately 30 per cent of the long-term un-employed, that is persons without work for at least 27 consecutive weeks (O'Hare *et al.*, 1991: 23). This figure is actually an under-estimate as it excluded persons in prison – with Blacks adding up to nearly half of the inmates in state and federal prisons (ibid.: 24).

These patterns were reflected in particular areas of employment. For example, in education, data from the Tenth Annual Status Report on Minorities in Higher education published in 1992 by the American Council on Education presents a 'bleak commentary' on the lack of progress of minorities into senior posts. In particular African-American faculty continued to be confined to the lower end of the professional ladder in positions such as assistant professor, instructor and lecturer.[9] Between 1979 and 1989 the total number of full-time employees in higher education increased by 20.8 per cent from 1.5 million to 1.8 million. The number of minorities overall went up in the same period from 17.7 per cent to 20.3 per cent. Within faculty positions (teaching) there has been little change, from 9 per cent at the end of the 1970s to 11.5 per cent in 1989. There have been major differences between minorities with least progress made by African-Americans. In 1989 African-Americans were 4.5 per cent of full-time faculty compared with 4.3 per cent in 1979. Nearly half of all African-American Faculty (47.7 per cent) are employed at historically Black colleges and universities.

African-Americans' share of the US labour force is projected to increase from 10 to 12 per cent by the year 2000, and they will contribute up to 20 per cent of the new entrants to the labour force (O'Hare *et al.*, 1991: 26). These jobs will not, however, be in managerial, professional, and technical occupations and the fear is that the US economy will become more and more a two-tier economy.

**Educational attainment**

The circumstances of African-Americans reveal patterns of segregation, concentration in inferior facilities with limited resources, and limited records of attainment. Black children add up to about 16 per cent of the nation's public-school students and they constitute a majority in many of the nation's public-school districts. At the end of the 1980s they were around 90 per cent in Atlanta, Detroit, and Washington, DC, and nearly 40 per cent in New York City (O'Hare *et al.*, 1991: 20). For example:

> In 1986, fully 27.5 per cent of all black school children, and 30 percent of all Hispanic school children, were enrolled in the twenty-five largest central-city school districts. Only 3.3 percent of all white students were in these same twenty-five districts.
>
> (Edsall and Edsall, 1991a: 228)

By 1987 about 83 per cent of young black adults, and 86 per cent of young whites, had finished high school.[10] Those Blacks that do stay on at school tend to earn lower grades, score below the national average on standardised tests, and are much more likely to be suspended or expelled because of discipline problems than are white students.

The percentage of Blacks in college throughout the 1980s stayed steady at around 20 per cent while the college attendance among whites continued to expand. In 1988, 21 per cent of Blacks were enrolled in college compared with 31 per cent of whites (O'Hare *et al.*, 1991: 22). By the late 1980s Black women were more likely to attend college than Black men. The figure for Blacks at college in the 1970s was around 23 per cent. And while about 20 per cent of whites ultimately earned a degree, only 11 per cent of Blacks did so (ibid.: 22).

### Health

While average life expectancy for white Americans continued to improve in the 1980s, it became stagnant for Black women and actually dropped among Black men. O'Hare *et al.* report that 'overall life expectancy for black males was 64.9 years, more than eight years short of that for black women (73.4 years), and seven years below that of white men (72.3)' (1991: 12). They add 'An African-American child born in 1988 can expect to live, on average, 69.2 years. This is six years less than the average for a white child born the same year – 75.6 years' (ibid.: 12). The situation reflected in other data was even more grim. For example:

> Blacks die at higher rates than whites at every age below age 85. Most of the excess black mortality is attributed to higher black infant mortality plus higher rates of death from eight major causes: accidents, homicides, heart disease, stroke, liver disease, cancer, diabetes, and Aids.
>
> (O'Hare *et al.*, 1991: 13)

Furthermore, Black babies are twice as likely to die as white babies: 'In 1988, the infant mortality rate (IMR) for blacks was 17.6 infant deaths per 1,000 live births, compared with 8.5 for whites' (O'Hare *et al.*, 1991: 13).

The diet and lifestyle of African-Americans also contribute to the risk of heart disease in ways that it does not for white Americans. O'Hare *et al.* report that 'Blacks are more likely than whites to die from 13 of the 15 major causes of death. . . . Heart disease and cancer are the leading causes of death for both blacks and whites' (1991: 14). They add:

> The most striking mortality difference between blacks and whites

is for homicide. The homicide death rate is six times higher for blacks than for whites, with black men especially vulnerable. The chances of a black man being murdered are 4 times higher than for a black woman, 7 times higher than for a white man, and 20 times higher than for a white woman. Homicide is the leading cause of death for younger black men. In 1988, nearly 5,000 African-American men 15 to 29 years old were murdered. For whites, Asians and other races, accidents, primarily automobile-related, are the major cause of death among young men.

(O'Hare *et al.*, 1991: 14)

While some of these differences can be explained in relation to the young age structure of African-Americans most stem from chronic social and economic problems. Alcohol and drug abuse, access to handguns and firearms, a higher death rate from Aids (three times higher than for whites), cigarette smoking and obesity.

**Housing circumstances**

Throughout the 1980s there was a clear pattern of disparity in the ownership of homes, and in their values. A smaller proportion of Blacks than whites were likely to own their homes, and among those that owned homes, Blacks owned houses of inferior quality. For example, at the start of the 1980s '68% of white households, and only 44% of black households owned their own homes' (Farley and Allen, 1989: 155). Although ownership of a home is the 'single largest asset for most Americans' nevertheless, the rate of home ownership among African-Americans was two-thirds that of the population generally throughout the 1980s and amongst this group the equity in their homes was only 60 per cent of the national average (O'Hare *et al.*, 1991: 30). In 1987 the media value of homes owned by whites was $69,300, while for African-Americans it was $48,800 (O'Hare *et al.*, 1991: 30). Furthermore, Black people paid more on average for their housing than whites (Blackwell, 1985); and substantial numbers of Black people were homeless.

Income differentials and personal preferences explained part of these disparities, but the major explanation for them is to be found in the factors underlying residential segregation (as described above) and in the animosity expressed by non-Blacks towards Black people living outside certain restricted areas.

## Political representation and participation

African-Americans were virtually excluded from political office in the United States until the 1950s and 1960s, the long list of recent 'firsts' (including first Black mayor of New York in 1989) reflecting this fact. Dramatic increases were made in the 1960s to 1990s when the proportion of Blacks holding political office increased by several thousand per cent. This phenomenal increase has now ended and though huge gains were still made in the 1980s, the overall advance was slow. By the end of the 1980s, African-Americans represented only a tiny fraction of the membership in city, state, and federal legislative bodies. The number of Blacks holding elective office went up from 4,311 (0.9 per cent of all elected officials in the country) in 1977 to 6,681 (1.3 per cent of all elected officials) in 1987 (O'Hare *et al.*, 1991: 34). This number increased to 7, 226 by 1989 (ibid.: 34). At the same time there were about two dozen black mayors of cities larger than 100,000 people by the mid-1980s (Polhmann, 1990: 142). The political colour of Black elected officials tends to be Democrat, but there are some key, and highly publicised, Black Republicans, as will be seen in Chapter 4.

The first thing to note about voting in the United States is that both Black and white Americans vote at lower rates than their counterparts in virtually every other democracy in the world (Pohlmann, 1990: 134). For example, Black turnout was lower than 50 per cent in the 1988 presidential elections (ibid.: 135). In addition,

> Less than one-half of all registered blacks voted in the most recent presidential elections; scarcely more than one-third normally vote in either congressional primaries or congressional general elections. . .the numbers normally fall somewhere in between for elections at the state and local levels.
>
> (Pohlmann, 1990: 134)

Black people are less likely to be politically active than whites, and 'their overall voting rate has continued to lag some 5 percentage points behind that of whites' (Pohlmann, 1990: 134). But the story is different when account is taken of Black and white socioeconomic status. When socioeconomic status is compared, 'blacks register and vote at higher rates' (ibid.: 134).

African-Americans 'are overwhelmingly allied with the Democratic party, and they tend to support African-American candidates'

(O'Hare *et al.*, 1991: 33). For example, in 1986 more than half of all Blacks over thirty years of age expressed a 'strong' commitment to the Democratic party, as did one third of those under thirty (Pohlmann, 1990: 140). By the end of the 1980s Blacks were casting a full 25 per cent of Democratic presidential candidate votes (Pohlmann, 1990: 142). Jesse Jackson played a crucial role in mobilising Black votes for the Democrats in the 1980s. In 1984, he garnered 16 per cent of the Democratic primary vote (more than 3 million votes) and gained nearly 400 convention delegates. In 1988, he did even better, winning more than 29 per cent of the primary vote (nearly 7 million votes) and gaining over 1,000 convention delegates (ibid.: 141).

**Racialised interpretations of the 'Colour Line'**

A further major dimension of the 'Colour Line' as experienced in the two nations concerns how Blacks and whites interpret and explain these very real differences in their circumstances and experiences. Are Blacks and whites aware of the sharp disparities that exist? Where they are aware, how do they explain them and how far are there common points of view and interpretations? Though there are variations across surveys, there is clear evidence of commonalities across the United States. Blacks and whites clearly express attitudes that suggest they are living in quite different worlds.

A national survey carried out in 1989 showed that there is a major gulf which divides how white and Black Americans understand the realities of 'racialised relations' in their nation. For example, when asked about incomes 'two-thirds of the whites surveyed believe black people get equal pay for equal work, while two-thirds of blacks believe just the opposite' (*San Francisco Tribune*, 1989: A-4). With regard to housing '55 per cent of whites said blacks are not worse off than other groups with comparable education and income, but 64 per cent of blacks believe they are worse off' (*San Francisco Tribune*, 1989: A-4). When asked about the police 'half of the black people surveyed say local police keep blacks down, while an equal percentage of white people say police are more helpful than harmful to blacks' (*San Francisco Tribune*, 1989: A-4). A national poll carried out by *Newsweek* revealed that 29 per cent of whites and 71 per cent of Blacks said that the federal government was doing too little to help Blacks (*Newsweek*, 1988: 23). In addition, 34 per cent of whites and 66 per cent of Blacks believe Black people are charged with crimes more harshly than white people.

What the evidence suggests therefore is that there is sharp divergence in the kinds of assumptions whites and Blacks make about each other's circumstances in the United States. Where they are aware of major differences in their circumstances and experiences, they tend to explain them in very different ways. In general a greater proportion of whites locate the problem in Blacks, and a greater proportion of Blacks locate the problem in whites. That is, whites suggest that Blacks do not try hard enough, are responsible for their own failures in education and employment, are too quick to blame racialised discrimination, do not recognise the burdens and obstacles that whites themselves face, and are appealing to 'illegitimate' privileges such as affirmative action and preferential treatment. This is particulary evident among working-class whites. For example, such attitudes were common at the University of Massachusetts, Amherst, where the vast majority of white students hail from the Greater Boston area, and many of them are the first in their families to attend university (Student Affairs Research and Evaluation Office, 1987; Harvey and McArdle, 1989). One dimension to this is the fact that significant, if small, numbers of African-Americans are doing well, some very well. This is evident to whites in the areas noted below (sport and music) but also in areas such as business, the professions and politics. Walk down Wall Street in New York City and you will see Black lawyers, businessmen and women; watch the television and you can see Black people proclaiming that they made it to the top all on their own. All around are signs of Black success. These successes militate against any simplistic portrayal of Black circumstances, and indicate the kinds of problems likely to be encountered in getting whites to recognise the immense structural obstacles to Black survival and success.

These attitudes have been particularly fuelled by the opinionated stance taken by President Reagan and by his appointees, especially Black appointees, to policy positions. Reagan accused Civil Rights Leaders of inventing racialised discrimination in order to keep their jobs, and suggested Blacks should try harder and moan less (Omi and Winant, 1986). Key Black advisers like Thomas Sowell and Clarence Pendleton joined in the chorus. Sowell in particular argued that 'West Indian' immigrants to the United States were more successful than African-Americans and that this in part reflected the greater individual effort and initiative on their part, and the corresponding lethargy and inaction of African-Americans (Sowell, 1983). Shelby Steele echoed this chorus at the end of the 1980s (Steele, 1990).

Most Blacks claim that the main obstacles they must confront arise from the persistence of racialised hostility and discrimination, as well as from the legacy of past discrimination. They add that Black people of all classes continue to face obstacles which no white person must face. These divergent interpretations of racialised inequality mean that when it comes to tackling the problems, both groups start from very different points of view, and find very different policies appealing. This is taken up in Chapter 5, in the discussion of policies to achieve racialised integration, harmony and parity.

## BLACK PEOPLE IN ENGLAND

To whom are we referring exactly when we talk about 'Black people' in England? In this book reference to Black people in England means people of African origin, that is, African-Caribbeans and Africans.[11] Racialised data (usually referred to in England as 'ethnic' data) have only recently been collected in a comprehensive way. The first question on such data occurred in the 1991 Census. There have been a number of national and local surveys, and these provide detailed data, and offer the possibility for cross-checks (Brown, 1984; *Labour Force Survey, 1989*). Even more than with the United States, variations occur in definitions used in the collection of data. Most data have been collected for African-Caribbeans (usually referred to as West Indians/Guyanese) though account is increasingly being taken of Africans (people born in Africa, or of African origin without any family relationship with the Caribbean) (*Labour Force Survey, 1991*).[12] Some surveys provide data which draw distinctions between Africans and African-Caribbeans (Haskey, 1989; Skellington *et al.*, 1992); others exclude Africans (Brown, 1984). It is unusual for surveys of Black people to cover only Africans.[13] Most data on African-Caribbeans are for Britain as a whole, with few studies focusing only on England. The overwhelming majority of African-Caribbeans live in England.

In the following sections I indicate the definitions being used by the various sources of data collection in an attempt to indicate whether Africans are included or not. For the purposes of the analysis of racialised barriers, boundaries and identities being undertaken in this book, the inclusion of Africans in the overall data does not greatly distort the general picture. They may be better off in general than African-Caribbeans, but they are certainly subjected to similar kinds of racialised hostility as others defined as Black.

## Demographic profiles

In 1981 the total Black population was just about 700,000, including 550,000 African-Caribbeans, 123,000 Africans, and 26,000 so-called 'British Born Blacks', from England's long-standing Black communities such as Liverpool and Bristol (Bhat *et al.*, 1988). Most of the African-Caribbean population was from the British West Indies (Jamaica, Trinidad, Guyana, Barbados, etc.) while the Africans were mainly from West and East Africa. A closer look at African-Caribbeans reveals that 47 per cent of the African-Caribbean population in the early 1980s was born in the England (*Labour Force Survey, 1982*: 33). Data from the 1991 Census, the first to have a question on 'ethnicity' indicate the size of the Black population at the end of the 1980s (Owen, 1992).[14] These data indicate that there were 496,000 African-Caribbeans, 203,200 Africans, and 172,900 'other' Black people in England (Owen, 1992: 1). For all persons of African-Caribbean ancestry about 12 per cent were of 'mixed African-Caribbean/White ethnic group', with a much larger proportion of this mixed group being young (*Population Trends*, 1985: 8).[15]

As a group of largely recent immigration – over 97 per cent of Blacks in the United States were born there, but less than 50 per cent of Blacks in England were born there – Blacks in England have faced a number of distinct problems not faced by African-Americans. One problem is the racialised nature of immigration legislation which has increasingly restricted their entry to the country. The legislation is incredibly complex, but most analysts are agreed that the general intention has been to 'keep Blacks out' of the country (Ben-Tovim *et al.*, 1982; Miles and Phizacklea, 1984). Another problem is the perception on the part of white English people that Black people are somehow 'not English' even if born in England. Englishness and Blackness are seen as incompatible, though the English are sometimes ambivalent. American essayist Paul Theroux captured the contradictions and hypocrisy involved in English terminology about Blacks:

Policemen were 'colored', convicted criminals were 'West Indian', and purse-snatchers were 'nig-nogs'. But when a black runner came first in a race against foreigners, he was 'English'. If he came second, he was 'British'. If he lost, he was 'colored'. If he cheated, he was 'West Indian'.

(Paul Theroux, cited in Small, 1989c)

The problems facing Blacks as immigrants go much further than name-calling. The immigration legislation, designed unashamedly to block Black people's entry to England, reveals the venality and dishonesty of the English at its worst. The intricacies of the immigration legislation and the 'race relations' legislation are simplified in the slogan 'Love thy neighbour, who shouldn't be here in the first place'. The immigration legislation implies Blacks are a problem in and of themselves and should not be allowed into England; the 'race relations' legislations suggests they must be treated as equals (Miles and Phizacklea, 1984).

The Black population reveals a larger number of young people than the white population. In the first half of the 1980s, just under half of the African-Caribbeans were aged under 20 (Coleman, 1985: 8). By the end of the 1980s, 32 per cent of African-Caribbeans (and 29 per cent of Africans) were aged between 16 and 29. This was slightly higher than the total for all ethnic minority groups for this age group, which was 27 per cent (Labour Force Survey, 1989).

The total number of families in Great Britain in 1985–7 was 15,238,000 (Haskey, 1989: 12).[16] African-Caribbean families added up to less than one per cent of all families in Great Britain (ibid.: 12). The total number of African-Caribbean families was 144,000, while the total number of African families was 28,000 (ibid.: 12). A total of 112,000 (1 per cent) of all couples in Britain are ethnically mixed, of whom 29,000 have an African-Caribbean member of the couple, and 21,000 have a person of mixed origins (*Labour Force Survey, 1987*: 38). Brown reported that at the start of the 1980s one-third of African-Caribbean households were headed by women (Brown, 1984: 38). By the end of the 1980s, four in every ten African-Caribbean families, and two in every ten African families, were headed by a female (Haskey, 1989: 13). In general, households headed by persons of African-Caribbean and African ethnic origin each tend to contain approximately the same number of people as in white-headed households (ibid.: 10).

The composition of Black and white families differed significantly. While almost half of white families contained only two persons, only one-third of African-Caribbean families (and one-sixth of African families) had two persons (Haskey, 1989: 11). On average, Black families contained 2.2 dependent children, whereas white families contain 1.8 (Haskey, 1989: 12). By the late 1980s over 20 per cent of African-Caribbean couples were couples with dependent children (*Social Trends*, 1992: 42). The highest proportion of families which are lone parent families is among African-Caribbean families (42 per cent) while 24 per cent of African families were lone parent families (Haskey, 1989: 12–13). The lowest proportion of married couple families is found among African-Caribbeans; six in every ten African-Caribbean families are married couple families. The highest proportions of lone mother families was to be found amongst African-Caribbean, African (and mixed ethnic origin) families. It was also true that lone father families were relatively more common amongst these groups (ibid.: 15).

## Residential patterns

The residential distribution of the African-Caribbean population in the 1980s was more or less set by 1961 (Smith, 1989: 27). In general, Black people were more likely to be urban, and more likely to live in certain sections of the inner city. Urban residential segregation between Blacks and whites increased in the 1980s (Rex, 1988: 31). For example, Smith reported that only around 3 per cent of ethnic minorities (in contrast to the national average of 24 per cent) lived in rural enumeration districts. What this means is that around half of the white population lives in neighbourhoods which have no Black residents, while only about 1 in 16 whites live in an enumeration district with a 'coloured immigrant' population of 5 per cent or more (Smith, 1989: 33).

Compared to the overall numbers, the settlement of Blacks reveals quite a paradoxical pattern. While the total number of Black people is small, the fact that they are heavily concentrated in certain cities, especially London, gives the impression that there are many more in the country than is really the case. To begin with, in 1981 98 per cent of Blacks lived in England, with 1 per cent each in Scotland and Wales. At the same time around 65 per cent of Blacks (and 56 per cent of all minorities) lived in one area (the south-east, including London). London on its own is unique and its population makes the figures for the south-east high. Over half of all African-Caribbeans in the country live in London (Smith, 1989). Data from the *Labour Force Survey* are available for the Black population for the period 1987–91 (*Labour Force Survey, 1991*). In this period we see that 81 per cent of the African population and 81 per cent of the African-Caribbean population lived in the metropolitan counties (*Labour Force Survey, 1991*: 25).[17] At the same time, 58 per cent of the African-Caribbean population lived in Greater London, as did 74 per cent of the African population (*Labour Force Survey, 1991*: 25–6). By way of contrast, two-fifths of all 'Afro-Caribbeans' and merely 6 per cent of all whites lived in inner urban areas (Smith, 1989: 43). For example, 43 per cent of 'Afro-Caribbeans' but only 6 per cent of whites, lived in the inner city zones of London, Birmingham and Manchester (ibid.: 34).

Although a similar language is used in England to that of the United States to describe the residential settlement of Black people (for example, 'ghetto') the numbers are of a very different order (Rex, 1988). A distinctive feature of the US situation is the high concentration of Blacks in major cities. It has become expected and accepted that there are, and should continue to be, viable Black communities. Not so in England, where the areas reputed to have Black concentrations, and often called 'ghettos', invariably have more whites in them than Blacks. Brixton is regarded as the Harlem of London; yet only around 30 per cent of this small neighbourhood is minority (a significant proportion of them Asian). Despite the fact that the minority population is heavily concentrated in London it still adds up to less than 12 per cent of the city's 8 million people. The neighbourhood of Toxteth in Liverpool, which experienced the most destructive rioting in 1981, has no more than 20 per cent Blacks. If you want to find concentrations higher than that you have to come down to the level of blocks. There simply are no mass concentrations of Blacks in England like those found in the United States.

## Racialised wealth and poverty

There are no clear data distinguishing the proportion of whites and Blacks in poverty in England as there are in the United States. Estimates of their numbers must come from proxy indicators such as unemployment, low pay, and rates of claiming benefits (the data on unemployment are provided in the following sections).

Though they must be interpreted, their conclusions are all suggestive of circumstances of significant disadvantage for Black people in general, and a situation in which Black people are relatively worse off than whites. For example, Black males earned 10–15 per cent less than whites in the early 1980s (Brown, 1984). White men earned substantially more than Black men, with the median earnings for white men being about £20 higher than for African-Caribbean men (Brown, 1984).

Another indicator was that of dependence on social security benefits. Almost twice as many African-Caribbean households as compared with white households were likely to be reliant on child benefits during the 1980s. Brown found that 60 per cent of African-Caribbean households, as compared with 34 per cent of white households were more reliant on child benefits (Brown, 1984: 242). In general, Black people eligible for benefits were less likely to claim them than were whites, therefore this figure must be regarded as an underestimate.

**Patterns of employment**

During the 1980s white men and women were more likely to be in employment than Black men and women (Brown, 1984; *Labour Force Survey, 1991*: 27). When in employment, Black people typically occupied lower status jobs than their white counterparts. For example, Brown found that 67 per cent of white men were in work, compared with 64 per cent of African-Caribbeans (Brown, 1984: 150). And he relates that 35 per cent of African-Caribbean men as compared with only 16 per cent of whites were employed as semi- or unskilled manual workers (Brown, 1984). Around 85 per cent of African-Caribbean males were economically active in the late 1980s. The figure for females was 76 per cent (*Employment Gazette*, 1991: 61). In the late 1980s, 71 per cent of African-Caribbean men were to be found in manual jobs as opposed to 56 per cent of all ethnic groups (*Labour Force Survey, 1991*: 27).

In general the levels of jobs done by whites were much higher than those of African-Caribbeans (Brown, 1984: 157) though the 1980s saw some moderate advances into higher occupational categories by Black people. Most gains were made in the public sector with the opening up of jobs in local government, particularly those to do with 'race relations' units and related work. For example, a national minority ethnic group monitoring survey of the civil service in May 1990 found that only 2.3 per cent of ethnic minority employees were to be found in the grade of executive officer and above, while only 1.5 per cent were in the grade of principal officer and above. These data include all minorities (Skellington *et al.*, 1992: 133). A survey by MP Greville Janner found that minorities filled only 207 of the 18,644 posts in the top 7 civil service grades (Skellington *et al.*, 1992: 133). The Department of Employment reported the number of white and minority employees in managerial and professional occupational groups and gender, for the years 1987–9. For men, 35 per cent of white employees, as compared with 17 per cent of African-Caribbean employees occupied such categories. For women the equivalent figure was 27 per cent for white women, and 31 per cent for African-Caribbean women (Skellington *et al.*, 1992: 142). The reason there appears such a higher percentage of African-Caribbean women in such categories is explained by the fact that nurses are included. Brown reported the proportion in the top SEG category as 19 per cent for whites and only 5 per cent for African-Caribbeans. The proportion of whites in other 'non-manual' jobs was double that for African-Caribbeans (Brown, 1984: 157).

One indicator of high-ranking occupations is the category of self-employment, though it often hides more than it reveals (because it collapses such a disparate range of jobs and responsibilities). In his 1982 survey, Brown reported that for men, self-employment ran at the level of 14 per cent of whites and 7 per cent of African-Caribbeans (Brown, 1984). For women it was 7 per cent for whites and 1 per cent for African-Caribbeans (Brown, 1984: 165). Amongst the top categories of employees Brown reported for men 'the proportion in the top SEG category in the table (employers, managers and professional workers) is 19 per cent for whites and only five per cent for West Indians' (Brown, 1984). For women, the proportion in the top SEG was only 1 per cent (with 52 per cent in the 'other non-manual' category) (Brown, 1984: Table 92, 198).

Further data are available from the *Labour Force Survey* (*Employment Gazette*, 1983, 1987). For the years 1989–91 the *Labour Force Survey* reports the following findings: for African-Caribbean men there was 4 per cent in the professional category, 8 per cent in employers/ managers and 18 per cent for other non-manual. For women, the numbers were too small to report for the professional category, with 9 per cent for employers/managers and 51 per cent in other non-manual, the latter again reflecting the large numbers of such women in nursing (*Labour Force Survey, 1991*: Table 6.35, 36).

African-Caribbeans are over-represented at the other end of the occupational hierarchy. For example, only 58 per cent of white men were manual workers as compared with 83 per cent of African-Caribbeans (Brown, 1984: 157). Rates of unemployment among Black people were also higher than for whites (taking account of qualifications and experience) at all times during the 1980s. This is true for each age group, and for both genders. In the latter half of the 1980s, a period of very high general unemployment, the disparity was greatest. In general it was about twice as high among African-Caribbeans as amongst whites. Among men in the PSI survey, the unemployment rates were 13 per cent for whites, 25 per cent for African-Caribbeans (Brown, 1984: 151). The highest unemployment rates are for men in ethnic minority groups with no qualifications (*Labour Force Survey, 1991*: 27). Similar findings were reported for the late 1980s (ibid., 1991: 27).

**Educational attainment**

In general schools in England are not segregated in ways that compare with the United States. However, because of the over-whelming concentration of Black people in a small number of cities it is not unusual for there to be comparatively high concentrations of Black schoolchildren in certain areas. For example, in the inner city area of Handsworth over 90 per cent of pupils at all the secondary schools are from minority groups (though this figure includes other non-Black people of colour) (Rex, 1988: 32). Data on success in education once again reveals considerable racialised disparities. For example, only 38 per cent of African-Caribbean men have qualifications beyond CSE (Certificate of Secondary Education), and among these, relatively few go beyond Ordinary Level.[18] The comparable figures for African-Caribbean women are 41 per cent and 6 per cent (Brown, 1984: 147).

Among the age group 25–44 years, 13 per cent of African-Caribbean men and 18 per cent of African-Caribbean women had obtained Ordinary (O) Level qualifications; 5 per cent of both African-Caribbean men and women had obtained Advanced (A) Level qualifications, but not a degree; and 3 per cent of African-Caribbean men and 1 per cent of African-Caribbean women had a degree or higher degree (Brown, 1984: 147).[19] Among the age group 16–24 years, 32 per cent of African-Caribbean males had O Levels, and 6 per cent of males had A Levels. Among African-Caribbean men less than 0.5 per cent had a degree while for African-Caribbean women it was 0 per cent (Brown, 1984). More than twice as many minority young people stayed on in full-time education than did white people (this is all minorities, not just Blacks). For males aged 16–24 the figure was 33 per cent as compared with 11 per cent, for females in the same age group the figure was 24 per cent as compared with 12 per cent (Skellington *et al.*, 1992: 127). This higher than average figure disguises the fact that many do not go on to higher education – some are retaking courses for qualifications they have failed to get, and others are on 'low status' courses.

The Council for National Academic Awards carried out a survey of first degree graduates (excluding education degrees) in 1987 and found that 6 per cent of graduates were from minority groups (Skellington *et al.*, 1992: 127). It is unlikely that a significant proportion of these were Black. In 1990 the Polytechnic Central Admission System published its first breakdown of the ethnicity of its applicants that were permanently resident in the United Kingdom. A total of 76.7 per cent (131,452) were white, 1.4 per cent (2,441) Black Caribbean, 1.2 per cent (2,072) Black African, and 0.4 per cent other Black (653) (Skellington *et al.*, 1992: 128). These figures are especially low if one considers the higher proportion of young people among the Black population. The University Central Council on Admissions published the results of its first ethnic monitoring survey of university applicants in 1991. It revealed that minority students were just 1 per cent of the university population (inclusive of all minorities) (Skellington *et al.*, 1992: 129). Again, Blacks would be a tiny percentage of this figure. This emphasises that despite much larger numbers staying on in higher education, Black students are not well represented, and certainly not over-represented, in universities. In addition, research data reveal a high drop-out rate for African-Caribbean students: at least 25 per cent of African-Caribbean students taking degree courses did not take their final examinations (Skellington *et al.*, 1992: 129). This compares with a rate of white completion of around 97 per cent.

## Health

Successive research reports have revealed that for the Black population generally, there is clear evidence of inequality in the utilisation of health services, particularly preventative services (Bhat *et al.*,

1988: 201). In regard to the particular health obstacles that Black people confront (for example, sickle cell disease), the National Health Service and government response was either lukewarm or absent (ibid.: 202).

The average maternal mortality rate in the Black population is three times greater than that in the white population. The still birth perinatal and infant mortality rates were higher for Blacks than whites – even allowing for maternal age structure. Some of these rates have deteriorated for members of the African-Caribbean community (Bhat *et al.*, 1988: 201). In 1980, for example, there was a sharp increase in perinatal and infant mortality rates for mothers born in the Caribbean (ibid.: 181). These rates have also been decreasing faster for mothers born in England as compared with mothers born in countries from which most Black people in England originate (ibid.: 181). Overall perinatal mortality rate declined from approximately 96 in 1983 to about 93 in 1984. The comparable rates for African-Caribbean mothers were 83 and 84 (ibid.: 183). Males and females born in the African Commonwealth reveal the most strikingly high Standardized Mortality Ratios (SMRs) for all causes (ibid.: 179). It is also the case that complications in pregnancy are greater, as is the incidence of low birth weight, with its implications of aberrant child development (ibid.: 201). African-Caribbean women born in the Caribbean were more likely to consult for serious illnesses than were women born in England (*Population Trends*, 1990: 8).

## Housing circumstances

A series of studies have documented major disparities in the ownership of homes and evidence of direct and indirect racialised discrimination in mortgage lending throughout the 1980s (Smith, 1989; Ginsburg, 1992). Black people were also adversely affected by changes in the housing legislation, and were more likely to be homeless. In many instances Black women, particularly Black single mothers, were worse affected (Ginsburg, 1992). Overall, Black people were disproportionately likely to live in the country's most deprived and disadvantaged neighbourhoods (Brown, 1984).

At the start of the 1980s, over half of all white households but just a quarter of Black households lived in detached or semi-detached houses, while half the whites as compared with 60 per

cent of African-Caribbeans lived in dwellings built before 1945
(Smith, 1989: 41). In addition, Black people were two or three times
more likely than whites to live in homes without gardens (ibid.: 42).
This pattern of disadvantage is reflected in the expressed attitudes
of each group. Thus, over half the white population as compared
with only one-third of the African-Caribbean community claimed
to be very satisfied with their then present home (ibid.: 42).

These outcomes were not the result of choices or of uncontrollable
and impersonal market forces, but arose as a result of direct and
indirect discrimination practised by housing officials and estate
agents. For example, an investigation of the Liverpool City Housing
Department by the Commission for Racial Equality found clear
evidence of Black people being allocated to less desirable properties
(Commission for Racial Equality, 1989). Similar conclusions were
reached in Hackney (London), Nottingham and Bedford (Ginsburg,
1992: 114). Part of this was the result of 'informal administrative
discretion by housing officers' in ways which 'intentionally and
unintentionally disadvantaged black people' (ibid.: 116). There was
also evidence of stereotyping and assumptions that 'West Indians will
only want to buy in areas where their community is concentrated,
and that no whites will want to buy there or remain living there'
(ibid.: 119).

The Conservative government's policy of council house sales (via
the Housing Act 1988, and the Local Government and Housing Act
1989) also adversely affected Black people. This policy sought to
push privatisation of council properties by forcing the local authorities to sell them. Yet, because Black people are more dependent
on accessible and affordable rented accommodation, this access
was eroded (Ginsburg, 1992: 122).

**Political representation and participation**

During the 1980s Black support for the Labour Party was overwhelming, and Black people who ran as Labour candidates have
been more successful in winning local and national representation
in politics. Black voting for Labour increased as Black representatives increased in number during the 1980s. However, Black
people are still being denied representation and a voice commensurate with their numbers in the general population. This
problem is particularly acute when one takes account of the fact
that Black people add up to significant proportions of the voting

population in a number of key areas, including several boroughs in London and Birmingham (Anwar, 1986). In this context, it is not surprising that competition for Black votes from the Conservatives, and Liberals (and the Social Democrats for a while) has been strong.

The 1981 Census revealed that minorities made up over 40 per cent of the population in 3 constituencies (Brent South, Ealing Southall and Birmingham Ladywood). Most of these would be Asians. They made over 20 per cent of the population in 30 other constituencies. Polls in 1983 revealed that between 64 per cent and 81 per cent of minority voters voted for Labour (Fitzgerald, 1987). The pre-election poll carried out by *Caribbean Times* in 1987 found that 86 per cent of African-Caribbean voters intended to vote Labour, while 6 per cent intended to vote Conservative and 7 per cent intended to vote Alliance.

In 1986 there were 87 minority councillors elected in London, of whom 80 were Labour (Fitzgerald, 1987). At the same time 27 minority candidates ran for Parliament, of whom 14 were Labour. The four elected to Parliament at that time were all Labour, as were the two that narrowly lost in marginal constituencies. The House of Commons opened its door to the first Black members of parliament in 1987, when Dianne Abbott, Bernie Grant and Paul Boateng (along with Keith Vaz, an Asian) won seats for Labour. In a House of Commons with around 630 Members, this was hardly commensurate with the numbers of Black voters, but it was an important symbolic victory.

The establishment and growth of Black sections, and the ensuing conflict with senior figures in the Labour Party, including Neil Kinnock, the Party Leader at the time, reflected the major problems Black people continued to face within the Labour Party and the Labour movement (Shukra, 1990; Jeffers, 1991). Demanding a guarantee of seats for Black people on the Labour Party Executive Committee (in a way similar to the existing guaranteed seats for women) the Black Sections faced a complete rejection of Black people's rights to meet on their own, and a furious assault by the top echelons of the Labour Party.

### Racialised interpretations of the 'Colour Line'

How far were Blacks and whites aware of the inequalities just described and how did they explain various aspects of the Black experience of racialised barriers and boundaries, such as those described above? And are similar or divergent views expressed? The data are not abundant as in the United States but a similar pattern remains in which Blacks are more likely to see racialised barriers and hostility as a major determinant in their lives, while whites, though acknowledging it to a greater degree than whites in the United States, see it playing a more limited role. For example, white people in England are more likely than whites in the United States to acknowledge that Black people face 'prejudice'. When asked about the extent of 'racial prejudice' against Black people 55 per cent of those interviewed felt that there was a lot of prejudice against them (Jowell *et al.*, 1986). And 50 per cent of the white respondents felt that there was more 'racial prejudice' than 5 years ago (Jowell *et al.*, 1987).

But such beliefs did not extend towards their evaluations of the extent of discrimination against Black people. Almost twice as many Black people as white people believe that Black people faced discrimination in employment. For example, when asked if 'ethnic minorities' were treated worse by employers, 38 per cent of white respondents said 'yes', compared to 67 per cent of Blacks (Frow and Alibhai-Brown, 1992). There were also major differences between the two racialised groups when asked about the treatment Black people receive at the hands of the police. Around 48 per cent of whites and 75 per cent of Blacks felt that Blacks received worse treatment (ibid., 1992).

When asked what might be done about racialised inequality, twice as many Blacks as whites felt it was necessary to strengthen the laws to promote racialised equality. For example, when asked whether the 'race relations' laws should be made tougher, 31 per cent of whites felt this was needed, compared to 61 per cent of Blacks (Frow and Alibhai-Brown, 1992).

Other evidence confirms these general findings. The almost overwhelming opposition by white people to the policy of 'positive action' (Ball and Solomos, 1990); the indifference and often hostility towards equal opportunities policies of even a minimalist kind (Gordon, 1990; Jewson and Mason, 1992); the antagonism towards the Greater London Council's commitment to implement equal opportunities, all these indicate the lack of commitment to the policies necessary to achieve racialised equality (Jenkins and Solomos, 1987).

## EXCEPTIONS TO THE RULE

Alongside the dismal picture portrayed of the plight of Black people in the 1980s, a number of exceptions to the general situation have been listed above. For example, in the United States a significant section of Black workers and their families is matching and surpassing white achievement, and many Black young, educated, married couples are doing as well as and sometimes better, than their white counterparts (O'Hare *et al.*, 1991). In England, as well as the United States, some evidence suggests that Black women are achieving better than white women and even better than some white men (Farley and Allen, 1989; O'Hare *et al.*, 1991; Mirza, 1992). Blacks in both nations seem to stay on for higher education in greater proportions than their white counterparts. Similarly, impressions from the world of sport and the music industry suggest Black distinction, excellence and even superiority over non-Blacks.

Sports in general, and certain sports like athletics, boxing, American football and basketball, reflect these impressions of Black success. In 1983 Blacks won 14 of the 33 medals available in running races at the World Championships; in 1987 they won 19 (Burfoot, 1992: 89). Black sportsmen dominated athletics, boxing and basketball; Black sportswomen dominated athletics. Key successes in the 1980s included: in athletics those of Linford Christie, Jackie Joyner-Turner, Carl Lewis and Tessa Sanderson; in basketball Michael Jordan and Magic Johnson; in boxing Larry Holmes, Mike Tyson, Frank Bruno and Chris Eubanks. In sport some Black men (and smaller numbers of Black women) were the top salary earners. For example, at the end of the 1980s Blacks held 8 out of the top 10 National Basketball Association salaries, and Michael Jordan, the biggest attraction in the league, earned around $3 million (*Jet*, 1992: 47). Bruno, Tyson and Holmes earned millions for their fights.

In the area of music, from the successes of blues and jazz earlier this century to the success of Tamla Motown in the 1960s, and to the phenomenal success of Rap in the 1970s and 1980s, Black musicians seem to be unequalled and unsurpassed in earnings and popular appeal. International successes like Michael Jackson, Janet Jackson, Prince, Winston Marsalis and Miles Davis are overwhelming. In Rap music, LL Cool J and Hammer, Public Enemy and NWA have sold multi-million dollar records and held sell-out tours. Similar heights were reached in England by artists like Soul II Soul, Sade and Courtney Pine; and, to lesser degrees, in reggae by Aswad and Steel Pulse.

Successes in these areas tend to suggest the end of racialised barriers and the advent of a truly meritocratic society. But this is only one aspect of the picture, and a partial aspect at that. In those areas in which there is superior achievement Black people still continue to face additional obstacles compared to their white counterparts; and in areas like sport and music, closer inspection reveals phenomenal success for key individuals but limited success for Blacks as a whole. For example, in the United States Black businesses and self-employment are fraught with problems, and the positions of many Black professionals in the public sector remained precarious throughout the 1980s (Davis and Watson, 1985). Although Black women were more successful than some whites, this success was defined only in terms of earnings and conceals the extra hours worked and the additional costs involved in child care provisions.[20] In England Blacks stayed on in full-time education in greater proportions than whites, but they did not go on to universities, so we do not know what kinds of courses they were following, or how many were doing exams that they had failed once already. It seems reasonable to assume that they are taking longer to get the same qualifications, and/or that they are taking further educational qualifications rather than higher educational qualifications.

As will be seen in Chapter 3, Blacks dominate only certain sports, and certain fields of music; and where they are the top earners they amount to little more than a handful of individuals, often with less talented white competitors earning higher amounts (Cashmore, 1982). The fact is that most sport is dominated by whites, and it should come as no surprise that the wide range of sports in which we find few black competitors, and little evidence of success – car racing, yachting, equestrian events, gymnastics, and tennis – require large outlays of money. Moreover, Blacks occupy marginal roles in coaching and managerial positions, and there are still widespread racialised stereotypes and theories of sporting ability which impede Black aspirations because they lead to Blacks being channelled into sport and away from academic and intellectual activities (Cashmore, 1982; Hoose, 1989). Black people are not supreme in sport, we are simply the best in a tiny selection of sports, and our success can only be explained by a complex combination of opportunities, motivation, economics and role models (Roberts, 1983). Similarly in music, Black success is confined to a limited domain. There are no Blacks in country and western, few in folk music, even fewer in classical music, despite the successes of the Dance Theatre of Harlem. Again, looks are deceiving, and the highly publicised success of key individuals has few counterparts in the management of music, and is unrepresentative not only of Black demography generally, but of Black representation in the music industry. Blacks are there in numbers but they are behind the scenes usually in subordinate positions.

The highly publicised successes of some key Black individuals in sport and music, and anomalous patterns in the treadmill of racialised inequality, present a picture in contrast to the circumstances confronting most Black people. These facts cannot be ignored, and they are important for at least three reasons. First, they render analysis of racialised hostility that much more difficult than in the past when there was legal racialised discrimination in the United States and a 'colour bar' in England (Wilson, 1978; Rich, 1986). Second, the impression of success underlies many white people's views that racialised equality prevails, and racialised discrimination is slight. Third, they emphasise the determination of Black people to resist racialised barriers while also offering the limited benefits and inspiration of role models.

In fact there are few areas in which Blacks are doing better than non-Blacks, the individuals involved are tiny in number, and when compared to the numbers in the Black population as a whole, and to the total numbers involved in different areas of sport or music, they pale into relative insignificance. When we take account of other factors – the additional energies involved in being self-employed, the insecure nature of much Black employment, the problems which inhere in nuclear families, the additional costs of child care provisions for many Black women workers, and psychological problems created by racialised hostility – we must treat even these successes with caution. It may be true that in some highly circumscribed areas of life, some Blacks generally are not 'catchin' hell', but these are few and far between. While exceptions to the rule such as those presented here were interpreted throughout the 1980s as evidence of equal opportunities and the success of individualist culture, they must not be allowed to fuel the fires of those who would maintain the myth of equal opportunity in the United States and England.

## VICTIMS WITHOUT A VICTIM MENTALITY

The evidence indicates that racialised hostility (especially attacks, discrimination, abuse) remained high throughout the 1980s. In the United States most analyses of such hostility invariably take the pre-1960s period as a point of comparison (when legal segregation was entrenched) and usually end up saying that things are much improved (Wilson, 1978). But comparisons like these tend to ignore the continuing evidence of vicious and brutal attacks, rampant discrimination, and widespread abuse. This type of hostility occurred across many areas of life, and was both organised and individualistic. Its most extreme manifestations resulted in murders and maiming, which were usually reported. Less extreme, but equally violent and repugnant, manifestations did not always catch the headlines. Extremist groups continued their chant of 'white supremacy' orchestrated around life-threatening violence and assaults. Universities were a major site of racialised attacks, abuse and discrimination as the nation reeled in surprise over how its youngest and brightest white citizens embraced violence and hostility (Farrell *et al.*, 1988). Black students were frequently subjected to abuse and ridicule, and often faced violence and attack, while studying. Nor were the various agencies of the state free from such hostility. Political leaders, like Reagan and Thatcher, along with key politicians, manipulated white fears of Black competition for their political goals; and the police were often guilty of many crimes they were supposed to prevent (Krieger, 1986; Smith and Gray, 1983).

In England the National Front, the British National Party, and other extremist organisations, continued their assault on Black people's very existence (Thompson, 1988). Racialised violence and attacks took the lives and limbs of Black people, and bred fear and intimidation in Black communities (Greater London Council, 1984; Home Office, 1989). Much of this brutality and violence was perpetrated by the police (Hesse *et al.*, 1991). Studies of racialised discrimination indicated the continuing propensity of employers to discriminate against Black applicants for jobs, or those searching for housing and education (Brown and Gay, 1985). Various agencies of the state were not averse to capitalising on white fears of Black people, as successive governments raised questions about Black immigration and crime, condoned stereotypes and endorsed white notions of Blacks as an alien presence (Centre for Contemporary Cultural Studies, 1982; Gilroy, 1987a).

The picture presented in most analyses of the circumstances of Black people in each nation is dismal. Most books and reports end after they have presented an 'objective' or 'comprehensive' portrayal of the 'facts' (Brown, 1984; Hacker, 1992). But this is only half the picture. We cannot stop at simply describing the facts of inequality, as if facts and processes go unchallenged; we must also compare these facts with the spirit of striving against inequality and injustice. Despite the persistence of racialised barriers, discrimination and abuse, and the lack of opportunities, these processes are continually confronted with determination and perseverance by Black people. At each juncture in which hostility has been expressed against Black people, they have organised to contain and overcome it (Sivanandan, 1982; Marable, 1992). The fury of young Black men in England set off the decade with a bang – in riots in 1980 and 1981 (Benyon, 1984). Black people have developed cultures and communities of resistance from attempting institutional change from within, to community level organising; from ideological and cultural resistance to physical resistance, collectively and individually (Centre for Contemporary Cultural Studies, 1982; Gilroy, 1987a; Marable, 1992; Sivanandan, 1990). Sometimes such resistance has been organised around gaining greater access to mainstream provisions, as Black people campaigned against the established provisions, for example, in the work of local and national government; at other times it has had the goal of establishing separate provisions as Black people rejected the institutions and practices of non-Blacks (Liverpool Black Caucus, 1986; T'Shaka, 1990).

Key individuals and groups have attempted change from within, such as the work in England of 'race relations units' like those led by Herman Ouseley, firstly in Lambeth, London and then at the Greater London Council's Ethnic Minorities Unit (Ouseley, 1981, 1984); or in the United States with Jesse Jackson's 1984 and 1988 presidential campaigns (Collins, 1986). And, of course, the formal political activities of Black Congress men and women, and Black Members of Parliament (Anwar, 1986; Pohlmann, 1990). Campaigns have been mounted against extremist groups to picket marches and headquarters, to protest discrimination and victimisation (Davis, 1989; Hesse *et al.*, 1991); an extensive, rich and diverse literature has developed in each nation including a range of books, journals, magazines and newspapers. Conferences have been organised to mobilise various sections of the community and political activities, both mainstream and otherwise, have been organised (Federation of Black Housing Associations, 1986; Brown, 1991). Black people on many occasions have fought with extremists – and even the police – to protect their communities (Sivanandan, 1990; Marable, 1992). Various types of 'anti-racism' have been developed, many in alliance with whites committed to ending racialised hostility (Ben-Tovim *et al.*, 1986; Collins, 1986).

As ever, Black women have been central to these activities, often at the vanguard of them; in the heart of mainstream institutions in politics, education, employment and health, as well as Black organisations and feminist groups (Bryan *et al.*, 1985; Davis, 1989). Active in a wide range of organisations – from the Children's Defense League and professional organisations as well as the NAACP and the Urban League in the United States (Amott and Matthaei, 1991); and from Camden Black Sisters and the National Association of Women of African Descent, to Black Sections and the Black Trade Union Solidarity Movement in England (Mama, 1984; Bryan *et al.*, 1985), Black women have mounted campaigns, organised boycotts and challenged institutional injustice (Collins, 1991; Sivanandan, 1982, 1990). If their numbers have been equal to those of men on the front line, and in the rear, then the struggles that they have faced were certainly greater. More exploited than Black men, and more oppressed than white women, they have usually found their racialised and gender allies wanting (Carby, 1982; Mama, 1989; Collins, 1991).

The many examples of resistance by exceptional individuals that hit the pages of the media were supported by the thousands and thousands that daily gave of their time and energies in building the community infrastructure, establishing and extending the networks. Needless to say, this larger scale community resistance went much less noted or noticed. Despite racialised hostilities and obstacles, Black people kept fighting back. They refused to accept the barriers that obstructed their way forward, or the boundaries that demarcated their activities. Racialised disadvantage and inequality did not culminate in dead minds or motivations, and Black people chanted, 'here to stay, here to fight' to the bitter end (Sivanandan, 1982).

## CONCLUSION

This chapter set out to delineate the key elements in patterns of racialised inequality in the 1980s, and to highlight some aspects of the Black response to them. Forced as I am to rely on official statistics and data – replete with limitations of conceptualisation, focus and collection – the full extent of racialised disadvantage cannot be conveyed (Bhat *et al.*, 1988). Nevertheless, the general patterns are beyond dispute. The 1980s have seen some fundamental changes in the circumstances in which Black people find themselves, and there are major differences within the Black population in the two nations that must be taken into account in any comparative analysis. Despite dramatic changes, essential continuities remain. As a racialised category, Black people still remain worse off, and confront more obstacles than non-Blacks. All Black people experience disadvantage and discrimination, but the forms they take vary with the particular circumstances and contexts in which they find themselves. Given the added expenses they must incur, the economic problems confronting Black women, particularly those with children, have even more serious material consequences than for men. Despite relentless constraints, Black people still excel in certain areas, while in others our strength and striving must be reason for celebration (though not exaggeration) and grounds for inspiration. It is the foundation upon which we must build.

Black people in the United States faced problems which Black people in England did not face to the same degree, including levels of violence, devastation to communities and greater extremities in economic and political circumstances. And Black people in England faced problems which Blacks in the United States did not, including problems of immigration control and no critical mass to be mobilised for political action. The specifics of the 'Colour Line' are important for understanding the relative impact of discrimination resulting from class inequalities, racialised animosities or other factors, and for developing policies of resistance – Blacks can elect town mayors or police chiefs on their own in the United States, but cannot do so in England. But the commonalities are important for emphasising the common role played by processes of 'racialisation', the management of economic crises, and political processes via the manipulation of minorities and of the racialised fears of the majority. These similarities also emphasise the commonalities across capitalist societies, and are explored in greater detail in the following chapters.

# Chapter 3

# Racialised ideologies, class relations and the state

## INTRODUCTION

The 1980s were a decade in which the economic and political climate proved fertile ground for the cultivation of various types of racialised ideologies and hostility, and for drawing back from the limited institutional mechanisms designed to challenge such attacks on Black people's humanity and rights.[1] In the United States in the early 1980s President Reagan opposed every major civil rights measure put forward by Congress, he called the 1964 Civil Rights Act a 'bad piece of legislation', reshaped the Civil Rights Commission to weaken its enforcement abilities and argued publicly that civil rights leaders were using spurious claims of racialised discrimination simply to justify their existence, (Omi and Winant, 1986: 131–5; Pohlmann, 1990). In December 1986 in the Howard Beach neighbourhood of Queens, New York, a crowd of white youths chased a Black man to his death under a car, while several Black men were viciously beaten (Wellman, 1993). In 1987, Al Campanis, Vice-President of Player Personnel for the Los Angeles Dodgers explained on a popular national television talk show that Blacks lacked the ability to be managers of sports teams, insisting that Blacks were gifted with muscle but deficient in the mental necessities for managerial decisions (Omi, 1989: 12; Hoose, 1989).

During his presidential campaign against Michael Dukakis in 1988, George Bush's campaign manager, Lee Atwater, manipulated historically generated fears held by non-Blacks of Black men raping white women in a decisive and successful attempt at victory (Piliawsky, 1989). Similar strategies – invoking non-Black fears of Black competition and sexuality – were employed successfully by Jessie Helms in North Carolina (Newsweek, 1991). In 1988 I

received an anonymous letter arguing that it was immoral to encourage 'miscegenation' at the University of Massachusetts and
calling for my active involvement in 'work to forward clean separation between the races' (Small, 1989: 2).[2] In 1989 a young Black
man, Yusef Hawkins, innocently going to purchase a car, was
mistaken by some whites in Bensonhurt for the boyfriend of a local
white woman and shot dead (Marable, 1992). After the despicable
rape of a white woman in New York's Central Park a furore broke
out and multi-millionaire Donald Trump took out a full-page
advert in the *New York Times*; in the weeks preceding and following
this incident a number of Black women were raped on the streets
of New York and no one said a word (Cose, 1989).

In England in 1980, Erroyl Madden, a Black teenager suffering
from mental problems, was charged with stealing two toy cars from
a store. During interrogation by the police his mother was called a
'prostitute' and the police ignored the receipts he had in his pocket
for the purchase of the cars. All charges against him were dropped
in court. In 1981 after a white man was seen making a throwing
motion in front of a house, thirteen Black teenagers died in a fire
in South London. No one was charged and the court returned a
verdict that the fire began inside the house. A massive protest was
organised in March of that year against police, media and political
indifference and insensitivity (Small, 1983b). All across England in
1981 young Black people rioted and rebelled against racialised
hostility, from London to Liverpool to Leeds (Benyon, 1984). In
the same year, the Nationality Act consolidated and simplified state
institutional discrimination against Black people (cementing the
distinction between 'patrial' and 'non-patrial' still further), while
immigration authorities continued to ensure that even the most
genuine immigrants and visitors would be hounded and harassed
at the point of entry to the country, and that women would be
humiliated (Miles and Phizacklea, 1984).

Margaret Thatcher's 1983 general election campaign furthered
the subtleties with which Black people were to be stereotyped and
added to the general tendency to consider notions of 'Black' and
'British' as incompatible when her campaign slogan portrayed a
Black man in a suit, and read 'Labour says he's black, we say he's
British' (Layton-Henry, 1984). Preoccupation with sexual relations,
especially between Black men and white women, continued to
command attention when Bernie Grant (first Black leader of a
council in England) and his partner, a white woman, were harassed

because of their relationship (*Guardian*, November, 1985). A national study on racialised discrimination in employment demonstrated that at least one in three employers continued to discriminate against Black applicants for jobs, and that the level of discrimination had not changed since the first national study in 1968 (Brown and Gay, 1985; Brown, 1992). While Black people continued to add colour (and contributions) to the rank and file of trade union members disproportionate to their numbers in the population, trades unions continued to mouth equality until their lips hurt, but positions of power and responsibility remained lily white (Small, 1984; Phizacklea and Miles, 1992). In Brixton, London, in 1985 Cherry Groce was shot in the back and left paralysed from the waist down, and in Tottenham, London, Cynthia Jarret died of heart failure. Both were elderly Caribbean women and each incident occurred during police raids on private homes (Mama, 1992: 95). In 1987 a party in East London was tear-gassed by a group of local whites and a Black man was savagely beaten and lost an eye when he pursued the attackers (Thompson, 1988: 17). When Bernie Grant ran for Member of Parliament in 1988 he was portrayed as a gorilla in thousands of leaflets handed out in his own constituency (Gilroy, 1990a).

For Black women in particular racialised hostility in its cultural, institutional and individual manifestations was an everyday affair (Essed, 1990; Mama, 1992). The obstacles imposed by racialised ideologies, in conjunction with those of gender subordination, have a double impact on Black women – from portrayals of 'welfare mothers' and 'whores', to 'Jezebels' and 'sluts', in the cinema, on television, and throughout popular culture, Black women were represented as sexual objects, burdens on the economy, and failures (Bryan *et al.*, 1985; Collins, 1991). The consequences of such images were often victimisation and violence, with some Black men contributing to a significant proportion of it (hooks, 1990; Mama, 1989).

Analysis of these issues has varied in both nations. Some authors have failed to discuss 'racism' at all, preferring to explain racialised inequality primarily in terms of class dynamics (Gordon *et al.*, 1982; Taaffe and Mulhearn, 1988). Others have acknowledged that 'racism' plays a role in these patterns and that important links exist between 'racism' and broader class and political factors but these relationships are infrequently explored and explained, and even less frequently considered to play a role of greater importance than these broader forces (Miles and Phizacklea, 1984; Miles, 1989a). Still others consider racialised ideologies as the primary or exclusive focus and as central to the larger crisis (Omi and Winant, 1986; Gilroy, 1987a; Small, 1991b). This latter group emphasises how 'racism' is intricately intertwined with class and broader factors in complex ways and goes on to examine the unfolding of such relationships.

Most analyses of racialised ideologies have employed a common language of 'racism': from 'biological racism' and 'scientific racism' to 'pseudo-scientific racism' (Banton, 1977; Gossett, 1965); from 'innate racism' to 'unconscious racism' (Rose, 1976; Fredrickson, 1988); from 'psychological racism' and 'cultural racism', to 'intellectual racism', 'populist racism' and 'working-class racism' (Sivanandan, 1988; Moore, 1989: 159; Sivanandan, 1990); from 'institutional racism' and 'individual racism' to 'implicit racism' and 'explicit racism'; (Carmichael and Hamilton, 1967; Wellman, 1977; Hall, 1978); and 'sexual racism' (Shyllon, 1977). Some of these 'racisms' are overt and obvious, others are inconspicuous and operate in a more clandestine manner. These latter types are incredibly slippery, and their advocates employ ingenuity to deny their vindictiveness; not only have some done a ventriloquist act (they remain malicious and vicious but are less conspicuous) but others have done a disappearing act (moved to the backstage). In most analyses the state maintains a pre-eminent role. Clearly such an array of ideologies cannot be reduced to a single-factor explanation and the problem in using the same term to refer to such a wide array of ideologies, and to both attitudes and actions, has been pointed out (Reeves, 1983: 242; Miles, 1989a). This has led to a move away from the notion of 'racism' as a single monolithic ideology, to 'racisms' as multiple ideologies. In particular, there has been more talk of a 'new racism', and of the 'rearticulation' of 'racism' (Barker, 1981; Omi and Winant, 1986; Sivanandan, 1988)[3].

Many useful contributions have been made and these approaches display many strengths. But there remain several limitations. Most analyses are preoccupied with the state and the formal political arena; there has been a failure to identify what is distinctly 'new' about the 'new racism' (and what is distinctive about the 'old' racism), or to recognise racialised images and ideas with a long historical existence; and a failure to look at 'racisms' not directly contingent on state activity and manipulation.[4] As will be seen, such ideologies play a significant role in the continuation of racialised barriers, boundaries and identities.

I have several goals in this chapter. First, to evaluate analyses of the multiple racialised ideologies common to both nations and argue that these are better conceptualised as a complex dynamic of racialised ideologies and attitudes rather than as 'old' and 'new' racisms.[5] Second, to argue that while the state continued to play a central role in the articulation of many of these ideologies, the strategies employed by its various branches became more sophisticated, the language more saturated with sophistry and they were thus able to extricate themselves from blame more easily. Not least of which because the maintenance of existing patterns of racialised inequality no longer required the explicit embracing of racialised ideologies. Third, to insist that many elements of this complex dynamic of racialised attitudes and ideologies are no longer directly contingent on state activities, the economy or politics, for example, ideologies about sexuality, sexual relations and sporting ability.[6] Far from being new, these ideologies are replete with ideas, images and notions from the past and are expressed by individuals and institutions influenced by, but not part of, the state. These reflect the historical continuity of biological beliefs and indicate the role of the working class in their reproduction.

In doing so I will emphasise how racialised ideologies and hostility are inextricably intertwined with other types of hostility and exclusion such as those grounded in class, gender, religious and national axes of stratification, many of which seem to have little to do with processes of racialisation; for example, the market forces and the invigorated enterprise culture emphasised by a capitalist society responding to the opportunities and challenges of the Single European Market or Japan, migration patterns, individualism, the resurgence of right-wing movements and neo-conservatism (Gamble, 1988; Hoover and Plant, 1989; Himmelstein, 1990). I thus reject the 'coat of paint theory' and suggest greater consideration be given to the causal role of racialised ideologies.[7]

## THE REARTICULATION OF 'RACISM' IN THE UNITED STATES

Race is no longer a straightforward, morally unambiguous force in American politics; instead, considerations of race are now deeply imbedded in the strategy and tactics of politics, in competing concepts of the function and responsibility of government, and in each voter's conceptual structure of moral and partisan identity. Race helps define liberal and conservative ideologies, shapes the presidential coalitions of the Democratic and Republican parties, provides a harsh new dimension to concern over taxes and crime, drives a wedge through alliances of the working classes and the poor, and gives both a momentum and vitality to the drive to establish a national majority inclined by income and demography to support policies benefiting the affluent and the upper-middle class.

(Edsall and Edsall, 1991b: 53)

The changing economic and political context of the 1980s in the United States has led to 'transformations and transmutations in racism' (Marable, 1992) and to discussions of 'new racisms' and the 'rearticulation of racism'.[8] From the declining economic strength of the United States, increasing unemployment, and fear of Japanese competition, the budget deficit, the savings and loan crisis, problems in education and demilitarisation (Krieger, 1986; Hoover and Plant, 1989). The proponents of these ideologies have rearticulated biological, cultural and economic themes, racialised beliefs, and a range of broader values and ideas in the American way of life, and have been at the centre of various movements in a broad right-wing resurgence in politics. Different elements have been emphasised in each of these rearticulations but the central aspects are the use of a new racialised linguistics, codewords, and images, accusations of 'reverse racism' and characterising policies to combat discrimination as 'anti-American' (e.g. anti-individualism) and a burden on the economy. Racialised discourse of this kind has dominated presidential elections in the 1980s, as well as a host of state elections during the decade, such as during the campaigns of Jessie Helms in North Carolina, and Massachusetts democratic nominee for Governor, Charles Silber (Piliawsky, 1989).

The first broad trend and the one which has commanded most attention was described in the work of Omi and Winant (1986). It has recently been discussed by others (Edsall and Edsall, 1991a, 1991b). The concept of rearticulation is central to this 'new racism'. Omi and Winant define rearticulation as:

a practice of discursive reorganisation or reinterpretation of ideological themes and interests already present in the subjects' consciousness, such that these elements obtain new meanings or coherence.

(1986: 173)

This rearrangement of ideas and assumptions 'produces new subjectivity by making use of information and knowledge already present in the subject's mind' which are then infused with new meanings (Omi and Winant, 1986: 93). A major rearticulation of racialised themes occurred during the social movements of the 1960s and African-Americans were central in the challenge to the prevailing orthodoxy of ethnicity. Minority social movements during this time were able to challenge the racialised ideologies that held Blacks to be inferior and undeserving of equal opportunities. Nation-based explanations dominated this period but have since been overwhelmed in the changing national economic and political climate of the 1970s and 1980s, and the United States' changing role in the world (ibid.: 110). In particular, these new conditions allowed new right movements to appropriate, distort and re-present certain themes in a new racialised manner. Three main strands are identified – the Far Right, the New Right and Neo-Conservatives (Omi and Winant, 1986: 110). In these movements common ideas, notions, beliefs and traditions – some at the very core of the 'American way of life' – have been rearticulated and infused with new racialised meanings. These include equality, group and individual rights, and the legitimate scope of state activity. The ideas of equality and equal opportunity have been transformed to mean preference for unqualified Blacks.

While the Far Right is part of the reaction to Black demands for equality I think it is best treated as a continuation of historically dominant types of racialised hostility because for the most part it has simply 'revived the racist ideologies of previous periods' and it remains openly hostile to the promotion of racialised equality (Omi and Winant, 1986: 114).[9] The movement includes groups based on hatred such as Ku Klux Klan, the White American Resistance (WAR), the Aryan Nations and the Silent Brotherhood. They see the state as weak and unfair, society as polluted by Blacks and minorities, and they seek to develop a new sense of white (racialised) identity. In addition to their extremist members they also find a following among disaffected whites who feel someone should stick up for 'white interests' now that the state has gone too far in privileging Blacks. Examples of this can be found in the formation of white student clubs on university campuses (Levine, 1990: 60). Though significant, the overall activity of the Far Right has failed to reach the proportions it did prior to the 1960s. The Far Right is hardly vanishing and may even degenerate into terrorism in face of its inability to mobilise generally (Omi and Winant, 1986: 117). Some individuals in this movement, such as David Duke, have formally dissociated themselves from extremist groups to become mainstream though it is as yet unclear how successful this strategy will be.

The remaining two strands – the New Right and the Neo-Conservatives – proclaim favour for racialised equality in the abstract but oppose, obstruct and impede its achievement in practice by a variety of means. In particular they reject group demands for equality in favour of individual demands. Their vision of such equality:

> is that of a 'colorblind' society where racial considerations are never entertained in the selection of leaders, in hiring decisions, and the distribution of goods and services in general.
>
> (Omi and Winant, 1986: 113)

Both see the state as part of the problem – not only does it grant privilege to minority groups by way of affirmative action and quotas but it is too large and meddlesome in the 'normal' workings of the market. The state has gone too far in attempts to eliminate discrimination, they argue, to such an extent that now the 'real' victims of discrimination are decent, hard-working whites who suffer as individuals while African-Americans benefit as a group. Vocal opposition to bussing and 'reverse discrimination' are central concerns.

The New Right amounts to a network of conservative organisations which have developed independently of the political parties. They are outspoken on religious and cultural traditionalism, and have a clear populist commitment. They include the American Conservative Union, the National Conservative Political Action Committee, Conservative Caucus and Young Americans for Freedom. The Heritage Foundation is a major think tank for this movement. They promote their ideologies via a series of journals including *Conservative Digest, Policy Review* and *New Guard*. Collectively it promises a well organised alternative to the moral chaos caused by the social movements of the 1950s and 1960s. The movement has precedents in previous decades, including Spiro

Agnew, Jessie Helms and Pat Buchanan. The Neo-Conservatives – whose central thinkers and promoters include Nathan Glazer of Harvard University, and President Reagan – are opposed to group rights in favour of individual rights, and have used the issue of affirmative action to disseminate their views. Reagan promoted himself as the 'white people's president', and launched a wholesale assault on the limited gains of the previous two decades in tackling racialised inequality. He eliminated record keeping, restructured and changed the priorities of the Civil Rights Commission, and implemented a number of changes in Affirmative Action. He also stacked the Supreme Court with conservatives and is primarily held responsible for the new climate of 'meanness' in which individualism thrives (Pohlmann, 1990; Edsall and Edsall, 1991a).

Several mechanisms and tactics are central to the rearticulation of racialised ideologies including the use of codewords and a new linguistics of 'racism', manipulation of the idea of a 'color blind' society, and charges of 'reverse racism' and the excesses of 'anti-racism' (Omi and Winant, 1986; Wellman, 1986; Edsall and Edsall, 1991a). In particular, evidence of continuing racialised discrimination was ignored, stereotypes of Blacks were encouraged and the economic and ideological insecurities of the non-Black majority pandered to. Codewords are 'nonracial rhetoric used to disguise racial issues'; they are 'phrases and symbols which refer indirectly to racial themes, but do not directly challenge popular democratic or egalitarian ideals (e.g. justice, equal opportunity)' (Omi and Winant, 1986: 114, 120). There are other aspects of the new linguistics of 'racism' (Wellman, 1986). For example, the notion of a colourblind society is manipulated by playing on the distinction between individual and groups rights. By denying policies to combat racialised discrimination and to help Blacks, advocates claim they are promoting only what is fair and reasonable and consistent with US values. They add that this is simply what Blacks have been demanding for years. They portray the 'real victims' of 'racism' as white people – who work hard to advance themselves only to find their rights steamrollered by preferences for African-Americans and other minorities; and American institutions and values – threatened by the economic and bureaucratic burdens of 'anti-racism', for example, ethnic records, exams and tests. As a result employers who fear lawsuits disregard merit, and hiring is carried out by quotas (Edsall and Edsall, 1991a: 253).

Collectively such strategies play on the historically generated fears held by whites of Black economic, political (and sexual) competition, and the prevalent stereotypes of Black people as a drain on the American economy (Edsall and Edsall, 1991a: 216). The promotion of Black women as sexually promiscuous 'breeders' and 'welfare mothers', and Black men as 'muggers' and 'rapists' were common currency cultivated in the images of these right-wing activists.[10] Such images gain a strong foothold in a climate in which the American economy is struggling to maintain its lead on other nations, and whites feel burdened by economic hardship.

The rearticulation of racialised ideologies has played a major role in American political life and examples of such manipulation abound. One of the most flagrant manipulations of racialised imagery was that employed by the campaign supporters of George Bush, in particular by Lee Atwater (his campaign director), in his presidential contest with Michael Dukakis in 1988. Willie Horton was a Black felon who had committed first degree murder and been sentenced to life without parole in Massachusetts (Edsall and Edsall, 1991a: 222). After spending several years in prison Horton was released on furlough in 1986. He disappeared after his tenth furlough and eight months later brutally beat a man, and raped his wife several times, before being caught. The incident made major national news and Dukakis, who had vetoed a bill to prohibit furloughs twelve years earlier, was linked to Horton's crime. The furlough programme in question had first been initiated in 1972. Atwater thrived on the promise that Horton presented for him and could hardly contain his glee (Estrich, 1989). The images of Horton that were promoted blurred the complexity of the issues as Black crime – and Black rape of white women – became generalised currency in the political campaign (Piliawsky, 1989; White, 1988; Edsall and Edsall, 1991a: 224). They have had an impact that reverberates throughout American society (Walton, 1989). Despite the despicable actions taken by Atwater, and other Republican officials and supporters, Bush never silenced them and Atwater vigorously denied any culpability throughout. In a strange twist of fate three years later, Atwater on his deathbed admitted his culpability.

David Duke, former Grand Wizard of the Ku Klux Klan, turned main-streamer, who managed to sneak into England in the early 1980s despite a government ban, provides a second example of the deception involved in rearticulating racialised themes. In 1991 he came very close to being elected state senator in Louisiana in a climate in which his competitors were weak. He had forgone the bare-faced viciousness of previous decades in favour of two-faced virulence, and his campaign style involved a 'conservative rhetoric peppered with racially loaded language' (*Newsweek*, 18 November, 1991: 25). In his campaign talks 'His coded distillations of white economic and racial resentment . . . include "crime in the street" (black-on-white crime), "welfare illegitimacy" (black, unwed mothers), "affirmative action" (black economic advancement) and "heritage" (whites first)' (*Newsweek*, 18 November, 1991: 27). Activities like these were not confined to those in the full limelight – the evidence suggests that they were central to numerous campaigns across the nation, and in local constituencies (Black and Black, 1987; Goldfield, 1990).[11]

A further confounding factor which should be noted in the United States concerns the show-casing of right-wing and conservative Blacks. Heralded by the press and media, thinkers and achievers who hold conservative political views have received top positions in political and policy circles, out of all proportion to their numbers in the Black population. Their views are certainly at variance with the views held by the majority of Black people (Boston, 1988). These include academics such as Thomas Sowell, Glen Loury and Shelby Steele and policymakers such as Clarence Pendleton.[12] Many of these individuals have published numerous books, and a host of articles in popular magazines (Sowell, 1975, 1983; Loury, 1984; Steele, 1990). Their views and achievements have been highlighted and manipulated to confound the arguments of those who criticised Reagan's, and then Bush's, policies. In particular, Shelby Steele was headlined on television and in the press across the country (*San Francisco Examiner*, October, 1990). This development is a racialised set of activities which might not be best described as 'racism' but which certainly contributes to racialised hostility. It is a trend which is likely to endure and become more salient.

Links between racialised ideologies, cultural values and the changing economic and political realities nationally and internationally are clear to all. In particular, the perceived threat posed by Black people gets tied into a tangled knot of attack on the American way of life – involving 'threats' to standards of education, of the right to choose (abortion), gay and lesbian rights. Economic competition, the free market, individualism and individual rights, pervade these rearticulations of racialised ideologies.

## THE 'NEW RACISM' IN ENGLAND

The changing economic and political climate of the 1970s and 1980s in England was also fruitful ground for the resurgence and consolidation of racialised ideologies and for their rearticulation as mechanisms for attaining political and economic ends. Rising unemployment, an inability to develop economic competitiveness and low productivity were all part of this climate (Hall and Jacques, 1983). It is closely tied in to the end of the British Empire, and a lingering ambivalence and prevarication over what to do with the colonies and the Commonwealth (Taylor, 1989). Thatcherism and the resurgence of the right wing have prevailed in a context which has seen the continued manipulation of nationalist (white) English identity (such as during the Falklands War) and efforts to restore Britain to its former material and psychological splendour – to put the 'Great' back in Britain (Gamble, 1988; Hoover and Plant, 1989). One aspect of this enterprise has been the realignment with the European Community, though this has not been without its political and economic consequences.

The idea of a 'new racism' commanded most attention in the work of Barker, though Stuart Hall had earlier introduced the notion of multiple, historically specific 'racisms' (Hall, 1978; Barker, 1981).[13] Others have developed it (Gilroy, 1987a). Barker focused on how a small group of Conservative thinkers had developed a set of ideas for which they could refer for scientific rationalisation to the work of sociobiologists. This was part of a revision of Conservative ideology in the climate of the 1980s – a climate in which fears of immigration (of people of colour) were central. This group consisted of a number of Conservative politicians, as well as other right-wing thinkers inside and outside the Conservative Party, including Enoch Powell, the right-wing Institute of Policy Studies, and a number of prominent journalists (Barker, 1981). 'Racism' was explained by this group in terms of 'territoriality' and 'tribal protection', and it was maintained that sociobiologists have found an explanation for the process of natural selection which gives rise to such feelings (Barker, 1981: 96–9).

The central premise of this 'new racism' is the argument that it is 'natural' for people to want to live amongst their own kind. At the 'core of the new racism. . .is a theory of human nature' (Barker, 1981: 21). Barker describes the theory:

Human nature is such that it is natural to form a bounded

community, a nation, aware of its differences from other nations. They are not better or worse. But feelings of antagonism will be aroused if outsiders are admitted.

(Barker, 1981: 21)

Racialised discrimination, especially in the context of the unprecedented levels of immigration, is thus defended as 'natural' and even positive. There is no mention of racialised groups or identities in this theory, and no advocacy of a hierarchy of biologically defined 'races'. In fact such a hierarchy is rejected (Barker, 1981: 20). One appeal of this 'new racism' is a claim to authority based on biological science along with its avoidance of crude and simplistic assumptions which natural science had long since discarded.

A variation on this idea of a 'new racism' was described by the Centre for Contemporary Cultural Studies (CCCS, 1982). While Barker stressed the biologism of the 'new racism', these authors emphasised its appeal to cultural integrity and rationales. This group argued that the 'new racism' reveals continuities with racialised ideologies historically, because it is part of the broader ideological apparatus of the state in maintaining political hegemony and economic dominance (Centre for Contemporary Cultural Studies, 1982: 11). Racialised ideologies are conceptualised primarily as a mechanism for managing the economic and political crises confronting the state. Focusing on a similar group of right-wing thinkers inside and outside the Conservative Party these analysts emphasised how notions of in-group and out-group membership were being defined in terms of the 'natural' differences of culture. But this was done in a way that made the imputed cultural differences immutable. This analysis has been developed in subsequent work by these writers, Gilroy in particular (Gilroy, 1987a; Gilroy, 1990a). Gilroy affirms that in this 'new racism', 'culture is conceived along ethnically absolute lines, not as something intrinsically fluid, changing, unstable, and dynamic, but as a fixed property of social groups' (Gilroy, 1990a: 266). The corollary is that 'England's black settlers are forever locked in the bastard culture of their enslaved ancestors, unable to break out into the "mainstream" alternative' (ibid: 267). No matter what values are inculcated, one is bound to fail.

A major aspect of this 'new racism' is the identification of 'anti-racism' as authoritarian, inflexible, and 'reverse racism'. The efforts of the Greater London Council to establish and fund institutional mechanisms to combat 'racism'– in particular the wholesale assault organised in 1984 as 'Anti-Racist Year' – were especially highlighted for attack by the government, and various sections of the media. But so too were those of other Labour-controlled councils, inside and outside London (Gordon, 1990). In this attack the movement to achieve racialised equality was successfully portrayed as an unjust, invalid (and thus morally illegitimate) struggle, and one which forced social engineering, indecent values and declining standards on decent hard-working people (i.e. whites). As in the United States, the 'average white citizen' was portrayed as the 'real victim' of 'reverse racism'. It was tied inextricably to broader issues and values such as multicultural-ism in education, gay rights, and the powers of local authorities (Solomos, 1989; Gordon, 1990).

A third type of 'new racism' believed to have emerged in the 1980s is the 'market-fuelled racism' described by Sivanandan, in his usual blunt and lyrical style. This 'new racism' was one which provided an organising mechanism for the continued exploitation of people of colour, in the light of the new economic and political realities confronting European capitalists. It was a 'Pan-European racism' shared in varying degrees (in accord with their specific needs) by the different countries across Europe (Sivanandan, 1990: 153). Sivanandan maintained:

> We are moving from an ethnocentric racism to a Eurocentric racism, from the different racisms of the different member states to a common, market racism.
>
> (Sivanandan, 1990: 159)

The primary motivation for this 'new racism' was the need felt by European capitalists to compete with American and Japanese capitalists in an international economic order dominated by multi-national companies, new methods of production, distribution and consumption, new technologies and the movement of capital to labour. In this international order European capitalists sought to maximise the economic benefits of 'Third World' labour, and minimise the political and social costs. Because their labour was needed, or at least some of it, the problem was how to get what was needed but keep most of it out: 'The problem for an open Europe, in other words, is how to close it against immigrants and refugees from the Third World. But not so their labour is entirely lost' (Sivandan, 1990: 155). The answer was to make it into a Fortress

Europe, with conditions of entry that suit the economic needs of capital, while totally disregarding the personal, social and economic needs of workers. Migrants, guest workers and illegal immigrants, who have no political or citizenship rights, constitute a new super-exploited workforce enduring conditions which would be unacceptable to an indigenous worker, Black or non-Black. They do the 'low-skilled, menial, dangerous and dirty jobs' in work that is 'temporary, flexible and casual' (ibid.: 155). The conditions are such that they are locked 'permanently into an underclass' (ibid.: 158).

There are more of these workers across Europe than in Britain, because the latter exploited its colonials under different conditions. But even their numbers in Britain are large and increasing – as 'hotel and catering workers, the contract cleaners in hospitals, airports and so on, the security guards in the private security firms, petrol-pump attendants, domestics, fast-food assistants, hospital auxiliaries and porters' (Sivanandan, 1990: 155). It is not this group alone which suffers the consequences: all people of colour suffer because this 'new racism' emphasises economic exploitation, and political and social control. Given the particular position of Black women in the labour market, the adverse impact on them is substantial (Bruegel, 1989). Furthermore, this is a 'racism' in which skin colour serves as the defining and organising mechanism. This is a:

> racism which cannot tell one black from another, a citizen from an immigrant, an immigrant from a refugee – and classes all Third World peoples as immigrants and refugees and all immigrants and refugees as terrorists and drug dealers.
>
> (Sivanandan, 1990: 160)

Consequently all people of colour carry their passports on their faces. The links between immigrant, illegal immigrant, asylum seeker, drug dealer and terrorist justify state and multi-state activity to monitor and suppress by any means. Sivanandan maintains the need to recognise that it is Western capital which forces them there in the first place – as a legacy of colonialism, and of the dictatorships established by Western powers.

Recognising a need to challenge Labour's monopoly of Black voting, Thatcher and the Conservatives launched a series of initiatives at local and national level. A major element of this was the large scale media campaign during the 1983 general election.

The campaign backfired as Britishness and Blackness were presented as mutually exclusive but efforts to recruit members of the Black population who have achieved some educational and occupational success to Conservative ranks continued into the 1990s.

## 'NEW RACISMS' FOR OLD

While these analyses provide new insights to understanding the changing economic and political landscape within which racialised ideologies of various kinds are rearticulated to meet the needs of those in positions of economic and political power, there remain some significant limitations. There are several problems with the concept of a 'new racism', and with the assumptions and scope of the idea of a rearticulation of 'racism'. First, there appears in each nation to be not one 'new racism' but several. These 'new racisms' combine elements of biology or sociobiology, culture and economics, and each nation reveals clear evidence of codewords, a changing political (and social) linguistics of 'racisms' and accusations of 'reverse racism'. Each of these racisms overlaps the other in content and in the groups that propound them. To call them by distinctive names is to impute to them a distinctiveness and uniqueness which they do not merit and for which there is no clear empirical referent.

A second problem is that if these are 'new racisms' why is it that so many elements are evident in earlier periods of English and American history? Clear evidence is available of biological, cultural and economic rationales feeding into one another in most periods of recent history, as are examples of subtle and indirect racialised ideologies (Walvin, 1973; Shyllon, 1977). Economic considerations were always central to slavery as an institution, from the migration of Europeans, to the forced abduction of Africans and the reinvigoration of slavery in the United States as a result of Whitney's Cotton Ginny (Berlin, 1974). There were always those who did not bother to concern themselves with Divine or scientific rationales – economic profit was sufficient (Williams, 1944). The benefits to white Americans from Jim Crow were certainly dictated as much by market profits – double taxation for Blacks and inferior institutions – as by the political and psychological benefits. Non-Blacks enjoyed unchallenged access to education, housing and electoral office (Woodward, 1966; Davis, 1989). The majority of anti-Black riots in the late nineteenth and early twentieth centuries were caused by fears of economic competition, as, for example, in East St Louis (Wilson, 1978). Laws preventing Black sailors from working on English ships early this century (despite the fact that they were British citizens), and the efforts taken to encourage migration from the Caribbean in the 1950s, were also dictated by economic interests (Miles and Phizacklea, 1984; Rich, 1986).

Cultural rationales were also present at all times, especially in the early decades – the distinction between Christian and heathen, savage and civilised – being central (Williams, 1944; Jordan, 1968). After all, one aspect of European rationalisation for slavery was its role as a 'rescue mission' to bring barbarians to the bosom of Christianity (Barker, 1978). Many slave-holders eschewed scientific explanations, subscribing wholeheartedly to a religious interpretation of the institution (Banton, 1983). To these slave-holders Blacks were culturally inferior, as Divinely ordained, and they often ignored biological rationalisations, or rejected them outright. Many Victorians rejected biological determinism, but held tenaciously and uncritically to their cultural superiority – over Africans, Asians, in fact over any 'others' whatsoever, and working-class whites in particular (Bolt, 1971; Lorimer, 1978; Biddiss, 1979). Fredrickson shows the saliency of notions of culture during slavery, and Steinberg has described their tenacity since (Steinberg, 1981; Fredrickson, 1988). Similarly, no one doubts that beliefs about physical variation and later biology were central to 'scientific racism' and 'pseudo-scientific racism' during most of the slave era (Banton, 1977); and social Darwinism, though it operated from a different set of assumptions, remained essentially biological (Gossett, 1965).

Neither is subtlety and circumlocution in racialised discourse unique to the 1980s. The White Citizens Councils established after the Brown vs Board of Education decision of 1954 reflected 'a more decorous, tidy and less conspicuous method' of racialised hostility (Goldfield, 1990: 82); while opposition to desegregation entailed 'lawsuits and countersuits, delaying tactics, humiliating application procedures, nullification edicts, and outright intimidation' (ibid.: 106). Wallace portrayed the Civil Rights Movement to disaffected working-class whites as examples of social engineering and coercive federal government; Nixon followed his lead (Edsall and Edsall, 1991a: 63). Harris has vividly portrayed the ingenuity of the English civil service between the 1940s and 1960s in discriminating without appearing to discriminate – and certainly without getting caught – as inconspicuous administrative measures were employed to keep

Black people out of England via 'circulars, instructions and guidance to government agencies' (Harris, 1991).[14] They also offered 'informal advice' to colonial governments to discourage migration and regulate the issuance of passports (Joshi and Carter, 1984). Even the 1962 Commonwealth Immigrants Act did not mention 'race' (Miles and Phizacklea, 1984). Reeves has documented the various techniques employed for evading accusations of 'racism' since then (1983). The particular victims of these ideologies, the impact that they have had, and the features emphasised certainly varied, but an examination of the historical record confirms that there is little of a fundamental nature that is new to any of these 'new racisms'. In fact, it is not the 'new' features that need to be analysed but rather the ways in which 'old' features are rearticulated.

Third, most discussions reveal almost exclusive focus on the state and the formal political realm. Other realms of society, and other actors, have garnered little attention in most studies, and are not discussed, except as reflecting political machinations. The working class is most often seen as secondary and as passively embracing state dictates. Omi and Winant mention them, so does Miles, but they are not discussed in any detail, and certainly not linked to these politically-based 'racisms' (Omi and Winant, 1986; Miles, 1989b). In contrast I argue that many racialised ideologies now have a limited relationship to the economic vicissitudes of the marketplace, the political whims and fancies of the state or the capitalist class. Such ideologies and ideas have become entrenched and institutionalised in literature, media, music, educational and vocational organisations, in the popular consciousness and conventional wisdom. Ideologies like these continue to be reproduced and articulated in ways that are complexly interwoven with state ideologies, as well as broader forces and agents, but are much less dependent on them, and much less predictable in their effects.

So while the state remains a primary site of political struggle, and struggle over which racialised discourse will prevail, there are other areas of society which are sites of antagonism, violent confrontation and deaths. Attitudes and beliefs towards sexuality, sexual relations and sport exemplify such sites. The evidence suggests that these ways of thinking are embraced widely and in a coherent if sometimes contradictory manner (Cashmore, 1982a; Bryan *et al.*, 1985; Hoose, 1989; hooks, 1990). Working-class actors are central to the promotion of many of these ideologies and while the state does exercise an influence it is not as clear that it plays a central manipulative role. The fact that they are articulated outside the state calls for a different type of response. Some of these are examined in the following section.

Fourth, discussions of 'new racisms' – subtle, circumspect, indirect – mean we have tended to forget historically entrenched racialised ideologies – crude, confrontational, direct – which might, by implication, be considered 'old' racisms; right-wing hatred, vicious attacks against Black families and homes, police violence, and more. The belief in the survival of the fittest, and the so-called rights of the 'white race' to obliterate the other are far from obsolete: the murders and maiming by the Ku Klux Klan, and of Bensonhurst and Howard Beach,[15] in the United States, of Colin Roach, Winston Rose and Roland Adams in England; the harassment and hounding of Black communities as exemplified by the Boston Stuart case in 1989, of Black young people under 'sus' and 'sas' in England (Small, 1983b; Smith, 1983; Carlson, 1990); attacks on college campuses (Farrell and Jones, 1988); racialised terrorism against Black homes (Greater London Council, 1984; Action Against Racial Terrorism Group, 1986; Marable, 1992). It is widely known that many white prison guards are members of the Ku Klux Klan and Aryan Brotherhood (Williams, 1991: 4). The Far Right is active in each nation (Omi and Winant, 1986; Thompson, 1988).

Activities and atrocities of these sorts remain palpable and nasty, as anyone in a Black community across either nation will tell you. These 'racisms', and their consequences, have great immediate and personal impact and are nonetheless serious because they are less frequent and less systematic than in the past. In the community or workplace, on the streets and in schools, even on college campuses, 'racism' is far from subtle and sophisticated – it is brutal, barbaric and bloody; vicious, vindictive and virulent. The victims of these 'racisms' do not have to worry about unravelling the subtleties or deciphering the 'real meaning' of someone throwing a firebomb into their homes, or their children being kicked in the teeth or stabbed in the back. If we are to understand this multiplicity of racialised ideologies, diverse in cause and content, we need to go beyond existing approaches.

## SOME NEGLECTED IDEOLOGIES

One area of society in which the expression of racialised ideologies has been neglected is that of sexuality. Throughout the 1980s Black men were commonly portrayed as sexually voracious and magnificently endowed, and as 'sexual threats to "white womanhood"' (Omi, 1989: 118). Black women were represented as sexually wanton and full of stamina, and were most often treated as 'exotic sex objects' (ibid.: 118). Both men and women were portrayed as promiscuous and immoral.[16] In the United States the historical legacy is central to understanding contemporary stereotypes of men and women which are differentially represented but linked in a necessary manner, because the 'mythical rapist implies the mythical whore' (Davis, 1981: 191; see also Davis, 1989). Since slavery 'Black women have been seen as "all body, no mind"' (hooks, 1990: 153). Having used Black women in the past as 'incubators for the breeding of other slaves' white culture has produced 'an iconography of Black female bodies that insisted on representing them as highly sexed, the perfect embodiment of primitive, unbridled eroticism' (ibid.: 153). This 'cultural currency' was pervasive in the 1980s as institutions of the mass media represented Black women as 'more sexual, as earthy freakish, out of control' and as 'savages, sluts, and/or prostitutes' (ibid.: 154).

The various images of Black women are linked through the common theme of sexuality, and this is promoted to achieve the various interests of the powerful in different historical periods (Collins, 1991: 70). The images of today are thus grounded in the racialised ramblings of the past, and the exploitation of the Black body – for labour, recreation and violence – in the past. Black women were portrayed as being sexually aggressive during slavery to justify the widespread sexual assaults by white men and the increased fertility required of them (ibid.: 77). Today 'the welfare mother. . .essentially an updated version of the breeder woman image created during slavery' and the 'Jezebel, whore, or sexually aggressive woman' are central to such power (ibid.: 76–7). Collectively such images shift the blame on to Black women, and away from the structural sources of poverty. All serve to enable the state to get off the hook:

> From the mammies, Jezebels and breeder women of slavery to the smiling Aunt Jemimas on pancake mix boxes, ubiquitous black prostitutes, and ever-present welfare mothers of contemporary popular culture.
>
> (Collins, 1991: 7)

Similarly in England 'racist sexist fantasies' set the ideological terrain for interactions between Black women and non-Blacks (as well as in relationships with Black men) and sexist stereotypes are pervasive (Mama, 1992: 87, 89). An 'animal like promiscuity' was portrayed as the primary characteristic of Black women, as were myths of Black women's sexuality and reproduction (Bryan *et al.*, 1985: 212). Once again, the media was the main disseminator and 'countless media images depicting the Black woman as "exotic whore" prevail' (ibid.: 213). The Black woman continued to be portrayed in film and on television as a hooker, prolific breeder, domestic, night-club singer or athlete. As in the United States, this was linked directly and indirectly, to the Black man as 'sexual brute' (ibid.: 213). Overall, such images not only structured the sexual relations of Black women, but also impacted upon provisions for their family planning and medical treatment (ibid.: 194).

Closely tied to sexuality are, of course, racialised sexual relations.[17] Beliefs about sexuality and sexual relations reflect notions of the distinctiveness of 'races'. The metaphors used to discuss them – purity and pollution – hide an underlying set of biological beliefs. We are less likely to hear of opposition to such sexual relations for reasons of culture or 'reverse racism'.[18] Three particular sets of beliefs prevailed: an assumption that Blacks and whites are separate 'races', with Blacks inferior and whites superior, each possessing a distinctive sexual nature; an assumption that Black men crave white women (the 'forbidden fruit' or a chance for revenge on white men) (Collins, 1991; Spickard, 1989); the representation of the children of such relationships as genetically, psychologically and socially problematic (Wilson, A., 1981, 1987; Alibhai-Brown and Montague, 1992; Root, 1992. Also, see Spickard, 1989).

A range of agencies – schools, media, corporations and government departments – were the main sites for transmitting images like these (Collins, 1991: 85). Films like *Mona Lisa* reduce Black women to sexual objects. While beliefs about sexuality and sexual relations are likely to be widespread, the symbolism and imagery have a resonance out of all proportion to the actual practices which are limited in extent. Beliefs of this kind were the basis for the success of Bush's manipulation of Willie Horton, and the murder of Yusef Hawkins, as described earlier. The depth of anxiety and despair experienced by those who have entered into such relationships is poignantly described by Alibhai-Brown and Montague (1992) and Spickard (1989).

Another area in which analysis of racialised discourse has been neglected, and one in which such discourse is also preoccupied with the Black body, is that of sport. Most recent research on Black people in sport has focused on the disjuncture between its image as a realm of equal opportunity and the reality of racialised stereotyping and discrimination (Edwards, 1973; Cashmore, 1982; Hargreaves, 1986; Mason, 1988; Johnson, 1991). These are not the areas of my concern here. My interest is with a different set of attitudes and belief systems which characterise the sporting world – the widespread assumptions, beliefs, even articulated theories, that Blacks and whites are naturally – biologically, genetically, mentally – suited for different sports. Most contemporary scientific knowledge evaluates the impact on sporting ability of any biological differences as might exist between Blacks and non-Blacks to be negligible:

> Biology is irrelevant. Some people still believe that African rhythms and even special sporting talents are programmed into particular races' genes, but so much that was once reputed to be natural has turned out to be cultural that we are entitled to instant suspicions of biological explanations.
>
> (Roberts, 1983: 145)

The research demonstrates that racialised groups vary in biological abilities and in strength and motor performance just as they do on other indices (Roberts, 1983).[19] So much for the facts. Regardless of this, the evidence suggests very strongly that such views remain widespread and crop up time and time again – among working-class peers, sports commentators and press, teachers and professional coaches (Cashmore, 1982; Sage, 1990).[20] Some of these have been well publicised and caused a stir.

Racialised 'stereotyping' is central in American sports – Blacks and non-Blacks are deemed to have differential abilities and to excel in different activities (Greendorfer, 1992: 59; Sage, 1990: 134). In studies of coaches' attitudes Blacks are identified as possessing qualities such as 'physical speed, physical quickness and motivation to achieve' while non-Blacks possess 'reliability, quick comprehension, and thinking ability' (Calhoun, 1987: 193–4). This most often results in 'stacking', which entails 'the linking of specific traits or skills to a minority group and treating all members of that group in the same fashion' (Greendorfer, 1992: 59). The historical impact of these beliefs is reflected in the segregated social structure of sports in the 1980s. Greendorfer adds, 'not only is racial stereotyping at the core of stacking, but racial stereotyping conditions teachers and coaches to expect to see certain skills in some players but not in others' (ibid.: 60). Consequently, 'data reveal consistent patterns of black over-representation in non-central positions. . .and under-representation in central positions' (ibid.: 59). Other authors agree about the incidence of racialised stereotyping:

> The most blatant examples are the frequent attributions of black athletes' achievements to their 'natural' abilities to run fast and jump high and their 'instincts' to react fast; at the same time – and sometimes during the same game – white athletes' achievements are typically attributed to their 'intelligence' and superior 'thinking ability'.
>
> (Sage, 1990: 134)

One of the most publicised examples of such attitudes in the 1980s in the United States was that of Al Campanis, Vice-President of Player Personnel for the Los Angeles Dodgers who, in an interview on American television said: 'I truly believe that "blacks" may not have some of the necessities to be, let's say, a field manager or perhaps a general manager' (Omi, 1989: 112; Hoose, 1989). He went on to talk of Blacks' natural abilities – 'gifted with great musculature and various other things. . . .fleet of foot' but not equipped for senior administrative or managerial positions (Omi, 1989: 112). Another well-cited example was that of Jimmy 'The Greek' Snyder who maintained that slavery had weeded out the weakest Blacks with the effect that in contemporary American sport Blacks had advantages over whites (Omi, 1989).

Similar evidence was available for England. One author comments:

> The predominant understanding of ethnic differences, as far as PE (physical education) is concerned, is in terms of ethnic groups' physical differences: blacks are said to be less buoyant in the water than whites . . . West Indian pupils' natural movement tendency is said to be located in the lower half of the body . . . and West Indian 'effort attitudes' are said to be towards 'fighting attitudes'.
>
> (Hargreaves, 1986: 180)

The author continues, 'PE teachers widely assume that blacks are naturally better at sports, and promote black participation as an alternative success system for these pupils, as a way of integrating

them into the school culture and of gaining prestige for themselves
and the school' (Hargreaves, 1986: 180). In the domain of competitive amateur and professional sport, research carried out by
Cashmore demonstrated that many officials believe Blacks are
'equipped for certain disciplines only', that coaches, trainers and
managers often subscribed to theories 'about black sporting pro-
clivities stemming from, among other things, natural talent and
that blacks "lack bottle"', that is, courage, determination or guts
(1982a: 177, 183). This research led Cashmore to conclude that the
'explain-all theory of "natural ability"' was 'prevalent amongst
sporting communities' (1982a: 43). Further, 'virtually everyone in
sport, to some extent, accepts that blacks have a natural ability at
sport which functions at both physical and intellectual levels'
including a wide array of top sports coaches (Cashmore, 1982a: 46).
He goes on, 'Some folk theories of sport have achieved a myth-like
status, and they are often seriously entertained and elaborated
upon by those in sport' (Cashmore, 1982a: 44). Such research has
been subjected to mockery. In an interview with Cashmore about
evidence contradicting theories about natural ability, the inter-
viewer frivolously dismissed his research, arguing 'looking at the
history of sport generally, it seems hard to dismiss the natural talent
theory. In cricket, West Indians display a seemingly natural flair,
litheness and grace of movement that seems beyond their English
counterparts' (Reyburn, 1990: 9).

The most well-cited incidence of such attitudes must be that of
Crystal Palace Chairman, Ron Noakes, at the end of the decade.
He maintained that Blacks lacked what was needed for decision-
making positions and that they had 'the bodies' but not 'the
brains' for football. Black players, he maintained, were good on
the ball, had nice skill but then chaos broke out. Furthermore
they had little aptitude or interest in management. After considerable media attention, he later apologised but added 'I am
not a racist' (Priscoll, 1991). These views were far from original,
as was evidenced by the numerous statements in support of such
views reiterated in the letter columns of daily tabloids in the
weeks during and following the controversy. One media com-
mentator noted about Noakes: 'as he well knows, it was the kind
of casually expressed opinion about black sportsmen and women
that you could hear a dozen times a week down at your local'
(Priscoll, 1991: 8. See also, Hill, 1989). The media not only airs
but furthers such views. In a national 'quality' newspaper, one

columnist in an article on cricket entitled 'Lifestyle may explain poor Test Record', reported:

> Generally speaking, players of Anglo-Saxon stock do not have the same natural flair as those of African or Asian origins, and physically the West Indians are stronger, partly because of their lifestyle when they are young. They tend to walk to school, not to go by car, and they spend more time in the open air. Lucky them!
> (Martin-Jenkins, 1991: 21)

He thus weaves together in a plausible way biology and culture, but with an almost complete disregard for the facts. (See also the examples cited in Walvin, 1986: 71.) Because of such beliefs, Black young people are directed into sport more often than non-Blacks, with some teachers playing an important role in encouraging them. Many Black young people are made to 'feel they are naturally gifted sportsmen' (Cashmore, 1982a: 106). The highly visible (if selective) success of Blacks in sports such as boxing, athletics, and football, clearly contributes to this. For example, of the 600 professional boxers in Britain, 30 per cent were Black, while the population (including all minorities) was around 4.5 per cent nationally (Mason, 1988: 14).

While the over-representation of Blacks in certain sports can only adequately be explained in conjunction with other factors – including the impact of successful Blacks on aspiring Black young people – nevertheless, 'it has almost certainly got something to do with the stereotypes which live in the minds of trainers, coaches and managers about "natural ability"' (Mason, 1988: 16). Mason reports that:

> Racist remarks fall easily from the tongues of white players, coaches and managers . . . (and) some stereotypes persist in spite of any amount of contradictory evidence. Two favourite ones among the football *cognoscenti* are that black players are lazy and they have 'no bottle', in other words, they will avoid the hard, physical challenge which is sometimes necessary to win the ball.
> (Mason, 1988: 17)

Schoolteachers are again cited as steering Blacks into roles best suited to their 'natural ability' (Mason, 1988: 18). Contradictions abound and are ignored: Blacks lack 'bottle' despite holding half the British boxing titles; they cannot run long distances, despite the success of the East Africans. In their estimations of Blacks' natural ability few are distracted from their myopia by considerations of Blacks infrequent entrées into angling, alpine climbing, bowls, darts, equestrian events, gymnastics, ice hockey, ice skating, rowing, snooker, synchronised swimming, tennis, or yachting. Where are all the 'graceful', 'lithe' African-Caribbean gymnasts? Apparently beating their heads against the wall of racialised ideologies and discrimination trying to get education and employment to put them into positions where they can enter such sports.

Racialised ideologies of varying elaborations are pervasive in the world of sport with complex, emotive issues explained casually in the allure of a simple racialised rhetoric of natural ability. The stereotyping involved is systematic, elaborated and based on assumptions of separate racialised groups possessing distinct mental and physical abilities. It takes little effort to formulate it as a doctrine of 'natural ability'. Nor is it done in any deliberately demeaning or disparaging fashion. We are not talking about racialised abuse, diatribes of invectives; but simple, plain, praiseworthy 'common sense'. It is as if the holders of such views are praising Black 'natural' superiority in much the same way that white slavemasters espoused the 'natural' superiority of Blacks in the plantation fields.

On the whole then, it seems, the experience of many working-class whites of Blacks in sport, or rather their selective perception of Blacks in sport, facilitates a world view which posits Blacks as 'naturally' more able in certain sports, and which thus lends itself to a crude, biologically-based racialised ideology. Whether in boxing and athletics in each nation, football and basketball in the United States, or in soccer and cricket in England, Blacks are viewed as unequalled. But is this to be called a racialised ideology or is it a 'simple prejudice'? I want to suggest that these ideas, notions and beliefs constitute a relatively coherent, if often contradictory, ideology which might be described as follows: Blacks and whites are different biological 'races' with different abilities; these abilities are manifested in the sports realm in consistent ways; whites are able to think and handle sports requiring planning, decision-making and judgement; they are also able to float better in swimming; Blacks perform better in sports requiring physical strength, speed and stamina, such as boxing. These ideas are not consistent over time, but are modified to take account of new developments, such as the increased number of Black-middle and long-distance runners, and (English) football players.

The outcome of all of this is equally adverse for Black people. Though the exponents of such views – working-class whites, school-teachers, coaches, trainers and managers of sports institutions – do not wield the political power of governments and politicians, the power that they wield is potent. They divert young people away from academic areas, encourage them to perpetuate the stereotypes and generate conflict. And, as is usual with much of the racialised hostility described in this book, the ideologies about Blacks held by non-Blacks 'reveal more about white attitudes than about black attainments or qualities' (Walvin, 1986: 75). They have to do with maintaining status quo in power relations, and in the distribution of resources within and outside the sporting world. Some writers believe that many of the basic aspects of 'scientific racism' remain believable to most whites, and even to many Blacks (Collins, 1991: 24). What I have said here about sport (and about sexuality and sexual relations) has counterparts in other areas, notably in the realms of music and art where Black natural ability is posited time and time again (Walvin, 1986: 72). The fact that Blacks embrace these ideologies is explained more by their need to claim some superiority in certain arenas than by any convincing evidence.

## CONCLUSION

In this chapter I have outlined how developments in the 1980s have led to new challenges to the ways in which we analyse racialised ideologies and inequality, as well as how we might develop effective political and policy responses to them. I have argued that along with the strengths of the best analyses are a number of limitations, including a problematic conceptualisation of the 'new racism' due to a preoccupation with state activities, and insufficient consideration of agencies and actors outside the state and the formal political arena. I have demonstrated that while the state is central to the dissemination of some racialised ideologies, other racialised ideologies are important and are embraced and disseminated by groups outside the formal political arena. I have suggested that a better approach is one which conceptualises 'racisms' not as 'old' and 'new' but as transformations and shifts in racialised discourse, (and seeks to relate them to other economic and political forces). This formulation means we can then specify the various components of these ideologies and the contexts in which each is brought to the foreground, and assess which is more salient and in which historical context, especially *vis-à-vis* broader economic forces and political attitudes. We do not have to get bogged down in the futile exercise of searching for the historical origin of 'racism'.[21] With the international landscape increasingly dominated by a new vortex of economic and political forces, such patterns are bound to become more complex in the 1990s.

One of the central shortcomings of most existing analyses is the failure to consider racialised ideologies not entirely contingent on state activities. An analysis of these ideologies is important for several reasons. First, they are grounded in the personal and daily experiences of working class non-Blacks and reflect continuities with the past, in particular, embracing the idea of discrete hierarchical 'races' with different abilities. This signifies the refusal of many to let go of biologically-based 'racisms' despite the emergence of new knowledge, and represents a hard base of racialised resistance which daily impacts on the lives of Black people. Second, many of these ideas are not very new, and frequently not at all subtle. Third, they emphasise the differential impact of ideologies on Black men and women (as well as the differential power relations involved) and the additional obstacles imposed as a result of gender hostility. Fourth, in the areas described here – sexuality, sexual relations and sporting ability – racialised ideologies are not primarily or exclusively those of disdain and condescension, but involve important elements of jealousy and resentment. This adds new dimensions.[22] Fifth, because they are less likely to occupy a central position in ideologies articulated by the state – though the state does contribute to them – they call for different strategies of challenge and confrontation.

The influence of racialised discourse in these areas is enormous, and the consequences both immediate and adverse. For example, the scope of involvement of Black people in sport, the fact that it provides an arena for substantial and sustained interaction between Blacks and non-Blacks, as well as its popular influence, means it is of the utmost importance to the generation and dissemination of the images being described here. Black young people are being encouraged to get on the fast track to sports success, rather than the educational track to academic success. Just as importantly, this imagery, and how Black people respond to it, has set in motion hostilities between Black men and women that will endure for some time, yet whose effects have not been fully acknowledged or documented. For example, Black women suffer greater injustice from the racialised sexuality generally associated with Black people by non-Blacks. As some Black men take on the sexual roles imputed to them, embracing a hyper-masculinity, Black women can be victims not only of white 'racism', but also of Black men's aggression. The outcomes of sexual violence are both vile and contemptible and even when Black women challenge racialised stereotypes they are in jeopardy of reinforcing them (Cose, 1989; Mama, 1989). We cannot afford to underestimate the role that they play in patterns of racialised hostility. These ideologies have yet to be exposed to any rigorous scrutiny or linked to the political subtleties of the 'new racisms'. They merit greater examination.

One of the strengths of the approach taken by Omi and Winant is their use of the concept of rearticulation (1986). This concept enables us to approach the different elements in a way responsive to the influence of many factors, and the different contexts (Omi and Winant, 1986). This emphasises that racialised ideologies are always dynamic, are moulded to meet different circumstances and take account of different factors, even as they are challenged. Omi and Winant have subsequently suggested how the concept might also be applied to the consideration of 'new racial subjects' (Omi and Winant, 1991). It has several other strengths. It highlights the underlying coherence of racialised ideologies, and it moves us away from simply describing a typology of 'racisms' to looking at other obstacles to racialised parity, for example, other conservative or right-wing ideologies. I would extend their analysis to include other types of 'racisms' than those promulgated primarily by the state, especially ideologies predicated on biological beliefs; I would give greater consideration to the role of the working class as a creator and perpetuator of such ideologies, rather than as passive actor; and I would look more at the influence of international forces. This approach could be used systematically to incorporate and explain the influence of patterns of racialised ideologies from the past; to explore further the differential impact on men and women; and to examine manifestations of 'racisms' in more narrowly defined historical contexts, institutional arenas and walks of life.

In sum then, the approach I have outlined enables us to investigate when and where various factors (economics, politics, class, as compared with racialised ideologies, stereotypes, and hostility) are important (and in light of the interplay between local, national and international contexts), rather than assuming whether or not one is more important than the others at all times and in all places. In particular it challenges the 'coat of paint theory', enables greater consideration to be given to the causal role of racialised ideologies in general (especially in class approaches) and requires that more sustained attention be given to racialised ideologies not currently discussed in references to state sponsored ideologies or the presumed 'new racisms'.

# Chapter 4

# Stratification and the Black 'middle class': talented tenth or Black bourgeoisie?

## INTRODUCTION

The goal of this chapter is to examine the nature, extent and implications of increasing inequality in the Black population in the United States and England. I do this by first raising a number of theoretical issues and then describing some of the recent trends in the United States as stratification has increased in the context of legal desegregation. I then turn to examine the trends in England, as signs of increasing stratification appeared during the 1980s. The theoretical issues involved in this debate on stratification within the Black population have a long history in the United States (the background is described in Wilson, 1978). A central feature is concern with the role of the Black 'middle class' in facilitating progress for other Blacks. My main concern is to highlight and elaborate some important issues, taking account of the available data, and to suggest a number of reasons why no simple evaluation is possible at present. A particular goal will be to differentiate the range of groups subsumed under the broad rubric of a Black 'middle class', to examine some data on their numbers and activities and to incorporate consideration of gender. Overall, I want to suggest that important contributions have been made but that a number of significant problems remain. An organising theme for this chapter is to address the question: Does the Black 'middle class' help or hinder progress towards equality for other Blacks? Are they a blessing or a curse?

One of the most distinctive characteristics of the African-American experience since the 1950s has been the dramatically increased pattern of economic and political stratification (Farley and Allen, 1989). The Black population in the United States is overwhelmingly indigenous and the majority of families have been there for many generations, some dating back to the first Africans enslaved there in the seventeenth century (Farley and Allen, 1989). There has always been stratification within the Black population – by linguistic, religious and national origins, as well as by economic, educational and political variables – though the extent of such stratification was greatly constrained during slavery and throughout the Jim Crow period. But Jim Crow in the twentieth century also saw significant evidence of increasing mobility as a Black 'middle class' developed, particularly around small businesses (Wilson, 1978).

Stratification and differentiation, often characterised as fragmentation and polarisation, have expanded substantially since the Civil Rights Movement in the 1950s (Wilson, 1978). Categorical discrimination – against all Blacks – has given way to statistical discrimination – against sections of the Black population (Banton, 1983: 284). Though the balance towards paupers rather than princes, and towards mendicants rather than millionaires is indisputable, the 1980s revealed substantial variations in health, wealth and well-being (O'Hare *et al.*, 1991).

Discussion of the consolidation and expansion of a Black 'middle class' – and the increasing entrenchment of a Black 'underclass' – dominated analysis of Blacks in the United States in the 1980s (Murray, 1984; Wilson, W., 1987). The main tendency in these analyses has been to argue that the Black 'middle class' shares little in common with, and has abandoned, working-class and workless Black people, and that this process began in earnest with the success of the Civil Rights Movement in the 1950s and 1960s. One of the sour aspects of this 'success' was that desegregation led to the flight of many educated and talented Blacks to non-Black institutions from which they had historically been denied entry (Wilson, 1978; Wilson, W., 1987). This portrayal presents the Black 'middle class' somehow as deserting other Blacks. However, as usual, the picture is not that simple, and there is, as will be demonstrated, clear evidence contradicting it.

Although of very different dimensions, stratification among the Black population in England during the 1980s also increased as people of African origin became increasingly indigenous, and began to overcome some of the steadfast obstacles created by racialised discrimination.[1] Despite extensive racialised discrimination and hostility, the entry of small numbers of African-Caribbeans into some of the higher levels of the socio-economic hierarchy is clear. This group includes business owners, managers, self-employed, professionals such as academics, doctors and social workers, local and central government workers and civil servants. There are also politicians, and a number of miscellaneous rich individuals such as sport personalities and musicians.[2] The growth of professional associations and Black network associations (such as Rapport) reported in the Black media, reflect the self-directed activities of these groups. Though this is hardly of the order of the activity in the United States, it is significant and has led to a number of divergences in Black attitudes towards progress, has attracted attention from a number of scholars, and is bound to increase in significance (Gilroy, 1987a; Miles, 1982, 1989). This has been particularly important because of the greater popular and political concern with issues of class analysis. To some extent discussion of these issues is influenced by impressions and awareness of what is going on in the United States (Cashmore, 1991).

These developments raise a number of questions for each nation. What were the parameters of the Black 'middle class' in the 1980s? Who is to be included in this group and on the basis of what criteria? What was the economic basis of 'middle class' standing? What were the differences in the economic and status positions of sections of the Black 'middle class'? What developments suggested that the Black 'middle class' acted primarily or exclusively on the basis of class interests alone? What developments suggested the Black 'middle class' acted on the basis of a common racialised identity? To what extent did such actions contribute to the broader struggle being waged by working and workless Black people? And what evidence was offered to support these contentions?

There are other questions which need to be addressed. For example, there are common features with regard to conflict within the Black population over priorities and strategies; over how far the Black 'middle class' achieves its goals 'on the backs' of working and unemployed Black people; over how far sections of the white population, and the state, manipulate class differences within the Black population (Marable, 1983; Miles, 1989). During the 1980s did Black businesses provide jobs, role models and counter stereo-types? Did the Black 'middle class' vote and act on the basis of racialised affiliations, or on the basis of class interests? Did the Black 'middle class' act so as to confer benefits on other Blacks, that is, did they pay the 'Black Tax?'[3] Or did they simply feather their own

nests and thus abandon or 'sell out' other working (and unemployed) Blacks? A key underlying question is that in the creation
of a Black 'middle class' has the way been paved for changes in
the material circumstances of other Black people? Or has it simply
provided the state with additional mechanisms to suppress and
contain demands for more radical change?[4]

In interpreting these patterns I want to draw on a number of
theoretical issues, and construct a debate between two influential
African-Americans, about the role of the Black 'middle class' in
shaping the future for the Black population as a whole. These
contributions were made in different structural circumstances (by
Dubois at the end of the last century, and by Frazier in the 1950s,
both in the United States) but the central themes remain applicable
to the present day in both nations. The primary question concerns
the strategy to be embraced for overcoming the racialised hostility
and disadvantage confronted by Black people as a group, and the
role that the Black 'middle class' might play in this strategy. In
particular, in the United States, has the Black 'middle class' become
a 'Talented Tenth' leading other Black people to equality? Or
has it become a 'Black Bourgeoisie', uninterested in the problems
confronting other Black people and obsessed with its own self-
interest and conspicuous consumption? Finally, what are the
implications for racialised barriers, boundaries and identities as
we confront the 1990s?

An analysis of stratification and the Black 'middle class' in each
nation can help us evaluate further issues of racialised barriers,
boundaries and identities. There has always been a glass ceiling
which served as a barrier to Black aspirations but this has been
broken several times, and erected at higher (economic) levels. In
the transgression of such barriers, upwardly mobile Blacks have put
themselves into new situations which have involved crossing boundaries (social, sexual, political) and creating new tensions for
racialised identities. As with the other substantive issues discussed
in this book, developments in the United States offer insights on
the debates in England. Black people in England look to the United
States (as do Government and policymakers) to find insights on
policies to develop Black businesses and a Black 'middle class',
(Banton, 1985; *Voice* 5 February, 1991: 17; *Voice* 22 January 1991: 5,
23). There are many precedents in the United States, and the
absolute scale is much greater, so analysis in England can be
informed by an appreciation of patterns in the United States.

## TALENTED TENTH OR BLACK BOURGEOISIE?

Debate about the circumstances and activities of the African-American 'middle class' dates a long way back in the United States (Frazier, 1957). Drawing upon this debate enables us to outline a theoretical framework within which to evaluate the development of a Black 'middle class' in both the United States and England in the 1980s and 1990s. Consideration of the arguments made by W.E.B. Dubois and E. Franklin Frazier allows for the starkest characterisation of many of the issues at stake in discussions of the African-American and African-Caribbean 'middle class'. W.E.B. Dubois was a noted essayist, academic and political activist whose career spanned seven decades. He produced a vast array of writings – including detailed theoretical and empirical analyses of the circumstances of Africans throughout the diaspora – as well as editing and writing for numerous journals and magazines (Rudwick, 1968; Lester, 1971, vols I and II). His analyses responded to the rapidly changing circumstances of the United States – from the 1870s to the 1960s – and it does not make sense to pin down one set of theories as if he subscribed to them at all times. Writing in the early 1900s, in a context of segregation he produced a theory of the 'Talented Tenth' (Lester, 1971; vol. 1: 403). This was a general theory of civilisation and development, an attempt to characterise the growth of all societies.

Dubois argued that every civilisation produced a 'Talented Tenth' of its population – a group of the most talented and able thinkers, planners and analysts who contributed to the development of society in such a way as to lead the rest of the population forward. Dubois believed that the growth of a 'Talented Tenth' was the way forward for African-Americans. The 'Talented Tenth' constituted a group of intellectuals who would inspire and lead their own people forward on the basis of self-help and co-operation, while also seeking support from non-Blacks. They would become planners of African-American advancement, organising producer and consumer collectives and advancing the 'race'. African-Americans would thus build their own businesses, institutions and organisations on the basis of a self-help philosophy at the vanguard of which would be the brightest and most able African-American thinkers and intellectuals. This theoretical idea was put into practice by Dubois and is reflected in the phenomenal contribution that he made to African-American

schools, universities and education via publications and the training of teachers and educators.[5]

E. Franklin Frazier was a distinguished sociologist and educator,
a product of the renowned Chicago School of Sociology and a
student of Robert Park. He went on to produce an array of
sociology publications, and was elected President of the American
Sociological Society (now American Sociological Association) in
1948 (Edwards, 1968). While most of his work was scholarly, he
produced a polemical piece in the 1950s, while living and teaching
in Washington DC, at that time the African-American 'middle class'
capital of the United States. This book, *Black Bourgeoisie*, displayed
his contempt for a major section of the African-American 'middle
class' (Frazier, 1957). Although he was not responding directly to
Dubois, Frazier's position at its starkest was that the 'Black Bourgeoisie' was a total parody of a 'Talented Tenth'. He argued that
the 'Black Bourgeoisie' spent its life aping the habits and etiquette
of the white bourgeoisie, making a fool of itself, and living an
ostentatious and extravagant lifestyle for which it lacked sufficient
material basis. Most African-Americans in the 'middle class' at that
time were schoolteachers, professors in America's segregated Black
universities, or owners of small stores such as barber-shops, hairdressers and funeral parlours. Such jobs hardly paid a considerable
salary.

The 'Black Bourgeoisie', argued Frazier, had failed to play the
role of a responsible élite in the African-American community and
had shown no interest in the 'liberation' of African-Americans,
except where it affected their own status or acceptance by the non-
Black community (Frazier, 1957: 235). When the opportunity had
been present, the 'Black Bourgeoisie' had exploited the African-
American masses as ruthlessly as the whites and scorned the Black
pride and nationalism of Garvey, and the 'Negro Renaissance'
(ibid.: 236). They strove to forget the 'Negro's past' and 'have
attempted to conform to the behaviour and values of the white
community in the most minute details' (ibid.: 235). In fact, he
maintained, their entire mental outlook was dominated by an
obsession with the struggle for status. Rather than leading other
African-Americans to freedom, uplift and equality, the 'Black Bourgeoisie' was preoccupied with conspicuous consumption, sponged
off other African-Americans and squandered its wealth on petty
and superficial extravagances.

The key question for the 1980s is to identify patterns of activities of those in the Black 'middle class' and to assess whether the economic divisions within the Black population translated into political divisions – which is how we can begin to assess whether the Black 'middle class' is a blessing or a curse for other Black people. This is not so simple because the same action can be open to several interpretations. For example, does voting Republican or Conservative automatically constitute abandonment of Black people's interests? And does voting Democrat or Labour constitute commitment to such interests? Some people may wish to conclude that voting for a party which insists on a 'colour blind' approach, which reveals little Black representation or commitment of funds to the priorities of most Black people, is tantamount to a 'sell-out', whereas voting for a party which advocates affirmative action or positive action is the opposite. It would be presumptuous to conclude that any Black person voting Democrat or Labour neces-sarily has the interests of other Black people at heart. Similarly, it is tempting but a mistake, I believe, to define anyone who is rich and/ or votes Republican or Conservative, as being inimical to other Black people. Can we argue that someone relentlessly pursuing his or her own business, with complete disregard for the negative social effects constitutes a 'sell-out'? Can we conclude that any wealthy Black individual that eschews to discuss more general matters of racialised injustice, has foregone any commitment to the larger group? For example, consider W.E.B Dubois and Booker T. Washington: the former was largely portrayed as a nationalist, the latter as an integrationist, but was it that simple? (Meier, 1963). Both wanted black self-determination, but they had different visions and strat-egies about how that could be achieved.

How, therefore, are we to establish exactly what pursuing class interests amounts to? And can we presume that it automatically constitutes the abandonment of other Blacks? For some, pursuing class interests may be seen intentionally as the best strategy for all Blacks. During the 1980s this was the clear argument of Black people subscribing to Conservativism and Republicanism (Sowell, 1983, 1990; Steele, 1990). We need to establish criteria and anchor our evaluation somewhere: that is, we need to explore the lines of political demarcation and divergence within the Black population and to consider the evidence on both sets of arguments.

A central consideration has to be acknowledgement that many key organisations and groups, or their leaders, are usually 'middle class' by definition. In the United States this is as true of the Black

Congressional Caucus as it is of the Rainbow Coalition; it is as true of the National Association for the Advancement of Colored People (NAACP) as it is of the Urban League; and it is true of the Nation of Islam. In England it is as true of the Black Members of Parliament as it is of the Black Sections movement; it is as true of the Commission for Racial Equality as it is of the National Black Caucus; and it is as true of the Institute of Race Relations as it is of the Race Today Collective. So what can this tell us? In our analysis we need to address the question why rich or 'middle class' Black people should feel committed to other Black people? Why should they be judged to have sold out, when other non-Black 'middle class' people are not held up to the same expectations?

## FRAGMENTATION AND POLARISATION IN THE UNITED STATES

In the United States in the 1980s non-Blacks had more wealth and better incomes than Blacks as a whole, and for all socio-economic ranks taking account of education and work experience (see Chapter 2). But there was a significant minority of the Black population doing well – some of them extremely well – a section whose lifestyle matched that of non-Blacks. This was especially true for young educated Blacks. For example:

> Among (black) married-couple families where the head of household is 25 to 44 years old and a college graduate, the median income of blacks ($54,400) is 93 per cent that of whites ($58,800).
>
> (O'Hare *et al.*, 1991: 28)

By the end of the 1980s about one in seven black families had an income of $50,000 (as compared with nearly one in three non-Black families) while the percentage of Black men in professional and managerial occupations was 13 per cent in 1990 (O'Hare *et al.*, 1991: 29). These affluent African-Americans tended to be two-income families, well educated, in the prime, economically active age range, own their own homes, and live in the suburbs.

But how many African-Americans might be defined as 'middle class'? The concept of 'class' is defined in several different ways. Wilson defined a class as 'any group of people who have more or less similar goods, services, or skills to offer for income in a given

economic order and who therefore receive similar financial re-
muneration in the marketplace' and modifying Frazier's (1957)
approach, he identified the black 'middle class' as those employed
in white-collar jobs, craftsmen, and those in foreman positions
(Wilson, 1978: ix, 7). Landry defines classes as 'groups differing
from each other by the average market situation or rewards of
the positions their members occupy' (1987: 3). Focusing on the
most economically successful of the African-American population,
Boston distinguished a 'capitalist class' and a 'middle class',
each having two sections (Boston, 1988). He distinguished an old
Black capitalist class and a new one in terms of the basis of their
wealth and the extent of their connections with, and dependence
on, the rest of the Black population (ibid.: 33). The former is
long-established, derives its money from businesses in the Black
community and is thus dependent on it. The latter has its origins
in the 1950s and 1960s, is derived from Civil Rights actions, and is
employed largely by non-Blacks. The old Black 'middle class' is
based in Black communities and made up of self-employed people
such as doctors, lawyers, shop owners, barbers, beauticians, funeral
directors and carpenters (ibid.: 39) The new Black 'middle class'
consists of people whose 'skills are acquired usually through
advanced education, training, or specialized apprenticeships. Individuals possessing these abilities include scientists, engineers,
professors, technicians, professional athletes, and entertainers'
(ibid.: 39). Using this definition Boston calculates a Black 'middle
class' group for the 1980s of over 1.3 million, 'constituting approximately 15 per cent of the black employed population' (ibid.: 42).
He points out that the non-Black 'middle class' added up to 29.8
per cent of its employed population.

There are several reasons for suspecting that class affiliations
brought most to bear on the attitudes of the Black 'middle class' in
the 1980s. The first argument is the view that most people vote on
the basis of economic or class position, and support policies which
benefit them and their offspring, not someone else. The Black
'middle class' has different experiences and thus different priorities
from the Black working class. In other words, as Boston points out:

Social consciousness, political actions, and inactions are greatly
influenced by the institutional arrangements within which people
earn their means of livelihood.

(Boston, 1988: 9)

Having fled the ghettos and Black institutions (colleges, hospitals, businesses) when desegregation allowed them to do so, they now lead lifestyles in neighbourhoods and social institutions that are far removed from their Black working-class counterparts. Wilson argues that there has been an exodus of 'middle class' Blacks from the inner city (Wilson, 1987: 55–7, 143).

It is not that they are 'integrated' with non-Blacks, but that they socialise with one another in black-tie events and social functions rather than with the Black working class. While the Cosby show did not reflect the lifestyles of most African-Americans, there are hundreds of thousands of Black people who led a similar lifestyle. This group had common political, educational and economic interests and priorities, and voted and acted in its own interest.

A second argument is that the Black 'middle class', especially those that have emerged since the 1960s, are able to pursue their own interests unfettered by Black community concerns because they are often not dependent on Black workers for jobs, political support or custom. Many in the Black 'middle class' tend to be employed 'in mainstream occupations outside the black community' (Wilson, 1987: 143). In fact, many are more dependent on white patronage, their employers are white, including Federal and state governments, and they have to 'tow the line' (Boston, 1988). They may respond to some Black demands or requests but are not dependent upon them for direct business as was the case with the old Black 'middle class' in the segregated areas of the past. Given the firm commitment of the non-Black 'middle class' and government to free market mechanisms, and a philosophy of individualism, and their opposition to affirmative action, the Black 'middle class' can be expected to follow suit. No doubt a significant number of the Black 'middle class' are well represented in the ranks of the Blacks that oppose affirmative action (Marger, 1991).

Where there is support for affirmative action and other programmes by the Black 'middle class' that may seem like an expression of a common racialised agenda, it can be argued that this is because they are most likely to reap the benefits. Wilson argues that 'Race-specific programs' have led to greater success for 'advantaged blacks' than for poor Blacks (Wilson, 1978: 165; 1987: 111, 115). Black people applying to Harvard, Yale, Princeton or Berkeley, or for jobs in top corporations or law firms, are more likely to be 'middle class' or to have parents who are 'middle class'.

A third reason is that in politics it may be in the interest of some

Black politicians to play down or ignore key concerns of the Black masses. For example, some Black politicians have cast their net wider to win non-Black voters and gain bigger political office (Barnes, 1990). In some instances this has led to the abandonment of priorities cherished by Black working class people in their quest for a frontal attack on white 'racism'. Do such issues get played down? Thomas Bradly, Mayor of Los Angeles is a prime example. He has always appealed to a constituency much larger than Blacks, and had to do so given his state-wide aspirations. The same can be said of Andrew Young, and of Black politicians in constituencies with small numbers of Black voters. Several Black politicians say many of their colleagues do not feel obliged to Black constituencies (Barnes, 1990: 263).

Another example of the pursuit of self-interest can be found among Black businesses. Here it is suggested that the dog-eat-dog world of capitalism makes profit the pre-eminent motivating factor. Black entrepreneurs have little time for community benevolence and concern when trying 'to make a buck'. Who would doubt that Black entrepreneurs are as avaricious as white entrepreneurs (Boston, 1988: 38). Furthermore, promotion of Black businesses is part of the state's goal of incorporation and co-optation (Fusfeld and Bates, 1984: 215–235; Pinkney, 1984). In the South, in particular, the Black 'middle class' represented much of the hope for the Republican party (Goldfield, 1990: 242). The activities of many Black professionals also lend weight to this argument of enlightened group self-interest. Gaining access to the professions and élite educational institutions seemed to have little immediate benefit for Black people in poverty.

On top of all this we have the activities of Black conservatives. With the increasing numbers of the new Black 'middle class', the ideological trend of Black conservativism has been extended. There has always been a conservative stratum in the Black population but the 1980s reveals 'its most significant attempt to exert ideological influence over black society' (Boston, 1988: 46). It is unlikely that there are many Black conservatives among the working-class Black population. The distinguishing feature of this stratum is a social, cultural, political and organisational alienation from mainstream Black society and Black public opinion. Politically, this alienation forces it to the far right of the Black 'middle class' and Black society in general and has given rise to a new Black conservatism. During the 1980s many of its foremost spokespeople worked either for the government, white universities, or foundations and were closely affiliated with the conservative political tide sweeping mainstream politics in America. Because of this alliance, the stratum's ideologues enjoyed a notoriety far out of proportion to their actual influence within Black society (Boston, 1988: 46). Though small in number, Black conservatives are significant because of access to power and resources which were especially facilitated by the Reagan and Bush administrations. From Clarence Pendleton in the Civil Rights Commission to Thomas Sowell and Glen Loury in academia, Black conservatives have been resourced and highly publicised throughout the 1980s.

It is argued that this led the Black 'middle class' to have less sympathy with, or commitment to, the problems and priorities of the Black working class. They were more likely to be committed to the idea of individual effort and personal commitment, and more likely to subscribe to policies and politics which were out of tune with the wishes and needs of vast numbers of Black people that were unemployed, never-employed and in poverty. Wilson is convinced that the African-American 'middle class' got all the benefits and did not contribute to the uplift of other Black people.[6] He argues that the abandonment of the 'middle class' has led to the social isolation of the Black 'underclass' from skills, values, morality and aspirations (Wilson, 1987: 58). Interviews with many 'middle class' Blacks reveal that they feel many amongst their number have sold out the 'black masses' (Benjamin, 1991: 11).

If it is true that a disproportionately larger number of African-Caribbeans is to found among the ranks of the Black 'middle class', and that this group is an immigrant one, spurred on by personal sacrifice and initiative, then sentiments like these are likely to develop further (Farley and Allen, 1989). Examples such as Colin Powell may be extreme, but they illustrate the general point and lend great weight to the conservative leaning of successful Blacks.

Arguments like these suggest abandonment and betrayal for self-interest. An underlying theme, and one which dates back centuries but was highlighted most poignantly by E. Franklin Frazier in the 1950s, is the psychological malaise that the Black 'middle class' feels in a white 'racist' society. But is the Black 'middle class' pursuing a fleeting illusion? In a rhetorical flurry, Hare insists that the Black 'middle class' should 'abandon the unbridled pursuit of materialism and the all-engulfing frenzy for White approval and acceptance' because they will never get it (Hare, 1987: 86). The fact is, he argues that:

> For, after all is said and done, we are left with one indelible fact – and one thing members of the Black middle class will soon have to face – that no matter what else they may ever do, they will never get out of the Black race alive.
>
> (Hare, 1987: 86)

While several of these criticisms are persuasive, there remain significant problems. I outline here two broad sets of problems. The first set is theoretical, having to do with problems of conceptualisation and definition. Specifically, the Black 'middle class' is insufficiently defined, defined ambiguously or not at all and there is little attempt to differentiate the group. There is no consideration of the continued significance of racialised ideologies and hostility in maintaining racialised identities; and there is little attempt to take account of women among their numbers. The second set of problems is largely empirical, and has to do with details of the activities of the groups and individuals in question. While the arguments of critics are persuasive, they are not supported by any consistent data or by any determined effort to examine the actual lifestyles and activities in the 1980s of those defined as 'middle class'. There are data which contradict the characterisations offered.

On the first issue, Boston criticises the tendency to classify the 'middle class' arbitrarily by an income boundary, and to classify the entire family when the occupations of husbands and wives are very different (Boston, 1988: 7, 43). Wilson, the main proponent of many of these views, exemplifies many of these problems. He offers a definition of 'middle class' but it is broad and vague; he pays little attention to differences within the Black 'middle class' and he simply ignores women. Empirically he overlooks substantial evidence that many community activists and professionals contribute to programmes that have goals far greater than self-interest, including, among others, branches of the NAACP, PUSH (People United to Save Humanity) and the Urban League (Frazier, 1987). These groups did not have great power to achieve significant goals, and they were largely ineffective at the start of the 1980s and the onslaught of Reagan (Marable, 1983) – but that is different from accusing them of being entirely self-serving.

We cannot come to a fully informed analysis until we

differentiate the different sections of the rubric category of Black 'middle class' and assess their distinctive activities in terms of goals, priorities and strategies. For example, Marable argues there are different sections of Black leadership and the Black 'middle class', each struggling with others over accommodation in the larger fight for fairness for the Black majority, and the wider non-Black majority (Marable, 1983). For Marable, whose goal is socialism, one section of the Black 'middle class' poses the most problems:

> Black entrepreneurs and executives are the greatest internal barrier to the achievement of a socialist political consensus within the Black community.
>
> (Marable, 1983: 194)

A second theoretical consideration is that these arguments ignore the convincing evidence of continuing racialised discrimination in employment, education and housing throughout the 1980s (Landry, 1987; Wellman, 1993). The continued devastation caused by racialised ideologies, hostility and violence was outlined in Chapter 3. Wilson acknowledges some continuing discrimination but he reveals no recognition of how pervasive it is, and affords it little importance as a determinant of Black people's lives, when compared with class hostility (1978: 150; 1987). This amounts to an almost complete denial. Wilson and others also ignore the continued significance given by Black people to the racialised hostility in their lives (see Chapter 5). Because of the extent to which Black people, regardless of class position, share a view that racialised hostility is a major determinant of their situation they continue to organise around racialised identities with racialised agendas and priorities. Members of the Black 'middle class' are reminded of this all the time and there are many personal testimonies of racialised stigma and stereotypes that they face along with other Blacks (Graham, 1991: 116).

The third theoretical matter, and the most flagrant defect in most analyses, is the failure to differentiate the Black 'middle class' by gender. Although they share much in common with Black men, Black women occupy different structural positions which give rise to different priorities. For example, a greater proportion of Black women than men are likely to be single-parent families, while high proportions of Black women are in the professions. Thus, in 1990, '19 per cent of black women were in managerial and professional occupations, and 39 per cent were in technical or administrative.

While these percentages are well below those of non-Black women in higher paying jobs, the gaps are narrower than they are for men' (O'Hare *et al.*, 1990: 25). In addition more African-American managerial and professional women continue to be employed in the public sector, where there is less discrimination (Amott and Matthaei, 1991: 187).

We must look at the numbers and roles of Black women for several reasons. First, and axiomatically, the problems Black women face structurally are not synonymous with those facing Black men. They have to be assessed in terms of gender hostilities. We cannot assume that Black women will follow the same paths, and share the same priorities as Black men. It is not that they have bigger hearts and better morals than men, but the different structural locations which they occupy and different constituencies to which they respond, are likely to lead to different priorities. For example, most Black women professionals are found in jobs that serve Black, mostly poor and working-class clients. They are likely to be subjected to greater pressures and may respond accordingly (Amott and Matthaei, 1991). Once again, it is imperative that we identify the positions that women (and women's organisations) occupy in the socio-economic order, the roles that they have played in advancing political and policy causes, and the successes that they have achieved.

Second, the work and contribution of Black women in challenging and surmounting the obstacles confronting Black people generally has never been fully explored. In fact Black women employ a range of strategies to confront the multiple types of oppression they face, and they do so while recognising the complicity of Black men, but seeking to maintain bonds with them (Amott and Matthaei, 1992). These activities occur in three settings – 'political and economic institutions, Black extended families, and the African-American community as "family"' (Collins, 1991: 146). They reflect an activist tradition with 'two primary dimensions', a struggle for group survival, and a struggle for institutional transformation (Collins, 1991: 141–2). The former consists of 'actions taken to create Black female spheres of influence within existing structures of oppression' (ibid.: 141); the latter includes taking part in 'civil rights organisations, labour unions, feminist groups, boycotts, and revolts' (ibid.: 142). The contributions of Black women have yet to be fully assessed – whether in the National Association for Coloured Women, the Montgomery Bus Boycott and the Southern Christian Leadership Conference, the Children's Defense League, The Coalition of 100 Black Women, or the National Association of Business and Professional Women's Clubs. In their evaluations of the Black 'middle class' Wilson and other scholars simply ignore them (Wilson, W. 1987; Boston, 1988). We have yet to provide a full account of Black women's contributions, though frameworks have been established and some initial excavations carried out (Collins, 1991).

There is other evidence which suggests the potential for a common racialised identity and agenda between those in the Black 'middle class' and other Black people. While significant numbers of the Black 'middle class' are independent of the rest of the Black community, it is also clear that many remain economically dependent on Black customers and Black votes, locally and nationally. Most members of the Congressional Black Caucus, most Black mayors and others elected to political office, and the many thousands of small Black businesses in segregated Black communities, fall into this category. Jesse Jackson is perhaps the most notable example. This constitutes a structural overlap in their interests, and there is the continued manipulation of 'tokens' by white institutions. Blacks in prominent positions in white institutions – professors, businessmen and women, doctors – are hardly allowed to forget their Blackness, either by non-Blacks or Blacks. They are often forced to be Black spokespersons by non-Blacks, and are expected and pressured to take on such roles by Blacks in business and other domains.

The position of the Black 'middle class' is hardly secure and they have a vested interest in pursuing goals in common with other Black people. For example, it was more difficult for Blacks than non-Blacks to become 'middle class'. Their position was more tenuous with living standards clearly below that of non-Black counterparts (Wilson, 1978: 175; Landry, 1987; O'Hare *et al.*, 1991). For example, in the 1980s 'even among those in the highest income quintile, blacks have less than half the wealth of whites' (O'Hare *et al.*, 1991: 30). The Black 'middle class' faced problems which the white 'middle class' did not, including discrimination and lower earnings at every occupational level (Benjamin, 1991). In fact the Black 'middle class' declined in size during the economic stress of the 1980s. For example, one study found that:

The shrinking of the Black middle-class population in the inner cities . . . has been caused by their downward economic mobility, as more and more Blacks have lost their middle class jobs in the midst of the economic decline of their neighbourhoods.

(Amott and Matthaei, 1991: 183)

Furthermore, to reduce the goals embraced by Black people simply to class and materialistic goals is to ignore other factors such as psychology, ideology and culture. Blacks share common goals outside the materialist realm, including overcoming the lingering psychological effects of slavery, the continued degradation of Africa and Blackness, the persistent pejorative stereotypes of Black abilities and capabilities (see Chapter 3). The persistence of such problems causes psychological problems for Black people (Akbar, 1984). Their existence insists on a common racialised agenda, even common Black nationalist orientations, at least for substantial elements of the Black population. So Black people pursue many other goals and they can expect to be successful only in co-ordination around a racialised identity. The white 'middle class' neither shares such goals, nor supports them.

Turning to empirical issues, Regina Jollivette Frazier suggests that evaluation of Black 'middle class' commitment is characterised by conceptual confusion because 'there is a widespread misconception that unless assistance is visibly materialistic and produces a recognizable and measurable direct economic benefit, the middle class is not worthy of its "status" in life' (Frazier, 1987: 89). In fact a wide range of 'civic, professional, fraternal and religious organizations' have made contributions 'both monetary and in kind' (ibid.: 89). The Black 'middle class' has organised 'massive voter and registration drives . . . sponsored seminars, held rallies, waged battles in the courts . . . in education, they have tutored for endless hours, . . . marched, boycotted, sat in, been jailed, and many have died' (ibid.: 90). Numerous organisations have acted far beyond the parameters of self-interest. The Links Inc. made donations of more than a million dollars to the United Negro College fund; sororities and fraternities abound, as do other Black organisations such as the Legal Defense and Educational Fund, the Joint Centre for Political Studies and the Southern Christian Leadership Conference. Professional associations such as the National Bar Association, National Medical Association and Black Nurses Association organise conferences, raise funds and co-ordinate mentor programmes. Women's organisations are central here, including The Coalition of 100 Black Women, and the National Association of Business and Professional Women's Clubs.

As I suggested at the start of this chapter, I believe we need to consider the activities of at least the following distinctive groups: business owners and managers, the self-employed; professionals such as academics, doctors and social workers, and local and central government workers and civil servants; politicians, and the many miscellaneous rich individuals such as sports personalities and musicians. It seems to me we must disaggregate them, collect data and identify who is doing what and with what goals. An indispensable requirement would be to focus more on structural and institutional groupings and activities, rather than individuals. Much work has already been done but little is organised around addressing the questions raised here in a detailed way, and by examining the activities of the 1980s (Wilson, 1987; Cashmore, 1991). For example, both Marable and T'Shaka argue the need to differentiate the Black 'middle class' (Marable, 1983; T'Shaka, 1990). As a minimum we can say there is sufficient ground for suspecting a much more uneven picture than Wilson and others suggest.

A second concern of an empirical nature is that the general criticisms of the Black 'middle class' outlined above do not allow for regional variations because they are presented in such global terms, as either/or arguments. That is, as if the Black 'middle class' nationally was monolithic and acted monolithically, rather than there being different sections with different commitments and persuasions in different locations. Boston points out that there has always been a tug of war for leadership within the Black 'middle class' (Boston, 1988: 45; see also Marable, 1983). This is historically true, for example, between NAACP, SCLC and Urban League with the leaders of Black Power movement, and, for example, with Jesse Jackson, in the 1980s. The arguments are therefore on a too grand and macro level to withstand scrutiny.

## CLASS CLEAVAGE IN ENGLAND

> There is no such thing as a black-qua-black movement any more. There are middle-class blacks fighting for a place in the (white) middle-class sun and there are workless and working-class blacks fighting for survival and basic freedoms.
>
> (Sivanandan, 1990: 125)

There has been increasing interest in the growing stratification in the Black population in England during the 1980s. Initially most analysts concentrated on the dire circumstances of working-class and workless Blacks, particularly the young and those in poverty (Rex, 1988). But attention has now turned to the growth of Black businesses and the segment of the African-Caribbean population that has established their own businesses or broken through the glass ceiling into management and professional occupations (Ward and Jenkins, 1984; Platt, 1986).[7]

Data are not collected specifically on the Black 'middle class' in England, they are inferred from more general data on socio-economic status, such as self-employed workers, professionals, and non-manual workers. These data are limited though consistent. In his 1982 survey, Brown reported that for men, self-employment ran at the level of 14 per cent of whites and 7 per cent of African-Caribbeans (Brown, 1984). For women it was 7 per cent for whites and 1 per cent for African-Caribbeans (ibid.: 165). Among the top categories of employees Brown reported that for men 'the proportion in the top SEG category in the table (employers, managers and professional workers) is 19 per cent for whites and only five per cent for West Indians' (ibid.). For women, the proportion in the top SEG was only 1 per cent (with 52 per cent in the 'other non-manual' category) (ibid.: Table 92, 198). Further data are available from the Labour Force Survey (*Employment Gazette*, 1989). For the years 1989–91 the Labour Force Survey reported the following findings: for West Indian and Guyanese men there was 4 per cent in the professional category, 8 per cent in employers/ managers and 18 per cent for other non-manual. For women, the numbers were too small to report for the professional category, with 9 per cent for employers/managers and 51 per cent in other non-manual, the latter clearly reflecting the large numbers of African-Caribbean women in nursing (Labour Force Survey, 1992: Table 6.35, 36).[8]

Regarding the African-Caribbean 'middle class' in general in the 1980s we can therefore arrive at several main conclusions: the numbers were small but steadily increasing; the group was considerably smaller proportionately than that of its white counterparts; there were small but significant numbers of women in this group. It is unclear whether, in the present economic climate, the numbers will grow to any significant extent. While we can reasonably assume that their numbers will not increase dramatically we can also be sure that members of this group will strive to confer the various advantages they enjoy upon their offspring.

The African-Caribbean population generally seemed to rush to embrace the growth of a 'middle class' group. Having experienced substantial discrimination in their efforts to survive and succeed, and displaying many of the values of the capitalist society into which they have been socialised – though tempered by racialised hostility – many African-Caribbeans saw business and 'middle-class' membership as the best or only way forward (Sawyerr, 1983). There are numerous examples of central and local government support for the promotion of Black business and a Black 'middle class' (see, for example, Scarman, 1982: 167–8).[9] The mutual interest is reflected in the seminars and networks, and in the establishment of business directories, as reported in the African-Caribbean media (for example, *Voice*, 27 October, 1992: 8). Examples of this are evident across the nation, from Bristol to Birmingham, and Leicester to London. Strong indicators of this trend are evident in Liverpool, the nation's longest standing and most disadvantaged Black community (Small, 1991b).

Those few who have managed to establish businesses or become members of the African-Caribbean 'middle class' are ardent advocates of its consolidation and expansion. They seek redress to the discrimination they face, and strive to take advantage of the limited government initiatives providing funds and resources to establish businesses. They believe that their success will make a significant contribution to helping other Black people in Britain. Interviews with members of this group suggest three main arguments: that they will create jobs for Black people excluded by racialised discrimination from jobs elsewhere; that they will counter 'racist' stereotypes held by non-Blacks (such as the view that Blacks lack the wherewithal to succeed in anything except sports and music); and that they will provide role modes for Black young people to encourage and motivate them to excel academically and intellectually (Cashmore, 1991). Clearly, as the group most likely to take advantage of any resources available, they will support such initiatives, and they are hardly likely to reject the system that is helping them (ibid.).

There are several reasons why a Black 'middle class' in England is more likely to become a Black Bourgeoisie interested only in its own problems and priorities. First of all, it is suggested that the Black 'middle class' simply confuse analysis of the problems confronting most Black people, deflect attention from more serious issues, monopolise attention around their own less important concerns, and thus delay progress for the Black working class (Sivanandan, 1982, 1990; Howe, 1985). Sivanandan's position is reflected in what he has to say about Black sections in the Labour Party.[10] He maintains that Black sections did not arise from the struggles of working-class Blacks, but simply served the Black 'middle class' to overcome the problems it faced in joining the upper levels of the white 'middle class'. The priorities of the Black sections were 'middle class' priorities not Black working-class priorities, which were 'fundamental issues of life and liberty' and 'racial attacks, arson and murder' (Sivanandan, 1990: 126). Black sections were simply 'the demand of a handful of aspiring middle-class blacks' (ibid.). The media focus on Black sections when they should be looking at fascists (ibid.).

Sivanandan rejects the notion that to help 'middle-class' Blacks would benefit others: 'That would be to subscribe to the IMF/World Bank "trickle-down" theory that aid given to Third World bourgeoisies gradually finds its way down to the people' (Sivanandan, 1990: 125). They make him uncomfortable because, like the demand for Black representation elsewhere, they are like 'the reserved seats in the Executive and Legislative Council system in the British colonies' (ibid.: 125). In fact, he maintains, 'Black sections will neither "blacken" the Labour Party nor benefit the black working class. And the changes they can make from within will be cosmetic' (ibid.: 125). Consequently 'Black sections belong in the Labour Party, not to the black movement' (ibid.: 123–4). Similarly, Howe maintains that the Black 'middle class' in general, and those in Black sections in the Labour Party in particular, have no programme other than the Labour Party programme, and no wish other than to serve their own interests (Howe, 1985). In the film, *Blacks Britannica*, he had argued that anyone who thought that replacing 'bad whites' with 'good Blacks' – in the courts, police, business, government – would lead to significant improvement for all Blacks, was grossly wrong. Such significant changes require systemic changes. Paradoxically, Howe believes that while the Black 'middle class' will continue to grow in England, and will not help the working class, there is no alternative other than to suffer on and await the larger, more transparent class struggle. He suggests they should be allowed to pursue their own interests, as this will lead to progress of other sorts:

Once they remain shut out from the centres of power, they will continue to confuse, deform and corrupt the issues facing the black working classes with their own preoccupations. Let them be Members of Parliament, I say. Let them be judges, magistrates, bureaucrats in local and central governments, directors of this, managers of that. I say let them go forth into the centres of power, so that the real battle lines can be drawn between classes here, there and everywhere, uncluttered and free from the preoccupations of the black petty bourgeoisie.

(Howe, 1985: 16)

Miles has been one of the most consistent critics of all 'middle-class' groups, Black and non-Black (Miles, 1982, 1984; 1988; Miles and Phizacklea, 1984). His position is theoretically grounded, conceptually clear, and consistent over the years in his definitions, concepts, and in the questions he raises about gender and racialised unity (Miles, 1982, 1989). While he continues to concentrate on the economic and political power wielded by the (white) capitalist class, he has noted the small but growing number of Black people joining its ranks. His arguments overlap those of Sivanandan and Howe but he argues more explicitly that a Black '*petite bourgeoisie*' will inhibit efforts at a broader attack on the inequities of capitalist society. He raises important questions, questions which demand answers. But on the topic of the Black 'middle class' he is more incisive in the asking than the answering. He has yet to substantiate his theoretical arguments with detailed empirical data about the unfolding of the activities and attitudes of the Black 'middle class' in the 1980s. In fact, it is around the question of the Black 'middle class' that Miles reveals his greatest weaknesses, particularly empirically.

For Miles, 'the Marxist concept of class refers primarily but not exclusively to the location of groups in production relations' from which he reasonably infers that a Black bourgeoisie (i.e. small business owners) will act primarily in its own class interest (Miles, 1982: 302). For the state, the growth of a Black 'middle class' is a blessing because 'one dimension of the state's strategy to incorporate and defuse dissent is the creation and support for such a class fraction' (Miles, 1984: 224). During the 1980s in particular, the Conservatives worried about this dismal showing of Black representation and tried to woo Black candidates (Platt, 1986: 11). For example, in the 1986 local elections in May, the

Conservatives elected 6 Black councillors while Labour got 120 (both figures include Asians) (Platt, 1986: 11). Lurline Champagnie, an African-Caribbean from the Harrow West Constituency Party, and Conservative councillor for Brent, received the 'loudest, and most spontaneous, ovation' at the 1985 Conservative Party conference (Platt, 1986: 9). By the mid-1980s, the Anglo West Indian Conservative society had around 500 members in 10 branches, all of them in London (Platt, 1986: 13).

One of Miles's goals is to demonstrate the problems of portraying 'the population of Caribbean and Asian origin in Britain in the 1980s as occupying a unitary class position' (Miles, 1989: 128, see also 55). He is critical of analysts who seem to write as if Blacks are homogeneous, or who ignore the implications of developing class differences. In 1984 Miles noted that '"black" agents are to be found not only in the ranks of the reserve army of labour, but also within the proletariat and the petite-bourgeoisie' (Miles, 1984: 224). Miles also cites evidence from other studies about one section on Blacks and Asians 'whose political ideology and practice can only be described as conservative' (ibid.: 226). He maintains that many Asians came to Britain specifically to join the '*petite bourgeoisie*' and that some Asians and Caribbeans retain property ownership in India, Pakistan, Bangladesh and the Caribbean which constitutes 'the material foundation for the reproduction of conservative politics and ideology' (ibid.: 227).

Miles thus raises a series of questions based on his premise that it is the class position of Black people, determined historically and structurally, that will directly influence 'their political class struggle' (Miles, 1984: 224). First, 'I therefore continue to believe that it is necessary to analyze structurally the distribution of Asian and Caribbean people to different positions in class relations' (Miles, 1988: 447). Second, for those who see Blacks 'as a necessarily homogeneous political force, determined in the realm of the political and ideological' he simply asks that they indicate why a Black bourgeoisie would act in the interests of the Black working classes (Miles, 1984: 223). He wants to know why and how the common experience of 'racism' will be sufficient 'to prevent the black petite bourgeoisie from undertaking the function of social control over his "black brothers and sisters" in revolt?' (ibid.: 225). Miles points to South Africa, where some Blacks have aided and abetted the policy of the homelands (ibid.: 225). He has pointed out similar developments in the United States (Miles, 1989). Third, he consistently raises issues of gender. The existence of an 'Asian and Caribbean bourgeoisie, especially where it is engaged in the exploitation of Asian and Caribbean workers (and where those workers are also women)' merits serious attention, but is ignored by those who talk of 'black solidarity' and posit a view of Blacks constituting 'an "inclusive community"' (Miles, 1988: 447). In contrast he highlights the distortions in our analysis likely to be caused if we ignore the significance of gender and domestic labour (Miles, 1988: 457).

As with the United States there remain a number of both theoretical and empirical questions to be resolved. Once again there is a lack of clarity about exactly who is in the Black 'middle class' and (except for Miles) gender is ignored. The persistence of racialised hostility in maintaining racialised identities is also neglected or down played. Nor are there sufficient data about the activities of the groups and individuals in the Black 'middle class'. When we look at these issues, and at the some of the data for the 1980s, we must again raise doubts about some of these conclusions. Some of the evidence suggests reasons strong enough to sustain shared interests between the Black 'middle class' and the Black 'working class'. First, there is the problem of conceptualisation, classification and definition reflected in the failure to provide a suitable (or shared) definition of the African-Caribbean 'middle class'. The group being discussed broadly refers to almost all African-Caribbeans in the upper echelons of the Black population but they are described in several terms, with insufficient clarity, and there is (with the exception of Miles) only a limited attempt to link them to a clear theoretical framework. The terms used include 'Black professionals' (Gilroy, 1987a: 237); 'black bureaucrats' (Gilroy, 1987b: 24, 1990: 271); 'Black petite bourgeoisie' (Howe, 1985: 16); 'middle-class blacks' (Sivanandan, 1982: 124); 'the new black bourgeoisie' (Cashmore, 1992: 171, 172). In some instances, Asians are included as members of this group (Cashmore, 1992).

We have an amorphous array of individuals whose lowest common denominator is that they are the best or the worst off in the African-Caribbean population. Beyond this we cannot assume much else. Several problems come to mind. To begin with, is there any advantage in lumping together several structurally distinctive groups – owners of businesses, managers and executives, professionals, and others who, by virtue of income alone, might be called 'middle class'? Next, there is the problem of restricting membership of the Black 'middle class' to those in the 'self-employed' category of occupational groups. In fact the *Labour Force Survey* collects only a small sample of such economically active individuals and many of the African-Caribbeans included actually work in the construction industry. In addition a significant number of Black women (especially Asians) who are homeworkers are classified as self-employed. This is hardly 'middle-class' status. There is obviously a need for conceptual clarification on this matter.

In the definition of the Black 'middle class' the fact that women generally are ignored constitutes a fundamental problem and consequently there is no attempt to look at the implications of gender differences. The failure to address issues of gender is consistently highlighted by several analysts (Bryan *et al.*, 1985; Phizacklea, 1988). As with their counterparts in the United States, the problems Black women face 'are not equatable with or reducible to those of Black men, or subsumable to those of the Black community' (Mama, 1984: 25). They have to be assessed in terms of gender hostilities. Second, because the work and con-tributions of Black women in challenging and surmounting the obstacles confronting Black people generally has never been fully explored, whether through the League of Coloured People, the Campaign Against Racial Discrimination, the West Indian Stand-ing Conference, Southall Black Sisters or the Organisation of Woman of Asian and African Descent. As with Wilson in the United States, Sivanandan and others ignore them in England (Wilson, W, 1987; Sivanandan 1990). Like the United States we have yet to provide a full account of the contributions of Black women (Bryan *et al.*, 1985).

There are at least three major issues which demand attention here. First, the extent to which the 'success' of the African-Caribbean 'middle class' is based on the oppression and exploita-tion of Black (and white) women as workers. The evidence makes clear the continued discrimination built throughout the economic institutions of England, for example, long hours, poor pay, no unions. Second, we must raise the issue of whether African-Caribbean women in the 'middle class' are likely to act in the same way as men with regard to class and/or racialised identities. There is evidence to suggest that African-Caribbean women are less likely to vote Conservative than African-Caribbean men (Layton-Henry, 1984: 55). Third, there is a point often made at a popular level –

though not yet picked up in the literature – that African-Caribbean women are offered greater opportunities than African-Caribbean men, and that this is because whites in power fear them less than men. This belief has created some tension between African-Caribbean women and men – the latter expressing resentment – and may become increasingly problematic.

If the growth of a Black 'middle class' business sector is taken as evidence of 'improvement' for Black people generally, then we are bound to ask how much of the achievements of African-Caribbean businesses are built on the exploitation of Black (and white) women? The limited data that are available for the 1980s suggest that Black women continue to be exploited, both directly and indirectly, in laying the foundation for Black businesses, and in maintaining their survival and leading to their expansion. There is some evidence to indicate that African-Caribbean women are more likely to become professionals than men and that Black women are doing better in higher education (Mirza, 1992). Implicit in the notion of 'middle-class' status is a mentality and attitude to life which, in the business world, suggests the acquisition of a dog-eat-dog, cut-throat competitive nature. Can we expect African-Caribbean women to adopt such attitudes, or is there any evidence to suggest otherwise?

With regard to empirical issues there is a limited attempt to go beyond simply stating the size and numbers in the African-Caribbean 'middle class', by going on to explore the size of the different sections or looking at the size of capital involved, and the potential for expansion. Cashmore calls them 'a fast growing class of entrepreneurs' and talks of 'the new black bourgeoisie's glittering success' (Cashmore, 1992: 171, 172), but he offers no numbers and little evidence of success. In fact during the 1980s most Black businesses were small, and employed only a couple of workers (Ward and Jenkins, 1984; Ward, 1988). The African-Caribbean business-owning group was not a large one, nor did it reflect substantial financial turnover. For example, in 1982, 18 per cent of African-Caribbean businesses were in manufacturing and 46 per cent were in construction (Ward, 1988: 207). Between 11 per cent and 25 per cent of African-Caribbean businesses were involved in hair-care and beauty products. A full 60 per cent were in the service sector (Ward, 1988: 211). This suggests that many were individual workers. We would hardly consider such businesses to be at the forefront of capitalist activity, nor would we find it especially helpful to consider a market stall at Dalston Junction, London, Moss Side, Manchester, or on the Soho Road in Birmingham, in the same category as Dyke and Drydon hair products.

It seems unlikely that such businesses will grow much larger in the economic climate of the 1990s. For example, many draw on Black customers only and therefore their potential for expansion is limited. They must often compete with one other, as, for example, with hairdressers, hairdressing products, barbers, and vendors of cultural artefacts. Once we disaggregate and take into account some of these issues we are talking about very small numbers. For the early to mid-1980s Ward calculates a total of around 12,000 'West Indian businesses', the vast majority of them (72 per cent) tending to be run by people 'working for themselves without using a professional skill' (Ward, 1988: 207).

Nor have there been sustained efforts to develop a discussion of the political and ideological differences within the African-Caribbean 'middle class'; for example, what political stance is adopted by the different groups, and can they be assessed as friends or foes? Cashmore maintains that 'few of Britain's new ethnic élite are overly interested in challenging a system in which they have prospered' but provides neither the evidence to support this view, nor a definition of exactly who he means by the 'new ethnic élite' (Cashmore, 1991: 356). While the argument that Black business owners have little interest in the broader political concerns of Black people is persuasive, the peremptory dismissal of Black sections as simply self-serving and self-interested by Howe and Sivanandan is contradicted by evidence from the struggles in which some of them have taken part (see Shukra, 1990; Jeffers, 1991). Though Black sections reflected a firm commitment to working within the system, it is also clear that many items on their agenda extended to fighting for the rights of all Black people, even where that may have led to considerable personal loss for individual members. Here we see evidence of complex issues being tackled, and clear indications of a commitment to Black people beyond the immediate group.

Shukra indicates that even within the Black sections, it is not useful to lump them all together, some joined Labour to demonstrate the limitations of the party machine, others to extract resources, or build up networks, still others as a means to secure Labour positions (Shukra, 1990: 182). Shukra's own conclusion is that Black sections were bound to fail because they were preoccupied with 'representation and amelioration' rather than 'mobilisation and social transformation' and because Black sections tried 'to reconcile the irreconcilable' (ibid.: 188). This suggests that Blacks will find no joy in parliamentary efforts to promote parity. Gilroy himself says Black people should always turn their backs on the state (1987a). What Shukra, Jeffers and Gilroy do not show is why and how extra parliamentary activity will be more effective, especially if carried out on its own.

In addition, there was a wide array of Black organisations and associations established throughout the 1980s, groups with broader constituencies and goals (Ramdin, 1987; Goulbourne, 1990). Many Black professional organisations were also established for the first time. The National Black Caucus is a prime example. In Liverpool, the Federation of Liverpool Black Organisations (FLBO) was established in the mid-1980s (Liverpool Black Caucus, 1986). It extended activities organised around the Liverpool Black Organisation of the 1970s, and the Black Caucus of the early 1980s. The Militant campaign of working-class domination precipitated a dramatic increase in Black political activity (ibid.). Under the banner of the 'Granby People's Party' the FLBO ran the first independent Black councillor, and forced the Labour Party to field its own first ever Black candidate, Liz Drysdale. The FLBO lost the seat but Drysdale won.

Gilroy is critical of the activities of the Black 'middle class' but is unprepared to dismiss them in their entirety, suggesting several reasons why they might contribute to helping other African-Caribbeans (Gilroy, 1987a, 1987b, 1990). His focus is primarily around Black professionals and he discusses the continuing consolidation of power by 'black professionals' in 'local government agencies' (Gilroy, 1990: 270); and of the 'emergent black petite bourgeoisie' and 'their intrinsically problematic relationships to those they are supposed to serve' (Gilroy, 1990: 271). He describes three broad sections of 'middle-class' Blacks (including Asians) as the 'equal opportunities' section, the nationalists and the 'race is class' section (1987b: 13–14). He argues that by embracing notions of a 'transcendental racial essence' around the idea of Black nationalism and the Black 'race' the individuals involved have been able to ignore and wish away the 'conspicuous divergence of interests between the never-employed and the cadre of black bureaucrats employed by the local state to salve their misery' (Gilroy, 1990: 271). Many tensions remain as 'part of a political struggle within the black communities over what "race" adds up to' (Gilroy, 1987a: 236). The outcome of this contestation, however, is not a foregone conclusion. The processes of racialisation continue to bind together the different sections of the Black population in ways that offer hope for broad alliances:

> Despite their differences, the 'black professional' in a local authority social services department, the Afro-Caribbean ancillary in a hospital and the hip-hopping Asian youth of West London may all discover within that colour a medium through which to articulate their own experiences and make sense of their common exclusion from Britain and Britishness.
>
> (Gilroy, 1987a: 236)

It may seem that they are there to contain and constrain, to ameliorate rather than mobilise, but 'it would be foolish to deny the black petit bourgeois the capacity to "change sides"' precisely because a 'common history, culture and language, as well as the effects of racism, may all enhance this possibility' (Gilroy, 1987a: 24). He locates his analysis theoretically by reference to the intimation by Marx and Engels that in certain circumstances the 'middle classes' might abandon their commitment to capital and join ranks with the proletariat (Gilroy, 1987a: 24). He also argues that Black people's struggles have always been for more than simply a stake in the capitalist system – they have been more critical and more egalitarian in their appeals (Gilroy, 1987a).

The goals, agendas, activities and strategies of these groups have yet to be fully documented and evaluated. But it is easy to identify significant groups which advance more than a narrow self-interested agenda and we simply cannot dismiss them all as lackeys to the capitalist state. One point of this chapter is to begin to differentiate the African-Caribbean 'middle class', and to begin to assess how far they adopt class or racialised affiliations. When we examine the different groups, link them to the array of Black organisations and institutions in England, and examine the content of their political positions the picture becomes more complex. When we look at the activities of the 'petit bourgeois' professionals, politicians and conservative voters we see great divergence. We clearly cannot equate the activities of the Society of Black Lawyers with those of the Association of Black Journalists. Nor would we equate the Institute of Race Relations or Race Today Collective with the West Indian Conservative Association. I doubt that many would want to put Bernie Grant or Dianne Abbott in the same category as John Taylor or Lurline Champagnie. The growing work on Black political activity will be invaluable here (Shukra, 1990; Goulbourne, 1990; Jeffers, 1991). Gilroy's consideration of those involved in anti-racist struggles, and Shukra's work on Black sections, provide an example of how we might carry this further (Gilroy, 1987b). We need to assess exactly how the different sections of the African-Caribbean 'middle class' act for common goals, particularly in terms of criticism of the system beyond its refusal to allow them equal opportunities to become 'middle class'.

## MOVING THE DEBATE FORWARD

Analysis of the role and activities of the Black 'middle class' in the United States, has many precedents. The long history of a Black presence there, the large numbers, and the evidence of differential economic and political positions from the start has given rise to detailed assessments of what role Black 'middle-class' groups might play. In the 1980s the breakdown of racialised barriers and boundaries, the economic parity reached by some sections of the Black population, the saliency of Republicanism, and the show-casing of Black conservatives has led to some oversimplifications. Many analysts have suggested that class has become the pre-eminent factor in the lives of the Black 'middle class' and that they have abandoned other Black people. Wilson's critics would insist that he differentiate the various sections of the African-American 'middle class', that he account for his neglect of gender, and that he demonstrate why racialised hostility is insufficient to maintain common racialised identities regardless of class position (Boston, 1988; T'Shaka, 1990; Collins, 1991). Supporters of his 'betrayal thesis' would also be expected to account for the vital role played by sections of the Black 'middle class' in African-American struggles (Marable, 1983; Boston, 1988). His proposals for what policies might be introduced in place of those predicated on racialised identities (such as affirmative action) would need to be more persuasive (Duster, 1988).

In England, detailed analysis of this emerging group is in its infancy, and is characterised by a number of limitations. But many important issues have been raised. Miles has posed some incisive questions and he is far from the reductionist some make him out to be. However, he has not demonstrated that we can best benefit from seeing the African-Caribbean 'middle class' as a '*petite bourgeoisie*' in Marxist terms, or that he has taken sufficient account of how racialised hostility continues to bind this group's experiences and allegiances with those of their (racialised) working-class counterparts. He has not yet related the actions of the '*petite bourgeoisie*' to other Black professionals or bureaucrats (for example, those in local authorities) or offered a persuasive repudiation of the benefits of independent African-Caribbean political mobilisation and organisation. Despite this, we cannot dismiss some of the questions he raises. For example, he indicates how the problems Black people face are inextricably intertwined with class issues, identifies a number of the weaknesses in a politics predicated on racialised identities, leads us to question exactly what the Black 'middle class' shares with the Black working class and to inquire as to the precise circumstances in which alliances might be formed, and for whose benefit?

While Gilroy has challenged the assumptions and arguments of Miles for some time, and has raised key questions about the Black 'middle class', he too has yet to make a convincing case (Gilroy, 1987a: 24). A more persuasive argument would entail identifying how far racialised hostility will continue to serve as a binding agent for Black people which is greater than the evolving class differences. The debate on these issues would benefit greatly from a more detailed elaboration by Gilroy and Miles of their respective arguments.

If we choose to dismiss the many sections of the Black 'middle class' (especially if this is primarily on theoretical grounds) then we need to propose an alternative strategy for achieving and going beyond racialised parity. This will have to be one that engages with the prevailing conditions in the 1990s. Despite some grand dismissals, these issues are not unambiguous. For example, the establishment of Black businesses does not necessarily constitute the abandonment of other Blacks, nor does becoming a professional, or working within the system; nor does becoming a Conservative (though we would have to doubt how far anyone who upholds the principles of free market mechanisms could honestly expect any good to come of it for most other Black people). These patterns reflect differential priorities and strategies, individual and collective. They entail different strategies for individual uplift and for contributing to group uplift, and they reflect different assumptions and priorities of how to go about this. This is reflected in the debates between W.E.B. Dubois and Booker T. Washington, between Manning Marable and Glen Loury, between Bernie Grant and John Taylor, between Dianne Abbott and Lurline Champagnie. We need clearer criteria about how to evaluate what sections of the Black 'middle class' and their organisations are doing and in what ways this contributes to helping other Blacks.

In England the critics of Miles would insist that just as he demands evidence that 'middle-class' African-Caribbeans would aid their working-class brothers and sisters, he must demonstrate why a white working class socialised in a culture saturated with racialised ideologies and hostility would help Black working-class brothers and sisters (Sivanandan, 1982: 93). Chapter 3 demonstrated that many of the racialised ideologies to which the non-Black working class subscribes, and the benefits which they gain from them, cannot be explained as the exclusive work of the state or ruling class. He must also confront the very real problem of persuading the African-Caribbean working population to oppose their entrepreneurs. How will he convince a group decimated by discrimination that they should give up efforts to enter the realms of economic activity? It may well be that the African-Caribbean working class is not prepared to look beyond the pros and cons of a capitalist society, nor to forego benefits now for some promised gains in the distant future. Again, the climate of the 1990s – the fall of communism, Fortress Europe, rampant individualism – must be confronted.

If racialised hostility means that Black people face problems which non-Black people never face, then gender discrimination creates obstacles for Black women that Black men never face. While Black men are confined to unskilled and low-paid jobs, Black women are confined to unskilled, low-paid, and part-time jobs with less security (Amott and Matthaei, 1991; Mama, 1984, 1992). Black women receive less pay than men, are more likely to incur greater costs (resulting from responsibilities for the upkeep of homes and for child care, invariably expected of them by men), and, where their employer is a man, may be subjected to gender hostility. All women are potential victims of domestic and sexual violence, and, as was demonstrated in Chapter 3, Black women are more likely to be victimised by both Black and non-Black men, and face less likelihood that this victimisation will be acknowledged and responded to (Cose, 1989; Mama, 1989). The complexities of these relationships frequently create tensions, anxiety and hostility between Black men and women.

The obstacles confronting women are greater than those confronting men, and the options for dealing with them and making alliances are more problematic. We cannot presume that the growth of Black business has equal benefits for men and women, especially given the discrimination against women woven into the fabric of each society. More work must be done to identify the structural positions occupied by Black women (and Black women's organisations), to evaluate the intricacies of the multiple obstacles that they face, to describe their contributions in advancing political and policy causes, and to outline the successes which they have achieved.

If my analysis is at all persuasive then we need to do several things. We must reject the idea that the alleviation of the disadvantages currently endured by most Black working-class people, and the never-employeds, will be significantly changed as a result of the simple existence of a Black 'middle class'. There will certainly be marginal improvements, and we can expect several reasons for expecting some common alliances. Beyond that there is little evidence to suggest that on its own it will confer any significant or long lasting benefits for most working-class Blacks. Promotion of a Black 'middle class' would lead to racialised equality only in the sense that the extent of inequality in the Black and non-Black population will be roughly the same (see Small, 1991a: 39–40). We must also recognise that its existence will complicate matters greatly, for example, by confusing the relative impact of racialised, class and gender obstacles, in perpetuating inequality. We need to identify what political goals members of the Black 'middle class' are actually fighting for, if any, in each nation. Some members of the Black 'middle class' will simply be fighting for their own personal 'place in the (white) middle class sun', that is, for individual economic success and lifestyle (Sivanandan, 1990: 125). Others have broader political goals. How do such goals tie in to inequities beyond racialised hostility?

Furthermore, the growth of a Black 'middle class' will not, by achieving a reasonable material status, help redress any of the psychological problems associated with white capitalist culture and its derogation of 'the other' (Akbar, 1984). The vilification of African culture, the undervaluing of Black history, the stereotypes of Black life and culture, will not be greatly inhibited merely by the presence of Black entrepreneurs, especially if they simply emulate the values and ideals – individualism and competition – of the white 'middle class' on their road to business success (see, for example, Sivanandan, 1982: 96). Of course, many might ask why should Black people not have this, or aim for it in the short run? Many want this, and accept, broadly, the contours of capitalist society, but its pursuit leads to the foregoing of other goals and may create greater strife within the Black population. Some might doubt that this can be avoided, in the short run (see Howe, 1985). Experience from the United States offers insights, as with so many issues in this book, into the processes of antagonism and acrimony associated with class differences which beleaguer the African-American community, and which promise to develop in England.

I believe that gains could be made if we were to tie in our analysis of the Black 'middle class' to broader analysis of the 'middle-class' and to the sociology of professions, as well as to the analysis of women in stratification and politics. For example, Savage maintains that it is difficult to specify exactly what a 'middle-class' political position and activity entails (Savage, 1991: 26). This is because there are no organisations dedicated specifically to 'middle-class' goals (like those that are working class) and few, if any, organisations have leaders that are not 'middle class', whether right- or left-wing (ibid.: 26). He points out that other authors have argued about the ambiguous position of the 'middle class' – some maintaining that it is radical, while others see it as a conservative force (Goldthorpe, 1982; Graetz, 1991).

He explores some of the differences between different sections of the 'middle class' – public and private sectors, occupational differences, professions versus managers (we can add owners versus 'middle class') and examines voting patterns. He concludes that we must 'take for granted that it is fragmented and divided' and seek to account for the divisions (Savage, 1991: 27). He identifies a growing antagonism in the ranks of the 'middle class' between 'those who rely upon the state for the reproduction of their class positions, and those who do not' (ibid.: 51). This leads to conflicts along several axes – public/private, professionals/managers, young/old and men/women (ibid.: 51). Though such divisions are not as entrenched for Blacks as for non-Blacks, nevertheless they are bound to grow, especially in a context in which Black 'middle- class' members are fighting for scarce resources.

## CONCLUSION

Stratification in the Black populations of the United States and England is here to stay. There are reasons to expect that the Black 'middle class' will continue to grow as it consolidates its childrens' future, and will continue to be wooed by white mainstream economic opportunities; it is also likely that the 'underclass' will become significantly worse off. There are grounds for suspecting that many in the Black 'middle class' will pose problems for other Black people, that they will act only in their own interest, especially in light of the 1990s climate, the increased enterprise culture, conservatism and de facto withdrawal of support for 'equal opportunities' initiatives. But there are also reasons why we should not simply dismiss Black 'middle-class' groups with the cast of a deterministic hand. Several pressures remain which are conducive to sustaining racialised identities as a means to common goals. We need to assess the situation closely, taking on board clearer definitions and a fuller estimate of numbers, differentiating by political position and taking full account of gender.

Stratification will undoubtedly increase in the near future and we shall see a further dissolution of racialised group affiliations. Of course these trends will differ under the Clinton and Major administrations. Though we may argue about the pattern, extent and speed of stratification, there can be no doubt about that general fact. It is unlikely that this can be avoided, either in the short or long run. The issue is not to block it, but how to respond to it. The development of Black businesses and professionals is necessary and important but must be tied to a progressive programme which goes beyond the limits of free market mechanisms. The question is how to ensure that this is done, and that efforts to go beyond such limits do not get lost in the momentum?

Some Black people consider the Black 'middle class' to be a 'Talented Tenth' that will act as a vanguard for advancing the interests of all Black people; others see them simply as a 'Black Bourgeoisie', interested only in their own self-aggrandisement. My concern has been to contribute to a more rigorous evaluation of the different sections of the Black 'middle class' the role they played in the 1980s, and might play in the 1990s, in creating improvements for other Black people. However they evaluate the Black 'middle class' most Black people simply want greater representation in all walks of life (for example, racialised parity). I simply argue that the growth of a Black 'middle class' will not necessarily change the plight of the majority of working-class Black people or challenge some of the fundamental inequities which characterise the United States and England.

It is important to note that no one is calling with such passion and fury for the white 'middle class' to help other whites, or, for that matter, to help Black people. Racialised identities are inextricably entwined with feelings of expectation, anticipation and betrayal, as demands by poor Blacks on affluent Blacks reflect the continuing struggle over 'what race adds up to' (Gilroy, 1987). Patterns of racialised inequality and hostility are largely attributable to the structures and ideologies erected by non-Blacks and it may be true that while non-Blacks put us in this mess we are the only ones who will get ourselves out of it. However, we must maintain pressure on non-Blacks, and be wary of allowing non-Black people to force such responsibilities on to Black people alone.

Black people who envisage a way forward in either nation on the basis of the strength of racialised identities as a mobilising force (as I do myself) must confront some difficult decisions. If we choose to embrace members of the Black 'middle class' then we should elaborate on why they will bypass their own class interests and help other Blacks. In theoretical terms, we must establish why affiliations determined in the ideological and political realms (racialised affiliations) will be more important than those determined in the economic areas (Miles, 1984: 223).[11] We should therefore identify factions and political positions, and explore how far it is worth organising efforts around them.

It would be unwise at this stage to embrace a Black 'middle class' as a blessing or to dismiss it as a curse, except on some problematic theoretical grounds. Before we jettison the Black 'middle class' we must take heed of the fact that in the United States 'every major improvement in the economic status of blacks was caused by coercive political intervention rather than by free market forces' (Boston, 1988: 98; see also Wilson, 1978: 135). Similar claims can be made for England. Sometimes this coercion came about because of riots, at other times it arose from multi-racialised political representation, the latter involving some key actors from the Black 'middle class'. Before we can be certain that the Black 'middle class' will feather nothing but its own nest we need to establish the size of this broad group, differentiate its sections, take full account of gender divisions, establish which political agendas they support and evaluate what contribution they are making to Black working-class people. We might then decide to support only those with a clear and progressive agenda which benefits more than a tiny handful of Blacks. I develop these issues further in Chapter 6.

# Chapter 5

# Racialised integration, harmony and parity

## INTRODUCTION

In England in 1967 the first national survey of racialised minorities, carried out by Political and Economic Planning, found evidence of extensive discrimination in employment and the provision of services (Daniel, 1968). This study focused on six towns and cities across England by carrying out tests in which Black people (and other minorities) attempted to get work, buy houses or obtain private accommodation. The study concluded that racialised discrimination varied from the massive to the substantial, and that it was greater against Black people than against other non-Blacks or (white) immigrants. Further surveys in the 1970s and 1980s confirmed continuing high levels of racialised discrimination in employment and other areas including mortgages and estate agents practices (McIntosh and Smith, 1974; Brown and Gay, 1985; McCruddon *et al.*, 1991). Alongside this discrimination in the 1980s the pattern of racialised inequality was substantial in the areas of employment, housing, education and health. Black people were worse off compared to non-Black people in all these areas, and considerably worse off in several of them (see Chapter 2). The evidence on racialised attacks and other conflicts demonstrated that racialised antagonism was a significant feature of contemporary British life (Home Office, 1989; Hesse *et al.*, 1991).

At the same time as the survey by Political and Economic Planning, a national survey of attitudes of racialised minorities and the non-Black majority, carried out by Rose and associates, found substantial evidence of 'good race relations' (Rose *et al.*, 1969). The views expressed in the surveys carried out during the 1960s led them to conclude that:

the majority of the population are tolerantly inclined and that
there is more tolerance among those who live near coloured
people.

(Rose *et al.*, 1969: 675)

They outlined some of the problems in defining the notion of
'integration', and gave several examples of political and policy
statements about 'integration' (Rose *et al.*, 1969). Successive surveys
of attitudes towards 'race relations' since then have demonstrated
even greater 'tolerance' towards racialised minorities on the part of
non-Black people (Smith, 1976). Putting aside for the moment the
question of whether such surveys reveal what people 'really' believe,
the evidence certainly suggests a decrease in rigid and hostile
attitudes towards Black people. Writing in 1985 Banton said 'over
the past thirty years in Britain there have been a veritable host of
committees and associations, official and unofficial, established to
promote racial harmony' (Banton, 1985: vii). He added that while
the input into such organisations had been substantial, 'the output
of actual achievement looks much smaller' (ibid.: vii). He argued
that we could not say for sure whether this was true because 'it is
difficult to obtain any satisfactory measure of output' (ibid.: vii).

In the United States in the 1960s evidence of racialised discrimination in employment, housing and education was substantial
(Wilson, 1978). Throughout the 1970s and 1980s there was evidence
of a decrease in patterns of discrimination, but it was still substantial
overall (Black and Black, 1987; Marable, 1992). An important study
in the 1980s, a follow-up to the Myrdal Report, found extensive
evidence of injustice and discrimination (Wilkerson, 1988). Evidence on racialised violence and attacks was also significant, the
violence around Bensonhurst and Howard Beach exemplifying such
evaluations (Levine, 1990; Wilkerson, 1988). Most commentators
invariably took this as an example of deteriorating 'race relations'.
But at a conference of Black and other minorities organised by
the Center for Law and Social Justice, participants argued that
incidents of violence, while important, were not the best indicators
of the state of 'race relations' in the United States. The best indicator
was the continuing pattern of racialised inequality and injustice
(French, 1988).

In the 1980s the University of California, Berkeley became the
first major non-Black university to have a majority of students of
colour (Institute for the Study of Social Change, 1991). It was and

continues to be hailed as a model in racialised integration. Despite such claims, there is considerable evidence of extensive 'balkanization' on campus (Shao, 1990; Institute for the Study of Social Change, 1991). Similar conditions and arguments prevail on other American campuses which are praised as exemplifying 'good race relations' (Farrell and Jones, 1988). When students at the University of California, Berkeley, were asked about their priorities in promoting 'good race relations' white students invariably said 'good race relations' meant having Black friends, and they were largely against affirmative action and other policies designed to redistribute resources (Institute for the Study of Social Change, 1991). These responses were framed in the context of notions of meritocracy, qualifications and ability, alongside the firm belief that 'the residues of historical discrimination are not relevant to today's social policy' (ibid.: 40). However, for Black students 'good race relations' invariably meant access to resources, especially support for affirmative action (ibid.)

Most of the American non-Black population revealed similar views to those expressed by non-Black students at the University of California, Berkeley, with increasing opposition to policies to tackle or make amends for racialised discrimination. By the end of the 1980s a clear majority (61 per cent) of white Americans argued that even where there was clear evidence of racialised discrimination in access to employment against African-Americans, there should be no preference in hiring or promotion afforded to African-Americans (*New York Times*, 1991: 4.1). This evidence demonstrates that throughout the 1980s there was a common notion in each country that policies were needed and efforts should be made to combat racialised discrimination and attacks, and promote 'good race relations' (Jenkins and Solomos, 1987; Wilson, W. 1987). Many in the United States believe that racialised integration has been achieved in England, that this has led to an improvement in 'race relations' and that the United States could improve its own 'race relations' by following in England's footsteps. This belief is particularly evident on American university campuses (Debley, 1989; Green, 1989).

But what the examples above also suggest is the complex, even contradictory, relationship between patterns of racialised inequality and discrimination, Black and non-Black attitudes to these patterns, and towards what should be done – policywise and politically – about them. The idea of achieving 'good race relations' involves

notions, indicators and criteria that allow for very different interpretations and emphasis. That is, substantial discrimination and
widespread inequality can persist while people can conclude that
'race relations' are improving; and people can be in favour of 'good
race relations' while steadfastly opposing the policies that might
lead to that end. We can expect such problems and conflicts when
they concern large numbers of the general population whose views
and assumptions are bound to be highly divergent. But this should
not be the case for governments and policymakers. However,
during the 1980s governments and policymakers pursued the
promotion of 'good race relations' or equal opportunities 'using
terms and concepts in a confused, arbitrary and contradictory
manner' (Jewson and Mason, 1992: 218; see also, McCruddon *et al.*,
1991). This was true of practitioners and of the advisory literature
in the field. The broad range of Black organisations also differed
concerning their goals, priorities and strategies (Sivanandan, 1982,
1990). I believe this is because of confusion about what 'good race
relations' comprises;[1] because of the different priorities of the
different groups; because power lies in the hands of the non-Black
majority so their priorities prevail; and because most non-Blacks
object to Black priorities due in part to the former's commitment to principles like individualism, 'free choice' and the free
market economy.[2]

In this chapter I examine the notion of 'good race relations' in
the 1980s in the context of continuing racialised inequality and
discrimination. I outline the expressed attitudes of Blacks and non-
Blacks to policies on racialised relations and describe government
policy initiatives undertaken in the 1980s. I examine various images
and policies around the idea of 'good race relations' and suggest
that it conflated three sets of goals or institutional interests: racialised
integration, racialised harmony, and racialised parity.[3] Racialised
integration usually suggests the physical and social interaction of
Blacks and non-Blacks in housing, education, employment and
other social spheres. Racialised harmony suggests non-antagonistic
social interaction, whether in conditions of integration or otherwise.
Racialised parity suggests similar access to, and/or ownership of
resources, economic, educational or otherwise.[4]

I suggest that the idea of 'good race relations' mystified both the
goals of policies organised around racialised relations, and the
means by which such goals might be achieved.[5] Clarification of
these issues would enable a clearer idea of what goals are being

pursued, and the methods by which they might be attained. My main focus will be on the fields of employment, housing and education, as I outline policies of affirmative action in the United States, and positive action in England. Though there are differences between the two nations in the evolution of these issues (Banton, 1985: 126), once again there are striking similarities and converging patterns which suggest commonalities.[6] A distinctive feature of the 1980s was the dominance of right-wing thinkers in representing policy and political measures to eliminate discrimination as unjust and illegitimate. I argue that during the 1980s – in a context of substantial racialised inequality, as described in Chapter 2 – the priority for most Blacks was that of racialised parity (usually meaning 'equal shares of resources'), while for most whites it was racialised integration or harmony. Where whites expressed commitment in principle to racialised parity (usually meaning 'equal access to resources') they strongly opposed the policies most conducive to achieving this. Similarly, among politicians and key policymakers (dominated, of course, by whites), least effort was made to achieve parity. Even where policies to achieve parity were promoted in principle they commanded limited resources, and limited political commitment in practice (Krieger, 1986; Shaw *et al.*, 1987).

## INTEGRATION, HARMONY AND PARITY IN THE UNITED STATES

The data outlined in Chapter 2 indicated the entrenched pattern of racialised segregation in the United States during the 1980s. Though some significant changes had occurred since the 1960s – particularly in employment and education – Blacks and non-Blacks continued to be segregated across the United States in fundamental ways. Blacks remained overwhelming urban, tended to live in neighbourhoods alongside one another (regardless of income) and Black schoolchildren attended schools (mainly public) which were overwhelmingly Black. While there were large numbers of Black students in white colleges, they often led largely separate social lives. Blacks and non-Blacks worked in different jobs, in an occupational hierarchy that favoured non-Blacks, and though some Blacks and whites dated or married (mainly Black men and white women) these represented a tiny proportion of all dating and marriage.

Significant numbers of Black people – in cities like Detroit, Michigan, Washington, DC, Gary, Indiana, Oakland, California, Birmingham, Alabama, and Richmond, Virginia – grew up in areas where they had little or no significant contact with the non-Black majority. Data from the 1980 Census confirm the continuing pattern of residential segregation, and the negative effects of such patterns on Black people in terms of housing costs, likelihood of home ownership, high rates of unemployment, educational segregation and adverse psychological consequences (Farley and Allen, 1989: 155). The authors from this study conclude:

> Segregated neighbourhoods continue to limit the social contracts of whites and blacks, and high proportions of blacks and whites in metropolitan areas now reach adulthood without ever having a close friend of the other race. Many may complete their education without ever attending a school which enrolled students of the other race and without living in a neighbourhood where the other race was well represented.
>
> (ibid., 1989: 157)

They add that trends established in the 1970s 'will leave blacks highly segregated in the foreseeable future' (ibid., 1987: 145). Data from the 1990 Census confirmed such conclusions (O'Hare *et al.*, 1991).

These conclusions also apply to employment and education. Half as many Black men (15 per cent) as white men (30 per cent) worked in executive, administrative, managerial or professional jobs, while the figure for Black women was 19 per cent compared with 26 per cent for white women. Black men were more likely to work as semi-skilled labourers and twice as likely as white men to hold service jobs. In universities and colleges African-American faculty continued to be found in relatively junior positions such as assistant professor, instructor and lecturer. During the mid-1980s, Black children totalled about 16 per cent of the public-school students in the United States and constituted a majority in many of the nation's public-school districts. They formed 90 per cent of school pupils in Atlanta, Detroit, and Washington, DC, and nearly 40 per cent in New York City (O'Hare *et al.*, 1991: 20).

Waters reports that in the United States, 19 states retained laws against 'inter-racial' marriage until 1967, and that although now officially allowed, the informal practice of marrying within one's own group remained strong. Waters points out that in the 1980s

Blacks aged 25–34 were '19,131 times more likely to marry a black than a white' (Waters, 1990: 104). She adds, 'Ninety-nine per cent of American-born black women in their first marriage have mates who are also black' (Waters, 1990: 103). Though these patterns reflect the tragedy of racialised inequality, they can often lead to farcical situations. One evening in 1986 my brother told me he had discovered an 'integrated' bar in Oakland, California. As he took me there I had an impression of Blacks and whites sitting and drinking together. When we entered I was taken aback to see one half of the bar full of whites, the other half full of Blacks, neither paying any attention to the other, and quietly getting on with the business of drinking. I turned to my brother and he laughed, 'This is an integrated bar ... for the United States!' This situation reflected many aspects of American thinking on such matters, where notions of 'integration' can be markedly different from England. For example, Goldfield describes how schools in Little Rock, New Orleans and Atlanta were integrated, but the actual numbers involved less than 10 Black children in each city school (Goldfield, 1990). The contrasting meanings of 'integration' to Blacks and whites is discussed shortly.

The United States was as far from racialised integration in the 1980s as it was in the 1960s. Efforts to achieve integration, for example via bussing, indicate the emotional significance of residential and educational segregation and integration in the lives of whites in that society. Conflict in South Boston, in Bensonhurst in Brooklyn, New York City, in the city of Yonkers in New York State, as well as in the South – re-emphasise the continued significance of the matter (Feron, 1988: B2). For example, in the South, the Supreme Court's directive that Southern institutions desegregate 'with all deliberate speed' was thwarted by many bureaucratic and legal measures (Black and Black, 1987; Goldfield, 1990). In Louisiana in 1987 the state's colleges found themselves largely segregated; the four 'traditionally black universities' had student populations that were 87 per cent to 97 per cent Black, while the 'traditionally white' colleges were 74 per cent to 96 per cent white (Marcus, 1988: B5). In the North there has been significant hostility to efforts at integration, often outmatching the South for the intensity and verocity of violence, especially in Boston and Chicago (Fusfeld and Bates, 1984; Pohlmann, 1990). Data from the 1980 Census indicated that many cities in the North were more segregated than those in the South (Farley and Allen, 1989).

Problems with racialised integration reflect problems with racial-ised harmony. I have defined racialised harmony as non-antagonistic social interaction, whether in conditions of integration or otherwise, entailing elimination of conflict, especially where that occurs around discrimination, and a notion of Blacks and non-Blacks socialising together. In its most anodyne form, the notion of racialised harmony is reflected in celebrations of carnivals and festivals, as well as in conditions at some university campuses, where Blacks and non-Blacks interact – in classes, in halls of residence, dining halls, sport, and recreational activities – in ways that are unparalleled elsewhere in American society. Visions of racialised harmony are broken by the racialised attacks and violence of extremist groups such as the Ku Klux Klan and the White Aryan League, and by apparently random attacks such as those at Howard Beach and Bensonhurst described in Chapter 3. This racialised 'disharmony' is believed to result from lack of interaction, lack of familiarity and from a climate of stereotyping and scapegoating. It was looked upon with regret in the 1980s because racialised conflict and violence of the sort that characterised earlier periods of United States' history were believed to have become largely a thing of the past (Wilson, 1978).

Once again the evidence in Chapter 2 demonstrated that racial-ised disparity – in health and wealth, education and employment, and health – was a fact of life in the United States in the 1980s. Black people were worst off by just about every major indicator. Racialised discrimination played a major role here, as well as the structural positions in which Black people found themselves (in ghettoes, away from jobs, without educational institutions) as a result of past racialised discrimination.

## Black and white attitudes to racialised policies

What about the attitudes of Blacks and whites towards one another, towards the pattern of racialised inequality and towards policies promoting 'good race relations'? Some of the evidence on these issues was outlined in Chapter 2. Overall, whites and Blacks explain racialised inequality in very different terms, and express marked differences in their willingness to support policies to eradicate it. Whites are in favour of equality of opportunity, but they see racialised inequality as a result of a failure on the part of Black people, not as a consequence of past or present discrimination, and they do not support policies to change this. Black people see their position as resulting largely from past and present discrimination and believe policies should be implemented to change this.

The evidence is consistent in revealing that white stereotypes of African-Americans have decreased, most whites are less likely to see African-Americans as inferior, and there is less support for blatant racialised discrimination. Most surveys reveal that whites display strong acceptance of the idea of integration, but equally strong rejection of policies (like bussing and affirmative action), which are designed to achieve this (Gilbert, 1988). Most whites display greater acceptance of integration in secondary social areas such as entertainment, public places, and other less personal areas. They may 'tolerate' a limited number of African-Americans in close proximity, but only in low numbers. But many whites still object to racialised dating – most of them object to it very strongly – and to integrated residential patterns (Schuman *et al.*, 1985). For example, a large proportion of both Blacks and whites say they desire to live in an integrated neighbourhood, but their perceptions differ on what actually constitutes integration. In a report on the 1980s:

> Black respondents in several large cities expressed a preference for neighbourhoods that were equally divided among black and white residents. Whites preferred to live in an 'integrated' neighbourhood in which 80 per cent of residents were white and only 20 per cent black. A neighbourhood that is 40 per cent black and 60 per cent white would not be considered fully integrated to the black residents, while white residents might think the same neighbourhood is past the 'tipping point' and is on the way to becoming all black. These fundamental differences in the perception of integration have not been widely recognized or fully appreciated.
>
> (O'Hare *et al.*, 1991: 31)

In light of this we might well ask exactly who wanted integration? Apparently most whites, especially working-class whites did not, while more affluent whites acceded to it only in certain circumstances. A greater proportion of Blacks seemed in favour of it but a significant element of this was the clear relationship between 'integration' and better resources, the realisation that most whites would not give Blacks resources, and aspirations of a 'colour-blind' society. It must also reflect some internalisation of racialised ideologies and an element of self-hatred and acceptance of white supremacist ideas (Akbar, 1984).

The disadvantaged position of African-Americans is explained by whites in terms of the former's lack of efforts: 'most whites continue to view the problems as the result of blacks' own shortcomings, not social conditions or institutional forms of discrimination' (Marger, 1991: 268). Blacks 'see their plight as deriving primarily from a lack of the same opportunities as whites' (ibid.: 269). A 1987 poll found that '59 per cent of whites but only 26 per cent of blacks believed that blacks had the same opportunities in employment as whites' (cited in Marger, 1991: 269). Similar divergences in views are evident in explanations of experiences with the police and in education.

## Policies and priorities in the 1980s

One of the primary goals of US policy since the 1960s has been to create equal opportunity by ending racialised discrimination, and it has been organised around the idea of policies that will ultimately create a 'colour-blind' meritocracy. Building on the legal framework established with the 1954 Supreme Court decision, Brown vs Board of Education, which ruled 'separate but equal' provisions unconstitutional, legal measures like the 1964 Civil Rights Act and the 1965 Voting Rights Act sought to further ensure equal opportunities (Goldfield, 1990). The essentials of these policies can be illustrated in the instances of bussing and affirmative action, each of which was introduced because equal opportunity in law did not lead to any significant changes in practice, and because for a period equality of outcome as a goal came to replace equality of opportunity (Wilson, W., 1987: 114). Affirmative action was a major plank of federal efforts, as were the 1972 US Office of Education guidelines for 'goals' for university admissions and hiring of faculty (Dye, 1992: 67). Policy goals like these resulted from the actions of the federal government, Supreme Court and senior policymakers, not from white popular support (ibid.). The origin of the policies is important because working-class whites have never supported them in any large number.

During the 1980s, the political climate was not conducive to strong legislative or policy measures to combat racialised discrimination or to promote racialised integration, harmony or parity. Ronald Reagan was against anything but minimalist policies designed to promote 'good race relations' for a variety of reasons. He believed that they inhibited the free play of the market, increased the interference by big government, diverted economic resources into social policies and hindered the 'free choice' of individuals to live, work and play where they wanted to, and with whom they wanted to.

The goal of bussing was to improve the access of Black school children to education, and to bring Black and non-Black children together to appreciate one another, to learn to live and work with one another. The goal numerically was to achieve a better racialised balance so that the numbers in schools became commensurate with the numbers in school districts. The evidence showed non-Blacks had better resourced schools and Black children in white schools did better educationally. Schools were officially desegregated from the 1950s, though this was limited in practice, due to the resistance mounted by non-Blacks, and because of continued segregation in housing in a context of neighbourhood schools. Integration in education did not work, even in schools where Black children were bussed in, as was made clear by the data provided in Chapter 2. It was massively opposed, especially in the South, where school districts waited for law suits, countersued themselves, then obstructed and hindered implementation (Goldfield, 1990). A tactic often employed was that of 'white flight' as white parents simply moved house, or moved children to private schools, thus leaving the schools more segregated than before. One of the most hotly contested situations was in Boston. In 1974 Federal District Court Judge Garrity ordered bussing and encountered massive resistance by whites. In 1973 Boston had 94,000 public-school students, 57 per cent of whom were white; in 1985 it was left with 57,000 students, of whom 27 per cent were white (Dye, 1992: 57). Even where relatively large numbers of Black and white kids attended the same schools they often sat in separate parts of the bus, and different areas in class rooms; even at college level 'balkanization' was widespread.

Opposition to bussing involved both working-class and middle-class whites, the latter especially when their children were required to go to predominantly Black schools (Dye, 1992: 58). This opposition reflected widespread acknowledgement of the inferior facilities in which Black people had been educated, as well as underlying presumptions of Black inferiority. Consequently, the United States remains as segregated as ever (Farley and Allen, 1989). Even in cities regarded as the most integrated, liberal and progressive, segregation is endemic and its consequences are immediate, palpable and nasty. For example, the city of Berkeley, California, is seen as the heart of radicalism and progressiveness. It had a Black progressive mayor when Reagan won his second sitting. But contrary to public wisdom, segregation is endemic.

Affirmative action was an attempt at legislative and policy initiatives to combat racialised disadvantage, and promote a better redistribution of resources. Introduced in 1963 under an executive order issued by John F. Kennedy, and strengthened and expanded by Lyndon B. Johnson in 1965, it had two goals: to curtail patterns of discrimination, individual and institutional; to repay Black people for previous discrimination, in particular by providing for quotas (Wilson, 1978; Claiburne *et al.*, 1979). Affirmative action contributed to the dramatic increase in the representation of Black people across a number of spheres in the 1960s, including education, the legal profession, medicine, and in the business world. Affirmative action stimulated the expansion of Black businesses and made a significant contribution to the Black middle class, hitherto confined to small Black businesses drawing almost exclusively upon Black customers in the long-established ghettos (Wilson, 1978; Landry, 1987). It was also responsible for guaranteeing Black people access to semi-skilled and unskilled areas of employment in which there was clear evidence of widespread racialised discrimination, in particular, in city councils, police departments and fire departments (Duster, 1988).

Despite these obvious and dramatic gains, there were severe limitations. For example, some of the gains attributed to affirmative action derived from the removal of legal and institutional barriers to resources, and even then, only relatively small numbers made any significant educational, occupational or income advances (Murray, 1984; Farley, 1984). Many of these breakthroughs were held in check, or even reversed during the 1970s and 1980s, as a series of Supreme Court decisions were influential, quotas and set asides were challenged or abandoned, and non-Blacks were given the go-ahead to sue for 'reverse discrimination' (Omi and Winant, 1986; Pohlmann, 1990). Affirmative action also created new problems and a series of negative consequences; for example, it led to Black institutions and neighbourhoods being deprived of their most talented residents, many professors and students taking up places at white universities, residents moving out of traditional areas of Black residence. There was also a widespread incidence of tokenism and Blacks new to white institutions faced greater psychological problems as they attempted to 'make it' in a white world (Davis and

Watson, 1985). Conflicts within the Black community developed as some benefited while others were left unaffected. The ensuing responsibilities and obligations were often catastrophic for the individuals involved, especially in academia (Banks, 1984). Furthermore, limited Black successes allowed many non-Blacks (as well as some conservative Blacks) to argue that unqualified Blacks, the beneficiaries of 'reverse discrimination' were the recipients of preferential treatment to the former's disadvantage, that discrimination was over and that such measures were no longer needed (Loury, 1984; Steele, 1990). This was a line of reasoning bound to resonate with whites in times of economic decline, which has exacerbated tensions between Blacks, and given right-wing non-Blacks – and Blacks such as Sowell – ammunition to blame the victims for lack of effort (Sowell, 1983; 1990).

A key example of these conflicts was the Supreme Court decision in the Baake case of 1978 (Bindman, 1980). Alan Baake, a white student, sued the University of California, Davis after he was refused admission to medical school, and Black students with lower scores were admitted under a quota policy. The Supreme Court struck down the university's special minority admissions policy, but said the objectives of the policy were legitimate. Baake was admitted to the medical school, and the university was told that it must end quotas but could use 'race' or 'ethnicity' as a factor in overall considerations, as was done, for example, at Harvard. The decision was interpreted by both opponents and advocates of affirmative action as an endorsement of their respective positions. In the 1980s Reagan encouraged non-Blacks to bring law suits against affirmative action policies, and restructured the Civil Rights Commission in accord with this sentiment (Omi and Winant, 1986). Although he is not a conservative, the strong opposition to affirmative action by William Julius Wilson, Professor of Sociology at the University of Chicago, and an African-American, has been highlighted widely (see Chapter 3). In all this debate there has never been any discussion of affirmative action policies for the children of university alumna, or for athletes, despite the fact that such groups have always had affirmative action and receive substantial funds (Larew, 1991). Of course, most recipients of such policies are non-Black.

Finally, there remains the problem that even if fully supported affirmative action remained essentially reformist and diversionary; it was not designed to challenge inequality *per se*, but to ensure that the pattern of Black inequality should be no worse than that for non-Blacks. Preoccupation with affirmative action has diverted attention away from more fundamental aspects of inequality, and led to conflict between non-Blacks and Blacks, as well as within the Black population. In particular, it has provided an acceptable issue for those who harbour more serious racialised animosity to have a vent for their hatred.

Government and policymakers in the United States have sought policies around 'good race relations' for a variety of reasons. There is clear evidence of state subterfuge, of a willingness to respond to, and encourage, racialised hostility by the non-Black electorate, or prevarication and delay. There is also the relentless commitment to individualism and minimal government intervention. Where genuine efforts are being made, the fact that so much attention has been given to integration over other priorities results from the idea that so much of the racialised antagonism that prevails arises from the strict separation of Blacks and non-Blacks in housing, education and employment. This belief is often reflected in the way England's less segregated society is viewed as being more harmonious (Glazer and Young, 1983). These attitudes are especially manifest at the nation's colleges, where Blacks and non-Blacks come together for the first time and where universities see 'integration' as part of their broader goals of social citizenship (Debley, 1989; Green, 1989). Once again, this reflects a lack of clarity over goals, priorities and policies.

## INTEGRATION, HARMONY AND PARITY IN ENGLAND

The available evidence on patterns of occupational, residential, educational and other social areas (especially patterns of racialised marriage) in the 1980s reveals that England is more socially integrated than the United States (Brown, 1984; Smith, 1989). Black people there are more likely to go to school with, live and work in greater proximity to the non-Black majority. It is almost impossible for Blacks in England to grow up without frequent and sustained exposure to non-Blacks of all classes and in a range of institutions. However, for those who see England as integrated, one of the most striking first facts that derive from a closer inspection is the pattern of settlement concentration. At no time in the 1980s did the minority population, including Asians and Chinese, exceed 5 per cent, so it is almost ridiculous to describe Britain as a 'multi-racial' society. The only 'multi-racial' areas are a tiny number of urban centres.

Black people in England are concentrated in urban areas, the overwhelming majority of them in the South-East and the Midlands. For example, over 65 per cent of African-Caribbeans live in Greater London (Smith, 1989: 32). In fact England is systematically segregated. But there are no ghettos in England in the American sense of areas in which the vast majority of residents are all Black. It is true that many areas are regarded as ghettos – Brixton, Hackney and Peckham in London, St Pauls in Bristol, Handsworth in Birmingham, Moss Side in Manchester, Toxteth in Liverpool – and Black people do live in the most deprived and disadvantaged neighbourhoods within these districts. However, these are all areas in which the majority of residents are in fact non-Black, and they are areas which are geographically very small.[7]

When housing patterns are examined Blacks do not stand out favourably (Brown, 1984; Smith, 1989). Smith provides data to show that 'discrepancies in the housing quality of white and black households are consistently found in all sectors of the housing system and cannot always be explained simply by income differentials'; and that half of white households but only one quarter of Blacks lived in detached or semi-detached houses, with similar disproportions indicated when comparing age of properties and housing density (Smith, 1989: 43). She also provides evidence on discrimination in housing markets, and argues that scholars have underestimated 'the potency (symbolic as well as material, political as well as economic) of housing and residential space in the racialization of social inequality' (ibid: 44).

In the workplace, although we find Black people disproportionately over-represented in lower-skilled and lower-paid jobs, and in jobs which require shift work, nevertheless, they are overwhelmingly to be found working alongside white workmates who are the majority (Brown, 1984; Labour Force Survey, 1987). There are few Black businesses or institutions owned, managed and staffed by Blacks, except at the level of small stores or shops (Ward, 1988). In education we confront a similar story; while Black people are less likely to acquire educational qualifications, or to go on to university, they still find themselves for the most part alongside majority non-Blacks (Killian, 1987a). There are some areas in which Blacks are a majority in schools but these are not large in number and the percentages are tiny (Rex, 1988).

In England, rates of racialised marriage, cohabiting and dating are high – as many as one quarter of all marriages involving a Black partner have a non-Black partner and Blacks and non-Blacks are believed to freely interact (Brown, 1984; Alibhai-Brown and Montague, 1992). The city of Liverpool is known to have the largest population of Blacks of mixed white and Black parentage and is often regarded as the epitome of harmony (examples of such views are cited in Liverpool Black Caucus, 1986). Frequent interaction, even if it is the experience of a minority, and even if it is often resented, has become a way of life in the city. One recent Liver-pudlian visitor to the United States commented to the author 'Yes, the States is a free country, you can do what you want, go where you want, buy what you want and all that. But you better not bring home a boyfriend or girlfriend of a different colour or all hell breaks out'.[8] While in England the matter remains an issue of considerable contention, and conflict often occurs, nevertheless, the evidence reveals a considerable incidence of this most often quoted indicator of harmonious 'race relations'.

Racialised attacks have a long history in England, with several examples of anti-Black riots dating to the start of the century, but greater public attention developed in the 1970s and 1980s (Fryer, 1984). Surveys demonstrate the 'widespread nature of these types of attacks' (Solomos, 1989: 133). The activities of far right groups have been central but so has a political climate which stigmatises Black people. Attacks and the climate of anxiety, unease, fear and feelings of siege they generate were widespread in the 1980s (Hesse *et al.*, 1991). Racialised harassment in many forms was a constant plague of Black residents (Greater London Council, 1984). There have been some horrendous attacks against Black people, including incidents in which the police were the perpetrators; for example, the deaths of Winston Rose and of Colin Roach (Hesse *et al.*, 1991); and the attacks on Mrs Cherry Groce and Mrs Cynthia Jarrett (see Chapter 3). Despite this, 'the policy response to racial attacks and related phenomena has been at best muted and at worst non-existent' (Solomos, 1989: 134).

Discrimination is institutionalised in immigration legislation, and is widespread in every other area of life from employment to education (Miles and Phizacklea, 1984; Brown and Gay, 1985; Gifford *et al.*, 1989). Blacks were more likely to be unemployed, and if they worked, earned less than non-Blacks, were less likely to be in non-manual or skilled positions and far more likely to work night shifts (Brown, 1984; Smith, 1989). Despite the comparatively

favourable pattern of housing integration in England, discrimination has often been at its most rampant, some of the most violent
confrontations have occurred, and deep-set animosities become
embedded, as a result of conflict over housing, especially council
housing (Smith, 1976).

## Black and white attitudes to racialised policies

No extensive surveys have been carried out on the attitudes of
Blacks and non-Blacks to past and present discrimination, or on the
policies designed to achieve 'good race relations' as there have
been in the United States. But there are several. In general the
attitudes of most non-Blacks in England have become less rigid
than they were in the past, but many stereotypes prevail. Some of
these stereotypes were outlined in Chapter 3. Whites were more
likely to acknowledge that racialised discrimination occurred –
some even admitted it occurred frequently – and they often
believed that Black people received unfavourable treatment at the
hands of the police and other agencies. For example, in surveys
carried out in the 1980s which asked about the incidence of 'racial
prejudice' against Black people, more than 40 per cent of respondents felt that there was a lot of prejudice against them (British
Social Attitudes, 1992: 1–2). And 50 per cent of the respondents
felt that 'racial prejudice' had increased over the previous five years
(British Social Attitudes, 1987). But when asked about policies to
combat such injustice, around twice as many Blacks as whites felt it
was necessary to strengthen the laws to promote racialised equality.
For example, 31 per cent of whites, compared to 61 per cent of
Blacks felt it was important to make 'the race relations laws tougher'
(Frow and Alibhai-Brown, 1992).

In general, attitudes in England, like those in the United States,
were shaped by a firm commitment to a 'colour-blind' meritocracy
when matters of access to resources such as education, employment
and housing, are concerned. But in light of the evidence on
racialised discrimination it is clear that, as in the United States,
most non-Black people support such policies much less in practice
than they do on paper. Attempts by the Commission for Racial
Equality and various local authorities to encourage the development of positive action and contract compliance measures as tools
for the promotion of racialised parity in employment (and elsewhere) have met with both legal and administrative resistance

(Burney, 1988; Solomos, 1989). In the 1988 Local Government Act, Thatcher imposed severe restraints on the ability of local authorities to implement contract compliance. The Act prohibited consideration of 'non-commercial' matters in the awarding of contracts (McCrudden *et al.*, 1991: 29–30).

## Policies and priorities in the 1980s

Legislation and policies designed to promote 'good race relations' date from the early 1960s in England. The first piece of legislation was the 1965 Race Relations Act and White Paper in which discrimination was 'confronted' by setting up conciliation machinery to deal with complaints of discrimination, and by outlawing discrimination on the grounds of 'race' colour, ethnic or national origin, in such places as hotels, restaurants, places of entertainment or on public transport (Daniel, 1968). Legislation to extend the areas prohibiting discrimination occurred in the 1968 Race Relations Act (Brown and Gay, 1985). This legislation proved to be conceptually weak and legally cumbersome to serve as a deterrent to racialised discrimination.

Most of it was oriented towards individual forms of behaviour and it failed to generate resources needed to implement effective programmes (Solomos, 1989: 72–5). The 1976 Race Relations Act, which introduced the concepts of institutional discrimination and positive action, sought to rectify this (Brown and Gay, 1985). The 1976 Act combined the Race Relations Board and Community Relations Council into the Commission for Racial Equality and thus combined the responsibilities for combating discrimination and promoting harmony in the same institution (Banton, 1988).

Legislative and policy measures from the 1960s and 1970s were based on concepts of disadvantage and deprivation (Rex, 1988: 35). In part governments did not wish to take responsibility for combating discrimination. Such polices also reflected and in turn reinforced the orientation towards 'colour blindedness'. This is true of the Urban Programme, Community Development Projects and Inner City Partnerships. It is ironic that the measures set out in Section 11 of the Local Government Act 1966 introduced resources, but in practice their use has been corrupted (Rex, 1988). On the whole the programmes just mentioned 'did very little to combat discrimination and ... they undermined rather than supported the development of independent political action' by Black people (Rex, 1988: 36).

Most agencies and organisations adopted a 'colour-blind' approach towards racialised relations at the start of the 1980s. The commonly held view was that mention of 'race' or 'racism' exacerbated problems and incited racialised animosities (Young and Connolly, 1981). The idea that 'racism' was a significant cause of racialised inequality contradicted the views held by many in the Labour Party that the primary problems confronting Black people were class based (Ben-Tovim *et al.*, 1986). The right wing felt that mention of 'race' inhibited the free workings of the market economy, especially where policies were needed to ensure equal opportunities. They took the view that the best person for the job, and the maximisation of equal opportunities, would be ensured by the free play of the market (Solomos, 1989).

The idea of racialised integration as a policy goal has a relatively short history in England. It dates directly from the 1960s, though there are debates pertaining to these matters in the 1950s. Until this time there were very few Black people in Britain, and no areas with large settlements of Black people. A key benchmark in this is the official acknowledgement of the 'multi-racial' nature of Britain, and the need for policy to recognise that (Miles and Phizacklea, 1984; Solomos, 1989). This policy was built on the twin pillars of immigration control, and the promotion of 'good race relations' and integration. The latter was to be achieved via 'welfare agencies' and legislation (Solomos, 1989: 72). Central to this was Roy Jenkins' statement 'without integration, limitation is inexcusable; without limitation, integration is impossible' (cited in Banton, 1985: 45). As Miles and Phizacklea make clear, this was really arguing that 'in order to eliminate racism within Britain, it is necessary to practise it at the point of entry into Britain' (Miles and Phizacklea, 1984: 57). This policy thus defines Black people *per se* as a problem. Miles and Phizacklea outline the slide down the slippery slope of the numbers game (ibid.: Chap. 4).

Roy Jenkins subsequently moved the goals of policy one stage further: 'I define integration, therefore, not as a flattening process of assimilation but as equal opportunity, accompanied by cultural diversity, in an atmosphere of mutual tolerance. This is the goal' (cited in Banton, 1985: 71). But when it comes to considering an evaluation of the relative circumstances of Blacks and non-Blacks in employment, education, housing and health, let alone many other areas, the goal is vague, and the means to attain it even more vague. The idea of 'racial harmony' pervades scholarly, policy and general writings on racialised relations (Banton, 1988). As a public good the idea has been enshrined in England since at least the 1960s and is stated time and time again as a goal or objective to be attained (Banton, 1985: 126). In the early establishment of British policy, the National Committee on Commonwealth Immigrants, established by the government in 1965 felt Community Relations Councils should promote 'racial harmony' for everyone, not just one section of the population (ibid.).

During the 1980s most of this changed. After some bickering, the vast majority of major organisations adopted equal opportunity policies, and, in principle at least, the notion of 'ethnic monitoring'. This was spurred on in large part by persistent pressure by Black organisations, and some non-Black organisations, by the riots of 1981, by extensive activities of 'anti-racist' groups (especially in the field of education) and by the efforts of the Commission for Racial Equality. A major player in getting these issues on the agenda was the Greater London Council under Ken Livingstone. They took a high profile on all issues of equal opportunity, including gender, and disability, and invested large amounts into mobilising around the promotion of these issues. This included organising major policy reviews, activities and funding around 1984 as 'anti-racist year', and the establishment of a contracts compliance unit (Ball and Solomos, 1986).

The Conservatives in general, and Thatcher in particular, were against institutional measures to achieve 'good race relations', and were content to play a minimalist role, assuming that a free market would ensure equal opportunities for all. Thatcher felt government interference in business practice inhibited the free play of the market, while policies designed to promote 'integration' were contrary to the needs of individuals for free choice of where to live and with whom and where to work. For example, major inner city initiatives, such as 'Action for Cities' in the late 1980s, said little about racialised inequality (Solomos, 1989). Thatcher simply sought Black votes via her campaign in 1983, and encouraged a few Black candidates to run. She strongly opposed positive action, and did everything she could to obstruct it. Her abolition of the Greater London Council, while broadly motivated by the desire to curtail Labour influence, was greatly influenced by the latter's high profile opposition to racialised discrimination (Ball and Solomos, 1990).

Some local authorities made key advances in establishing wide ranging 'race relations units' with extensive powers (mainly on paper, but many in practice), but most of them engaged in one-off high profile measures, rather than 'a sustained mainstream-oriented programme of action' (Ben-Tovim *et al.*, 1992: 205). Section 11 funding was more 'compensation' to local governments for extra burdens of minority presence, and was not designed to redress racialised injustice (Ben-Tovim *et al.*, 1992: 207). Senior officers and administrators were able to obstruct measures aimed at challenging institutional inertia and racialised obstacles.

This occurred in the context of significant economic changes, including harsh business realities, and changes in centralisation of policy management by government (Jewson and Mason, 1992). The official change of emphasis of Community Relations Councils into becoming Racial Equality Councils at the end of the 1980s, with a new emphasis on combating racialised discrimination, reflected a growing dissatisfaction with the slow pace of change, and the pressures to achieve big goals with limited resources. These limitations are manifest despite the fact that in no other European country are there such detailed, specific and wide-ranging legislative practices designed to achieve equal opportunities (Wrench, 1990: 578).

A legislative and policy initiative that reflects many such issues is that of positive action. It was introduced in the 1976 Race Relations Act, in recognition of the severe disadvantages caused by indirect and institutional racialised discrimination. Influenced by analysis of affirmative action in the United States it was very explicitly designed not to be concerned with quotas or with any notion of rectifying past discrimination (Burney, 1988). It allowed employers to introduce training for their current employees where the proportion of Black people in higher-rank jobs was lower than the proportion of Black people in the employer's recruitment area. It also allowed specific measures to be taken in trying to recruit Black people, for example by advertising in the Black press. The 1976 Act expressly forbade positive discrimination or quotas. Its take up has been highly uneven, with some authorities taking a very high profile on it, others almost totally neglecting it (Commission for Racial Equality, 1986). A number of independent agencies were established during the 1980s to develop and implement positive action policies, often in conjunction with local authorities, and these were influenced by developments in affirmative action in the

United States. A prime example is Merseyside Skills Training established in 1983 by the Liverpool City Council (Connolly *et al.*, 1992). Others include Positive Action Training in Housing (PATH) which has offices in London and several other cities.

In general positive action has received limited resources compared to other policies, and has generated most vocal opposition, even from those who favour equal opportunity policies (Burney, 1988). It is an example of how little support there is for policies likely to bring some significant change to the abject circumstances in which many Black people find themselves as a result of racialised hostility.

## CONTRASTING PRIORITIES, CONFLICTING OUTCOMES

When we consider the goals and policies to promote 'good race relations' in the United States and England during the 1980s, and the divergent institutional interests of different constituencies, we confront a complex picture, with conflicting assumptions, conflicting goals and priorities (group and individual) and confusing methods (law and morality). The goals of racialised integration, harmony and parity are not clearly spelt out either in theory or in practice. These notions reveal problems in definitions, in the different policy conflicts of trying to achieve all three, and in the policy and political priorities of Blacks and non-Blacks. Any attempt to achieve all three, without any clear priorities – as seems to have been the case throughout the 1980s – runs the risk of achieving none, and of creating considerable suspicion, distrust and resentment. Whichever one is chosen as a priority leaves some groups considerably displeased. How are we to unravel all of this?

When it comes to advocating policies, and considering goals and outcomes, most Blacks and non-Blacks started from very different assumptions. Non-Blacks assumed in much greater number that there was equal opportunity, Blacks disagreed. Non-Blacks considered past discrimination, and its legacy, to be secondary in its impact on current opportunities, Blacks disagreed. Most non-Blacks considered present discrimination to be relatively minor, Blacks disagreed. Most non-Blacks were interested primarily in equality of opportunity; Blacks were more interested in equality of outcomes, or at least in a dramatic diminution of the existing disparities. The different positions led to different policy preferences and priorities. The divergence in attitudes was more marked in the United States than in England (more non-Blacks in the latter concede current discrimination is significant) but the general conclusions hold. Government and policymakers navigate these murky waters and try to chart a course that takes account of conflicts and contradictions among the different constituencies, and of their own priorities. Any group or individual interested in understanding and/or acting on the issues must unravel some of these complexities.

Let us consider the notion of racialised integration. Given the marked differences in the patterns of social integration in the two nations, England provides examples of some of the strengths and limitations of the policy. If the priority was racialised integration alone then several problems must be confronted. First there is the problem of definition. The notion of racialised integration is defined vaguely which makes the policy difficult to formulate and implement. The term has a long history in both nations but there remains considerable confusion over its concrete implementation. In both nations it means primarily 'non-segregation'. In the 1950s and 1960s England used the policy of 'dispersal' when considering schooling and housing (Hiro, 1971; Killian, 1987a). While such a phrase is unlikely today, the assumption that somehow Blacks should not all be congregated in one place still prevails (Ball and Solomos, 1990). In the United States the society is so segregated that the general goal of integration seems clear enough, that is, to decrease the extent of segregation. But the situation in England shows that once you have gone beyond a certain level of integration, the goals seem confused. The concept of integration (like that of assimilation) causes confusion because it is applied 'both to individuals and to groups' (Banton, 1985: 48). Does integration mean some Blacks and non-Blacks interact? Or does it mean that 50 per cent of each population interacts? And given the marked differences in patterns of settlement – urban and rural, and within cities – what catchment area would be used? If so, can it ever be achieved and who would want that (Smith, 1989)? Would the integration of Black men and white women be evaluated in the same way as the integration of white men and Black women? Besides, it seems futile to aim for such numerical goals concurrently in employment, housing and education. Dispersal has not worked in England, nor did bussing in the United States, partly because there has been no clear statement of what exactly these policies were designed to achieve.

Second, there is strong opposition to the policies because neither Blacks nor non-Blacks want to be 'forced' to work, live or be educated with one other. Most Blacks and non-Blacks think of integration in very different terms and successive surveys demonstrate that though Blacks seem committed to the idea, there is opposition from non-Blacks, sometimes vigorous opposition. In the United States, Blacks will accept a greater degree of residential integration, non-Blacks will not; a similar situation prevails in England. Neither side will be happy. In all of this the cherished value of 'free choice' gets thrown out. Non-Blacks are more committed to this 'universalistic' notion, in principle and practice, than they are to notions of racialised goals. So whose definitions should prevail?

Third, even if integration could be attained the idea is limited in scope and would not dislodge many of the stereotypes about Black people. For example, in England there are still numerous areas in which Black people are totally absent, and in which the non-Black majority continues to be influenced by negative images of Black people in the media. Data provided by Smith indicate that for Britain as a whole 'about half the white population lives in neighbourhoods containing no black residents and only about 1 in 16 whites lives in an enumeration district with a "coloured immigrant" population of 5 per cent or more' (1989: 33). Many areas of Black settlement are considered ghettos, havens of drugs, violence and criminality and are seen as no-go areas for non-Black people and even the police (Gifford *et al.*, 1989; Smith, 1989). This is true despite the fact that non-Blacks outnumber Blacks in all these areas and crime rates are often higher in areas in which there are few Black residents (Smith and Gray, 1983). Integration would also leave direct and indirect discrimination widespread, because its achievement does not necessitate a reduction in levels of discrimination. The evidence from England confirms this, certainly in the area of employment where, despite patterns of increased residential and educational integration, discrimination has remained consistent; at least one-third of employers discriminate against Black people, including Asians (Brown, 1984; Brown and Gay, 1985). Nor has discrimination in housing and education gone down significantly (Greater London Council, 1984; Commission for Racial Equality, 1989). Overall, the limitations of integration are revealed when one considers gender inequality: men and women (Black and non-Black) have been integrated in all these realms and yet substantial disparities persist (Gatlin, 1987).

All of this leaves the primary concerns of Black people, for racialised parity, unaddressed. In England, neighbourhoods may be integrated, but the housing quality is fundamentally different (Smith, 1989); jobs may be integrated, but at different levels in the hierarchy (Bhat *et al.*, 1988); schools may be integrated but with continuing unequal outcomes for Black and non-Black pupils. The greater degree of integration in England has not led to economic, political or social equality. There is no equality of access or condition in employment, education or housing and certainly none in wealth (ibid.). As Rex points out:

> The notion that the main choice which we have to make in Britain is simply between segregation and integration is a comforting and unchallenging one because it suggests that no questions of inequality, exploitation and oppression are involved.
>
> (Rex, 1988: 28)

For all the benefits of racialised integration we still see evidence of rampant racialised discrimination, and a 'Colour Line' which remains stubbornly intact. This is not quite the picture of harmony often envisaged from across the Atlantic.

Beyond this, integration creates other problems, most notably of racialised sexual relations. Considerable stigma is attached to those involved in such relationships, resulting in conflicts for the partners, their families and their children. Individuals in such relationships are often stigmatised by their own communities, as well as by many in the communities which they join (Root, 1992; Alibhai-Brown and Montague, 1992). Conflicts arise not only between Blacks and non-Blacks, but also between Black men and Black women, and between non-Blacks, especially within families. There are psychological problems for the children which are a consequence of animosities between the two communities from which they are drawn, rather than from their own actions (Rich, 1986; Root *et al.*, 1992). The history of Liverpool provides the best example in England of these problems (Shyllon, 1977; Law and Henfry, 1981).

Finally, a fundamental problem in achieving integration is the underlying assumption that Black people are a problem *per se*. This assumption is captured in the numbers game of immigration and integration played out in England since the 1950s, as well as policy discussions in the United States where the idea of a 'tipping point' prevails (Miles and Phizacklea, 1984; O'Hare *et al.*, 1991). It is almost impossible to engage in discussion of racialised relations without the issue of 'how many Blacks' being raised by non-Blacks.

One outcome of all of this is that separate Black institutions are seen by many Black people as a primary goal. There is a long tradition of Black institutions in the United States (Wilson, 1978). In England Black people have become so frustrated by their experiences of living in an 'integrated' society that many efforts have been made to establish separate Black institutions where a motivating factor has been the need to secure room for the cultivation of a psychological state of mind uncontaminated by white 'racism' (Akbar, 1984). The 1980s saw particular efforts to establish separate Black institutions, many drawing on ideas and knowledge of precedents in the United States. This included the establishment of Black self-help groups, churches, schools, businesses, and Black sections within the Labour Party and trade unions. Organisations like the National Black Caucus, the Society of Black Lawyers, Kemetic Educational Guidance, the Association of Woman of African Descent, the Federation of Black Housing Organisations, and a range of Black professional groups exemplify this trend; as do the Consortium of Black Organisations, and the Federation of Liverpool Black Organisation in Liverpool.[9] The ideologies of Afrocentrism and Black nationalism are key here.[10] Developments like these emphasise how Black people conceptualise the problems they face not primarily as matters of segregation but as matters of inequality and disparity in access to and ownership and control of resources to shape their own lives.

Similar kinds of problems must be faced in any attempt to achieve racialised harmony. Problems of definitions, policies, support from Blacks and non-Blacks, and its limited scope arise, as do the other problems it causes, and the failure directly to tackle racialised disparities. Clearly, a central tenet is the need to eradicate racialised attacks and violence, and bring an end to racialised discrimination. But beyond that how can we ever tell when racialised harmony has been achieved? Even if substantial reductions were brought about, a single vicious outbreak of conflict or violence would challenge the overall notion. For example, one major incident, a murder or physical beating, is often held to be evidence of deterioration in racialised harmony when things may otherwise be fine for the majority of people. This is suggested by the Tawana Brawley case in the United States, or the case of Winston Rose in England. We may even wish to conclude that given the numbers involved, then there is considerable racialised harmony in both the United States and England. This is usually the emphasis of official representatives, who are quick to point out how few incidents occur. This is hardly a conclusion likely to find favour with Black victims of racialised abuse, and violence.

A second problem is that in seeking harmony we must pander to the whims of non-Blacks and forgo policies which aim to equip Black people with the resources to determine their own priorities. Most non-Blacks seem happy with racialised harmony because, like integration, it requires no discussion of access to resources or outcomes, and does not even have the perceived problems of integration, which requires non-Blacks to interact with Blacks. It may simply require interaction at carnivals, cultural events and other preoccupations with exotic ethnic difference. In fact racialised harmony can be achieved via non-action or non-interaction, that is, keeping considerable distance between Blacks and non-Blacks will leave harmony intact. Clearly, the notion needs to be spelt out better.

The idea of racialised harmony is also inextricable from the notion of a 'tipping point'. It assumes harmony can only be achieved if one keeps the numbers of Blacks in check. In the United States, racialised harmony for most non-Blacks seems to be a preoccupation with keeping Blacks out of non-Black neighbourhoods – if incidents during the 1980s were any indicator. In England they were most notably captured in the positions of Roy Jenkins and others outlined earlier, and in Mrs Thatcher's over-quoted speech that (white) 'people feel rather swamped' (Layton-Henry, 1984). Given the fact that Black people constitute little more than 1.5 per cent of the population, and all minorities add up to less than 5 per cent, this hardly augurs well for the future and suggests great difficulty in achieving racialised harmony in England. As will be clear, the goals of harmony are hardly likely to be achieved if there is any mention of resource distribution, and, as seems likely, if the increased patterns of integration lead to more racialised dating and marriage. The notion of harmony leads us to lose sight of the overall larger picture.

This brings us to the issue of racialised parity and its contradictions. The US policy of affirmative action, with its greater institutional resources and longer history, offers insights for England. Rampant disparity in resource distribution and access was a fact of life for Blacks in the 1980s and constituted the most fundamental problem of racialised relations in modern times; but for most non-Blacks it was not such a perplexing issue.

There are several problems concerning the definition of racialised parity. Is it to be defined at group level, or at the individual level? And how much inequality would be tolerated within racialised groups? For example, in the United States since the 1950s group access to resources has dramatically increased for African-Americans, but the benefits have gone disproportionately to those who were already better off (Murray, 1984). Many Black people, especially the young and educated, are already at parity with non-Blacks (O'Hare *et al.*, 1991). But this is hardly satisfactory as an indicator of progress towards parity for Blacks as a group, with one third of African-Americans in poverty and frightening rates of illiteracy, unemployment and ill-health. In light of the evidence provided in Chapter 4 about the disproportionate benefits which accrue to better-off sections of the Black population, how do we ensure that working-class and workless Blacks do not stay poor while the richer ones get even richer?

The most difficult problem for those who support racialised parity is the issue of how we get non-Black support from government, policymakers and the non-Black public. Government and policymakers have introduced clear legislative and policy initiatives, but they lack political will and the backing of resources commensurate with the dimensions of the obstacles. Anti-discrimination laws and positive action in England are regarded as the strongest in Europe, while England regards affirmative action in the United States as superior to positive action (McCruddon *et al.*, 1991). Hesitancy by the state arises from commitment to free market ideals, fear of international competition and fear of alienating non-Black voters. The state has shown its preparedness to condone, encourage and exploit white fears of racism and Black competition, and the formal commitment often voiced in favour of equal opportunities is belied by the insufficient resources committed, and key examples of retrogressive policies and laws. Even if there was political will there would be real constraints on action. If the state plays a part, so too do non-Blacks generally, and opposition to racialised parity also clearly results from racialised hostility and the belief on the part of most non-Blacks that any gains made by Blacks will be to the former's detriment. The evidence unequivocally demonstrates that this policy has least support among non-Blacks in each nation because it seems so entwined with equality of outcome and it challenges notions of free choice, individual initiative, hindering free market mechanisms. The opposition of most non-Blacks to redistributive policies in the United States is unambiguous. If racialised parity were to become a primary goal then immense power inequalities would have to be overcome to get non-Blacks to accept this goal. In England, Jenkins and Solomos point out:

> the white majority in Britain are unlikely, if left to their own devices, to do much about the social and economic disadvantage experienced by their black neighbours.

(1987: 219)

The evidence suggests a similar picture in the United States. In each nation key politicians have appealed to the racialised hostilities of the non-Black population to achieve their goals. These problems pose serious obstacles, and a set of issues to which I turn in the final chapter.

## CONCLUSION

Though they took different forms, and were institutionalised in different ways, racialised disparities, segregation and conflict were widespread throughout England and the United States in the 1980s. Attitudes of Blacks and non-Blacks towards the causes of these inequalities showed marked divergence, as did their attitudes towards what should and could be done about them. Policies designed to combat racialised hostility and discrimination were characterised by problematic assumptions, confusing definitions, divergent priorities and limited support. Underlying this confusion was the idea of 'good race relations'. Given these problems there is a clear need for clarity of goals, priorities and policies and a clear understanding of how each might be implemented. In any evaluation of the policy options which were embraced by different groups in the 1980s, Blacks and non-Blacks started from very different positions. Blacks and non-Blacks occupied dramatically different positions in terms of their ownership of and access to resources; and they explained these positions in very different terms – non-Blacks saw past and present discrimination as secondary, while Blacks regarded discrimination as a major determinant of their present predicament and wanted amends accordingly.

Most non-Blacks strongly opposed policies to redistribute re-sources, while Blacks were often in favour of them.[11] While non-Black opposition to redistributive policies derives in part from a commitment to the meritocratic ideals of individual effort, it is also clear that they will support redistributive policies whenever they are the beneficiaries of them, for example affirmative action for the children of university alumni, for athletes, equal oppor-tunities policies for women (Institute for the Study of Social Change 1991). The state did not take any vigorous action, or invest resources commensurate with the dimensions of the problems, and the mobilisation of right-wing and reactionary groups, including much activity by both Republican and Conservative parties, con-tributed to these situations.

When Americans conclude that 'race relations' in England are more harmonious there than in the United States they focus primarily on residential and educational integration and on several other areas of the social realm, in particular racialised marriage. The pattern of racialised integration which is believed to prevail in England is eagerly sought after because it is seen as a means by which to bridge the cultural divide between Blacks and non-Blacks, and to give rise to greater familiarity and the breakdown of crude racialised stereotypes. When England looks at the United States in terms of parity and Black success it sees only the tip of the iceberg. The successes remain inspirational in light of the struggles of African-Americans, but their overall impact is slight in terms of the hopes of the majority of Black people. American society cannot begin to claim that it has responded to the needs and demands of the vast majority of African-Americans.

One set of problems which arises in achieving and assessing progress derives from the competing assumptions about racialised relations (and equal opportunities) held by Blacks and non-Blacks generally, the state and policymakers, and the power differentials which these groups reveal. Another set of problems derives from our failure to clarify the criteria by which we might evaluate progress. Clarifying such criteria is all the more necessary given the multiple variables which might be drawn upon, and the fact that such variables are not co-terminous. Divergent policy initiatives are required to achieve racialised integration, racialised harmony and racialised parity. Black people and others committed to racialised parity must clarify their own goals and priorities at the policy and political level, if they are to challenge successfully the power differentials. Comparison of these issues enables us to demystify the notion of 'good race relations', and to distinguish racialised parity and racialised integration, both theoretically and as targets for policies.

# Chapter 6

# Still catchin' hell

> You don't catch hell because you're a Baptist, and you don't catch hell because you're a Methodist ... you don't catch hell because you're a Democrat or a Republican. You catch hell because you're a black man. You catch hell, all of us catch hell, for the same reason ... we're all black people, so-called Negroes, second class citizens, ex-slaves.
>
> (Malcolm X, in Breitman, 1965: 4)

When I first arrived in the United States in 1984 to begin graduate study at the University of California, Berkeley, I met an African-American graduate student named Clarence Spigner. Surprised that I had come to study in the United States, he said something to the effect of 'you must be mad coming to study here. Black people are catchin' hell in this racist society. In fact, things are so bad I even thought why not go to England to study.' 'Why not go to England to study?' I replied, 'I'll tell you why not! Because they probably won't let you into the country if you're Black. And if they do let you in then you'll have more trouble than any white person finding a job, a place to live and getting an education for your kids. Black people are getting kicked in the teeth in England.'

## INTRODUCTION

The goal of this book has been to provide a comparative con-textualised analysis of the Black experience in the United States and England during the 1980s. My concern was to describe patterns of convergence and divergence in the experiences of Black people during the 1980s, disentangling the intricate interconnections, and highlighting the multiple factors involved in contributing to the processes of 'racialisation'. The point of departure for this comparison was the existence of a 'Colour Line', that is, of systematic inequalities in the circumstances of Blacks and non-Blacks, with the former worse off in all major areas. After providing a contextualised overview of the main dimensions of this pattern of racialised inequality, I focused on several key areas in the 1980s; I examined the continuing role of racialised ideologies taking account of both covert and overt forms of hostility; I considered the increasing patterns of stratification within the Black population, assessing the extent to which such patterns gave rise to divergent political priorities and strategies; and I considered the main policy and political priorities that dominated government and policymakers' agendas during this period, the conceptualisations of 'good race relations' which underlay such goals, as well as the expressed attitudes of Black and non-Black people towards such goals.

Upon first inspection a comparison of the United States and England might not appear to be fruitful. In initial comparisons one is bound to be struck by the distinct differences between the two countries – structurally, culturally, ideologically and with regard to class, 'race' and ethnicity. Yet one is also overwhelmed by the simple striking similarity in the experience of people of African descent. In the studies that exist some analysts have chosen to emphasise the differences (Trow, 1988); others stress the similarities (Katznelson, 1973). I offered several reasons why a comparison of the Black experience which focuses on similarities in each nation is useful, and I argued that many benefits would accrue to those involved in attempts to combat racialised inequality.

I argued that historically the two nations reveal much in common, an evaluation of which reveals some perplexing parallels. Racialisation as a process has become entrenched in each nation, as a result of economic and political expansion via slavery and the exploitation of Black people. The racialised structures which were developed put institutionalised constraints on Black people's liberty, of an economic, political and social nature, including the entrenchment of a wide array of racialised images. An integral part of this process has been the development of racialised ideologies of various kinds – overt and covert, individual and institutional – which have served to differentiate 'Blacks' from 'whites' and to provide rationales for patterns of inequality. Whatever the differences between the forms of such ideologies they share that common feature of constraining Black people's lives. The state has played an integral part in these processes, giving rise to racialisation and multiple 'racisms', and containing and constraining resistance. Racialised ideologies and hostility have not gone unchallenged, as Black people have mobilised to confront and overcome them, and have demonstrated great resilience in the face of the odds against which they have struggled. I argued that though Blacks have undoubtedly been victims they have refused to submit to a victim mentality. They have utilised diverse tactics to attain their rights, tactics which attest to their humanity and assert community self-pride.

The overarching similarity in both nations is of course the 'Colour Line' – the inequality of wealth, income, employment, education, health and housing – which characterises the Black experience. This 'Colour Line' is both material (property, power and privilege) and mental (attitudes, ideologies and psychology). Racialised inequality at all levels is pervasive and profound, and Blacks and non-Blacks offer very divergent views of why inequality exists and subscribe to divergent ideologies of racialised abilities. In this chapter I provide an overview of the main arguments and findings, and link them to some of the recurrent themes of the book, in particular to the implications of the changing character of racialised barriers, boundaries and identities. I characterise some of the implications of these issues in light of the economic and political trends which have developed in the world order of the 1990s – an international context of spellbinding global transformations – and I outline some aspects of a strategy of resistance predicated on racialised identities.

## RACIALISED BARRIERS AND INEQUITIES

Chapters 1 and 2 provided an introduction to the key questions and a profile of the economic, political and social conditions of Black people in the 1980s. In Chapter 1 I asked how far have Black people come towards attaining racialised parity? And how far do they have to go? When William Julius Wilson raised similar types of questions he caused considerable controversy in 1978 (Wilson, 1978). He went so far as to argue that, in contemporary United States, class was more important than 'racial oppression' for most sections of the Black population and used as his framework a comparison of contemporary circumstances with historical systems of oppression, like slavery and Jim Crow (ibid.: 144). Within the context of such a framework, and a past in which Blacks were slaves and legally defined as inhuman, or where legal segregation was supported by the entire weight of white society, then the current situation may look like an improvement. But that has not been my primary framework of comparison for evaluating the circumstances of Black people in the United States and England in the 1980s. I found it more appropriate and useful to contextualise the Black experience by comparing their circumstances with those of their non-Black counterparts, economically, politically and socially.

The data provided in Chapter 2 indicate that Black people remain at a disadvantage on the basis of just about every major indicator of economic, political and social wellbeing. I described some of these disparities in a range of areas; I also highlighted some of the anomalous patterns, and some apparent exceptions to the rule. In this overview I provided demographic data on the Black population, described patterns of settlement and indicated owner-ship of, and access to, economic, political and social resources. While there was evidence of differences in size of population and length of residence, and while each group had arrived in different circumstances, there remained some striking similarities between the two nations. In the United States I described an African-American population that was overwhelmingly indigenous, while in England African-Caribbeans were a relatively small group, of relatively recent arrival. The pattern of stratification within the Black population was extensive in the United States, and on the increase in England.

I demonstrated that in England and the United States during the 1980s Black people remained systematically disadvantaged, enjoyed access to fewer resources and experienced greater inequality and inequities than the non-Black majority. This was differentially experienced by men and women and cannot be reduced to one cause alone. On the one hand broader forces had an immediate, encompassing and forceful impact, especially the context of rapidly changing economic and political circumstances characteristic of the decade. The US economy deteriorated during the 1970s, caught a second breath in the 1980s, and is currently in a state of crisis again. England suffered the oil crisis and trade union turmoil in the 1970s, the reverberations of the loss of Empire, and at the same time it joined the European Community. The Falklands War was a temporary return to imperial glory as Thatcherism promised to put the 'great' back in Britain in the 1980s, and national pride swung high. On the other hand, racialised violence, attacks and discrimination continued to contribute to the circumstances of deprivation, desolation and desperation in which Black people find themselves. Racialised hostility ensured that at whatever location Black people found themselves in the socio-economic and political hierarchy, they faced additional distinct obstacles to those faced by non-Blacks, and were at a greater disadvantage than non-Blacks. This discrimination occurred in immigration legislation and citizenship rights, and in the dispensation of power, property and privilege. In both nations, such patterns are likely to become more salient in the 1990s and beyond. This comparative overview provided a necessary context for any evaluation of the relative 'success' of the Black population in each nation, suggested that Black people in the 1980s continued to 'catch hell', and countered any simplistic notion that 'the grass is greener on the other side'.

Black people have boldly resisted the racialised hostility which has daily disrupted their lives. They have resisted by any and all means necessary – physical and cultural, ideological and institutional. Communities of resistance have reinforced the cultures of defiance, as well as alliances, movements and institutions established to achieve common goals. Sometimes they have been spontaneous and unorganised, other times planned and organised; sometimes individual, at other times collective. Some have joined the system to rise in its ranks; others have attempted to transform the system from within; still others have tried to dismantle it from outside. Some have sought success via a strategy of multi-racialised alliances; others have sought it via Black-only or Black-led organisations. Some Blacks have erected barriers to create an autonomous space within which to defend and assert their humanity; others believe such humanity can be found only in organisations that are shared with non-Blacks. Some believe the psychological difficulties facing them will be resolved only by ending economic and political inequalities; for others, psychological persecution must first be confronted before material inequalities can be addressed. Whatever the difficulties, however intractable the problems have been, Black people have sought to reach beyond a simple struggle for survival, in order to strive for success. This resistance continues in the 1990s.

For Black women the politics of resistance have always been far more difficult than for Black men, and their unwillingness to succumb to the consequences of adversity still more impressive.

Racialised hostility creates problems for Black people that non-Black people never have to face; but gender hostility creates obstacles for Black women that Black men never face. This creates complexities which are never recognised in analyses of resistance. For example, Black women pay a greater price for the racialised sexuality associated with Black people generally by non-Blacks. They are victims not only of white racism, but also of Black male aggression, where some Black men take on the sexual roles imputed to them and thus collude with the stereotype of hyper-masculinity (Wallace, 1978; hooks, 1990). Where Black women challenge this collusion they run the risk of reinforcing the racialised stereotypes, and of incurring the wrath of Black men (Amos and Parmar, 1984; Lourde, 1990).

But I also raised the question, how far do Blacks have to go to achieve racialised parity? Again, Chapter 2 has demonstrated that for Black people as a whole, disparities persist. Built as they are on historically entrenched structural patterns of discrimination, racialised barriers and discrimination have left Black people at substantial disadvantage compared to non-Blacks, at whatever occupational or political peg in the hierarchy one wishes to compare. This disadvantage will endure for some time to come as these disparities endure decades into the twenty-first century. The existing trends will produce Black populations that are even more highly diverse; continuing efforts at meritocracy will ensure that some sections of the Black population thrive and succeed, while continuing patterns of racialised hostility will entrench the remaining sections of the Black population more firmly in poverty. In the United States:

> By the year 2000, every black under age 40 (nearly 60 per cent of the black population) will have grown up in the more hospitable post-1960 racial climate. Yet racism – one of the major forces that led blacks to rely so heavily on one another – is still very evident.
> (O'Hare *et al.*, 1991: 35)

In England, there is little evidence to suggest that an alternative scenario is likely.

## RACIALISED IDEOLOGIES AND IMAGES

Chapter 3 considered some of the intricate ways in which racialised ideologies had unfolded and been manipulated. These racialised ideologies were considered in their various manifestations, and in terms of the groups that embraced and expounded them, as well as the goals of such groups. It was demonstrated there was clear evidence throughout the 1980s of multiple 'racisms' that reinforced patterns of racialised inequality, and that many of the activities of successive governments were central to all this. It was argued that despite increasing attention on transformations and transmutations in the forms and rationales of racialised ideologies – much of it articulated around the idea of a 'new racism' – there remained essential continuities. Existing analyses offered a number of strengths; they examined a range of racialised ideologies, attitudes, discrimination and hostility, individual and institutional, linked them to broader factors, and had moved from a notion of 'racism' as a single phenomenon, to studying multiple 'racisms'. But these approaches still revealed several limitations including a continued preoccupation with racialised ideologies articulated by the state and in the political arena, a failure to identify what was distinctly 'new' about the 'new racism' (and what was distinctive about the 'old racism'). There is insufficient analysis of continuities from the past and insufficient attention given to ideologies not directly contingent on state activity and manipulation. Though there was considerable evidence in the formal political realm of a shift from crude and blatant racialised ideologies to a variety of 'racisms', considerable evidence existed of the continuation of long-established traditions and exponents of racialised hostilities. These ideologies were illustrated in attitudes towards sexuality, sexual relations, and sporting ability where it was demonstrated that many non-Blacks still subscribed to the notion of distinctive 'races'.

Racialised ideologies in these areas were not dependent primarily on state activities, or the changing economic fortunes of each nation. They were entrenched in information and images disseminated by the media and other institutions, and reproduced and embraced by large sections of the white working class. They did not reflect any new linguistic codes or rationales, but appealed to long-established beliefs about the distinctiveness of 'races' and their divergent mental and physical abilities. I argued that analysis of these ideologies was indispensable because they were not very new and not at all subtle. They did not result directly from the activities of the state, vary in accord with the economic vicissitudes of the market place, or adapt to the whims and wishes of the powerful; they were grounded in the personal and daily experiences of working-class white people; they revealed the differential impact of ideologies on Black men and women (as well as the differential power relations involved) and the additional obstacles imposed as a result of gender hostility. Such ideologies were not primarily or exclusively those of disdain and condescension, but involved notable elements of jealousy and resentment.

In the light of these findings I argued that an approach was needed which conceptualised racialised ideologies not as 'old' and 'new' racisms but as transformations and shifts in racialised discourses. This approach was predicated on the idea that a wide array of ideologies revealed racialised content or lent themselves to racialised interpretations. Along with racialised prejudices and stereotypes, it was maintained that this constituted a complex dynamic of racialised attitudes and ideologies. While state activities and changing economic fortunes influenced them, these ideologies were transformed and manipulated in ways that were no longer determined or influenced primarily or exclusively by the state, the economy or politics.

I suggested that the concept of rearticulation should be central to understanding racialised ideologies, and that an approach based on this concept would enable us to investigate when and where various factors (economics, politics, class, deliberate racialised ideologies, institutional discrimination) were important (and in light of the interplay between local, national, international contexts) rather than assuming that one set of variables was always more important than all others.

## ECONOMIC STRATIFICATION AND POLITICAL AFFILIATION

Chapter 4 examined the nature, extent and implications of stratification and differentiation in the African-American population in the United States and the African-Caribbean population in England. My main concern was to describe the patterns of increasing stratification and assess the implications this might have for strategies to overcome racialised hostility and poverty. In particular I was concerned with the continued growth throughout the 1980s of sections of the Black population that occupied an educationally, occupationally and economically advantageous position – as compared with the rest of the Black population – and the role that this group might play in alleviating or exacerbating the conditions endured by others. I considered these issues by describing the pattern of stratification in both nations, raising a set of theoretical issues about these patterns and examining some of the available data.

Black people in the United States have a long history of confrontation of the economic and political differences within their ranks, and the 1980s continued this but with a new set of dimensions in light of the Republican domination of the political arena. In England, many African-Caribbeans rushed to embrace opportunities to become part of the 'middle class' – understandably in the light of the severe disadvantages faced there by Black people. This pattern was reflected in the mushrooming of events and seminars organised by African-Caribbean businesses, increased government funding, growth of regional and national networks, and the establishment of Black professional associations such as the Association for Black Social Workers and Allied Professions. Developments like these promised to increase access for African-Caribbeans to the corridors of business previously restricted – via racialised barriers – for non-Black people. Such developments force upon Black people the need to clarify our goals and to address the questions: do we simply want to construct an African-Caribbean class structure that approximates the white class structure – one which leaves intact other equally entrenched inequalities and oppressions, such as gender bias and homophobia – or do we want a more egalitarian social structure overall?

In the United States there is clear evidence of extensive stratification, and of divergent political priorities, strategies and tactics. In England, the evidence is less abundant but economic and educational differences are increasing, and there is evidence that political priorities are diverging. The existence of a Black 'middle class' in the United States and its growth in England has many implications for racialised barriers, boundaries and identities. First and foremost, it is evidence of a diminution of racialised barriers (as obstacles to equal opportunities). For example, it was suggested that categorical discrimination against all Black people has given way to statistical discrimination against specific sections of the Black population (see Banton, 1983). The divergent circumstances in which different sections of the Black population found themselves, and the different opportunities available to them, have broken down the strength of racialised identities and the potential for unity among Black people. In particular, stratification threatened racialised identities by giving rise to diverse experiences and explanations of the problems confronting Black people (for example, about law and order, welfare and dependency, white discrimination and Black efforts). Debates around these issues were evident over Jesse Jackson and Clarence Pendleton in the United States and John Taylor and Bernie Grant in England.

I argued that it makes little sense to talk about a Black 'middle class' as if it is constituted of a monolithic group embracing the same priorities and values. Each nation displayed evidence of different groupings within this broad rubric, whose position and status was secured by different economic or educational bases, and who responded in different ways to the problems confronting Black people as a racialised group. A number of factors were identified that suggested many within this rubric would simply feather their own nests, for example, by acting primarily in their own self-interest, by deriving the best benefits from the limited equal opportunity programmes, especially in light of the withdrawal of funds for equal opportunities in the climate of the 1990s. Their consolidation and expansion is bound to break down racialised barriers, confuse racialised boundaries and dissipate racialised identities.

But other factors indicated a continuing propensity to identify and work with other Black people and suggested reasons why many of them will not abandon other Black people, including the continuing severity of racialised hostility within each nation, the dire economic pressures, and the difficulties which all Black people continue to face. Their dependence on Black support for business and votes, and the pressures exerted on them (to represent Black constituencies) by both non-Blacks and Blacks will sustain such identities, not least because it is in their interests to do so. They will pay the 'Black tax' and contribute to Black working-class people's needs. Actions can be taken to ensure that they go further, that they confer some of their advantages on other Blacks, and that they push criticisms beyond the existing boundaries of the free market. Which set of factors is greater will vary from nation to nation, and across regions; and it will vary from city to city, and across families.

All members of this congeries of affluent Blacks were far from locked into one political line, but systematic evidence on their activities has not been collected and incorporated into theoretical analysis, so a great deal is open and struggle over directions is likely to be intense. This is why there can be no simple answer to the questions posed. What we can maintain for sure is simply this: Black people's political consciousness cannot be 'read off' from their economic, occupational or educational positions because the impact of racialised hostility and the articulation of racialised identities provides a basis for a politics which cuts across over-simplified class lines, and can act as the basis for broader political alliances. Those of us who see strength in racialised identities should not simply dismiss them with the cast of a deterministic hand. We need to assess the situation more closely.

I argued that it made little sense to analyse the Black 'middle class' without addressing the following issues: the need to provide clear definitions and conceptualisation, (distinguishing the *petite bourgeoisie*, professionals, and others) because if the Black 'middle class' is not defined then we cannot begin to measure who does what, when and where; the need to collect data about the different sections – their numbers, activities, affiliations, priorities; and the need to take account of gender differences, and the activities of Black women's organisations. I think analyses like these would benefit from comparisons of the two nations. In particular, we need to disseminate more information in England about the strengths and limitations of Black business and the Black 'middle class' in the United States.

Divisions will continue to give rise to conflicts over what are the best policies and politics to pursue and adopt, and which are the best strategies, for example, nationalist versus multi-racialised coalitions; and over who will benefit or ought to benefit most from the available policy options. These conflicts continued in the 1990s around the appointment of Clarence Thomas to the Supreme Court, and the election of Black members of parliament. Community activists must reject the notion that the various sections of the Black 'middle class' uncritically embrace free market individualism. They must begin to identify the different sections, and establish what their priorities and agendas are, assess how far they embrace the goals of the majority of Black people, goals which press for more than a piece of the capitalist cake, and which press for more egalitarian institutional arrangements and distribution of resources.

## CONTRADICTIONS AND CONFLICTS IN GOALS AND PRIORITIES

Chapter 5 set out to demystify some commonly held notions of 'race relations' by examining exactly what was meant by 'good race relations'. It was suggested that this notion conflated three distinctive goals, or institutional interests – those of racialised integration, harmony and parity – and these were defined and examined to clarify the strategies designed to achieve them. It was suggested that the conflicting methods required to achieve different goals left most people clambering for limited achievements, and few people happy about any of them. Policies designed to attain one set of goals seemed to conflict with the attainment of the others; and as we approached one set of goals, further problems of racialised antagonism and conflict arose in the other areas. In particular, the goals of integration and harmony did not necessarily tackle issues of resource distribution and allocation. For example, the pursuit of racialised harmony left racialised inequality unaddressed; racialised integration led to conflict in other respects, such as racialised dating and marriage; while making a priority of racialised parity led to substantial opposition from the non-Black majority (and the Conservative/Republican free-market lobby), and was usually only sought after in largely voluntaristic and piecemeal fashion.

I argued that all three goals could not be achieved simultaneously (if ever) and that there was thus a need to clarify which priority will prevail. Different institutional interests, not least those embraced by racialised categories, already clash over this matter. I doubt that it will be possible to drop any of the three in principle, but I argued that they must be prioritised in terms of the resources available to achieve each. It was also necessary to recognise the state's strategy in responding to and manipulating fears of non-Black electors, as well as the state's fundamental commitment to free market economics and politics. Central to this argument is my belief that during the 1980s most Black people wanted racialised parity, while most non-Black people did not, or were not prepared to countenance the policies which might promote such a goal as a priority. What still confronts Black people and Black organisations is how to get government and the white public to accept our priorities, as we seek to ensure that our items are on the agenda, and our needs are given full consideration.

In the light of such problems what goals can be advocated, and how can we ensure that they are implemented? Clearly we must reduce racialised conflict, attacks and violence; and we must reduce racialised discrimination. But what of integration and harmony? For those of us for whom racialised parity remains a priority how do we ensure that government takes on board Black priorities, especially if there is strong non-Black opposition to them? How do we ensure that more than a few Black people reap the benefits of such policies? And that in our obsession to secure something in the here and now, we do not lose sight of the need to act for goals that must go beyond capitalist society? I believe that a choice must be made between the different and conflicting goals and priorities. I believe most Black people want parity over the other goals and I believe that those of us committed to organising around racialised identities should press for racialised parity as a priority while recognising and seeking to go beyond some of its limitations. We should work to ensure that parity means more than making the existing Black 'middle class' even better off, and more than just material improvements; that is, it must also confront obstacles of psychological abuse.

One way of ensuring benefits for more than affluent Blacks is to ensure such policies are articulated around the interplay of racialised identities and class positions. Clearly also they must be differentiated by gender, so that Black women benefit. There are some clear precedents for this approach in each nation. In the United States, many equal opportunities policies take account of economic resources; as do similar policies in England. In order to tackle the worst manifestations of disparity we can seek to shape policies towards equipping those with least resources to get a first step on the ladder.

## THE CHANGING TERRAIN OF THE 1990s

The 1990s has seen a series of developments that will have significant impact on patterns of racialised relations in the United States and England. From the Gulf War and Middle East turmoil to the disintegration of the Soviet Union and the new configuration of military conflicts arising there; from the consolidation and expansion of Pacific Rim economies, to new developments in South Africa and Somalia; from chaos in the former Eastern bloc nations, the unification of Germany and unease over the consolidation of the European Community, the economic and political ramifications are immense. The role of the United States as policeman of the world, with military involvement in the Gulf, Somalia, and elsewhere, alongside substantial reductions in military armament, has become intricate and perplexing. This is likely to continue while the

United States envisages for itself a role of unilateral domination, while England maintains its illusion of international might.

Though these influences are complex and multifaceted, I believe that their impact on racialised barriers, boundaries and identities in the United States and England will be relatively straightforward. Patterns of racialised inequality will become exacerbated, the factors that maintain them will become more complex and difficult to pinpoint. Once again, the impact on Black women will be exceptionally adverse. These forces will relegate issues of racialised justice and equal opportunities in the United States and England to secondary status in a world in which concern with free trade and competition, individual initiative, the enterprise culture, and colour-blind policies, will prevail. Collectively they will provide new rationalisations for racialised hostility, and marginalise sustained efforts to combat racialised inequities (Small, 1993). Many of these influences reveal no apparent racialised content, and no apparent intentions of racialised hostility. But their impact is decidedly racialised because, as a result of racialised hostility in the past, Black people are already at a greater disadvantage compared to the non-Black majority, whatever their class position, or gender, and treating them as if they are equal is necessarily unfavourable. This will occur in several ways.

State action will become more circumspect – playing down direct and indirect discrimination, selectively highlighting equal opportunities legislation, emphasising the need to keep to the free play of the market, to meritocracy and to a colour-blind approach. The machinery is already in place to employ a political language saturated with racialised content, while professing commitment to oppose racialised hostility. In this way the state claims it is providing maximum opportunity for racialised equality, and is simply giving Black people what they want. Bush resorted to racialised imagery once again in his failed 1992 presidential campaign; Jesse Helms employed it in his successful state campaign. Clinton has taken a different profile, highlighting racialised injustice, putting Blacks into key government positions. Though he voices a concern for significant change, his policies are not about fundamental change. The British government has not hesitated to assert that its 'race relations' legislation is better than elsewhere in Europe. John Major has offered the kinder face of state 'racism' in Britain, but local Conservatives in Cheltenham did not want a 'bloody nigger' as their Member of Parliament;[1] Winston Churchill, MP (nephew

of Winston Churchill, the former Prime Minister), greatly exagger-
ated the size of the African-Caribbean and Asian population in
England to frighten white voters (*Weekly Journal*, 1991). At the 1993
Conservative Party Conference the Home Secretary warned of
'foreign scroungers' bleeding Britain dry. Language like this from
the government will continue alongside the more direct racialised
hostility associated with the election of British National Party
member Derek Beacon as a local councillor in East London. The
manipulation of the fears and insecurities of the non-Black population will continue to offer clear political gains.

Complications have been introduced by the confusion of racialised hostility with ethnicity and ethnic antagonism as if we are all
different now, all facing obstacles and prejudices, each and every
one of them meriting equal attention.[2] In Europe, racialised
hostility is being confused with ethnicity, and the 'ethnic cleansing'
of Bosnia, is being compared with the terror of slavery and
imperialism. While it is not useful to compare atrocities, it is
necessary to think about what the outcomes of these developments
might be. Greater national and international focus is on the
conflict in Bosnia, as funds have been diverted in that direction. In
the United States, the Los Angeles riots have highlighted the
increasingly complex relations between people of colour, while the
focus on difference in the arguments of 'European ethnics' has
continued into the 1990s (Waters, 1990). In England, Asians and
settlers from other European Community countries rub shoulders
uneasily with Black people, the latter being told by academics that
the term 'Black' makes no sense (Jones, 1993). Government and
policymakers maintain that the problems faced by Black people are
no greater than the problems faced by all immigrants. I believe that
such claims will increasingly be tied into the developing economic
and political differences within the Black population, and manipulated to our detriment.

At the same time, racialised activities outside the state will
continue as fears associated with the stereotyping of the Black body
– sexuality, sexual relations, sporting prowess – shape the attitudes
and actions of those who compete with Black people, as well as
those who are in positions to shape Black people's lives. Fuelled
on by media myths and sensationalism – such as the preoccupation
with what is between Linford Christie's legs rather than acclam-
ation of how fast his legs can carry him – Black people will find

the fast track to academic excellence blocked, and the fast track to sporting success open.

Affluent, socially mobile and politically prominent Blacks, particularly those that remain apolitical or align themselves with Republican and Conservative positions, will continue to complicate the overall picture, as will Black superstars in the sporting and music world. Their existence lends weight to the argument that the 'Colour Line' is a class line and encourages non-Blacks to reiterate the pre-eminence of individual effort, and to believe or argue that racialised inequality and discrimination are things of the past. It is ironic that Colin Powell, a significant political symbol of this whole charade in the United States, should receive an honorary aristocratic title from the Queen. Should he run on a Republican ticket for vice-president of the United States in 1996, tensions and conflicts within the African-American community will reach dimensions not even conceived of in the debate over Clarence Thomas and Anita Hill (Morrison, 1993).

These developments have added to the contradictions and confusion surrounding 'good race relations' and have already become the basis for the repudiation of the whole idea that racialised injustice should be combated by anything other than a colour-blind approach. Presented as anti-democratic, authoritarian or as silly 'political correctness', the many real efforts to oppose institutionalised inequality have been collapsed into some of the more ludicrous efforts, and the whole enterprise has been derogated (Gordon, 1990; Edsall and Edsall, 1991b). In the face of the conservative and free-market individualist climate of the 1990s, the hostility of most non-Blacks to policies to combat and redress discrimination, especially group-based policies, and a context of unequal power relations, the issue is not just what to do, but how to get it done?

## CONFRONTING BARRIERS, BOUNDARIES AND IDENTITIES

This book has demonstrated the continued significance of racialised hostility and ideologies in patterns of racialised inequality, and suggested the strength of racialised identities in seeking to challenge such patterns. It has been argued that while racialised inequality cannot simply be reduced to class issues, neither can it be eliminated without an offensive against other types of inequality. Ending racialised hostility and inequality – whether ideologies, attitudes and images, or attacks, discrimination and abuse – has always been the priority for Black people. And a central plank in most strategies has been a wish to act on racialised identities by mobilising through Black organisations and movements, ideologies and institutions. From my analysis, it becomes clear that Black people must choose between different strategies and different priorities. We have to confront the 1990s realities against their historical background. Exactly how this will be done is more likely to be determined in forums, meetings and campaigns, but here I offer one approach, an approach which takes mobilisation around racialised identities as a central feature. The remainder of the chapter elaborates this approach.

First of all, it is important to note that I do not intend to portray a full picture of likely developments during the 1990s, or of all the elements of a political strategy that might be found effective. This would require a greater consideration of the multiple factors involved than I devote here. My goal is to identify key features of a strategy that follow from the analysis developed throughout the book. However, I need to comment on a key issue which has been left undeveloped – the implications for my analysis created by the presence of Hispanics in the United States and Asians in England. The Los Angeles riots in 1992 have once again highlighted the fact that any analysis of racialised relations carried out within a framework of a Black–white polarity is bound to suffer limitations. Clearly, in order to carry out the comparative analysis that I set for myself in Chapter 1 – to highlight continuities in racialised barriers, boundaries and identities in the experiences of Black people in the two nations – it has been necessary to overlook the complexities introduced by reference to Hispanics and Asians, the other significant minority group in the two nations respectively. Yet each group is bound to play a decisive role in the future developments which affect Black people.

In the United States Hispanics are the fastest growing minority group – during the 1980s, primarily as a result of immigration, Hispanics (and Asian Americans) grew at rates that 'dwarfed the black growth rate' (O'Hare *et al.*, 1991: 6). By 1990 Hispanics numbered almost 22.5 million, and are expected to become the 'most numerous minority early in the 21st century' (ibid.: 7). Their concentration in specific areas – the south west, Florida, New York – has highlighted the significant role they will play in racialised politics (Sanchez-Jankowski, 1986). They have significant political power in certain areas and non-Black political leaders have sought to woo them, or to manipulate divisions, while conflicts with Blacks have also occurred (Suro, 1991).

In England Asians outnumber African-Caribbeans, and have a higher rate of population growth (Jones, 1993). There are substantial differences within the Asian population – between, for example, Indians, Pakistanis and Bangladeshis (ibid.). Indians in particular are more likely than African-Caribbeans to be self-employed, to occupy professional positions, and to have higher educational qualifications (Brown, 1984; Jones, 1993). Some Asians, particularly those from East Africa, are clearly located in the capitalist class, or that of small business owners. There is also evidence that Asians are more likely to vote Conservative (Anwar, 1986). Like the United States, conflicts have occurred between African-Caribbeans and Asians, and non-Blacks have once again sought to capitalise on the real economic and ethnic divisions. A pivotal symbolic issue in these antagonisms has been the issue of whether Asians identify themselves as Black (Modood, 1988). However, several key political organisations which campaign with a common banner of 'Black' – such as the Society of Black Lawyers, the National Black Caucus, the Federation of Black Housing Organisations and the National Association of Black Probation Officers – are headed by Asians, or have significant numbers of Asians in their ranks. This is especially the case for younger Asians born in England. So these issues are far from closed.

In sum, sizeable minority groups such as Hispanics and Asians add further complexities to an already complex situation. As racialised and ethnic communities in the United States and England become more diverse there is a greater need to identify the complex inter-relationships between economic and political variables, and racialised, religious and ethnic ones. Many non-Blacks want to foster divisions and will encourage antagonism around how such communities define themselves and relate to one another (Sivanandan, 1990; Marable, 1992). Black people have already begun to confront the problems raised by these relations – and they have not always been resolved with satisfaction. This is another set of issues that must be confronted. Some sections of these populations seek to establish a common language, and to achieve common goals, on the basis of shared priorities and strategies, while others seek their goals on the basis of class or ethnic lines. Though the activities of Hispanics and Asians will greatly affect the particular shape of the strategies developed by Black people, this does not pose any fundamental challenge to the main contours of the strategy. I now turn to its major elements.

Many analysts, as well as political and community activists, have argued that the best or only way to combat racialised inequality is via an approach which confronts economic and class inequality exclusively, or first and foremost, and which conceptualises racialised ideologies primarily as the work of the state and the powerful (Reich, 1981; Wilson, W., 1987; Taaffe and Mulhearn, 1988; Miles, 1989a).[3] Miles suggests that our political actions should be shaped by an analysis of capitalist development and class divisions, and of the process of racialisation within this (Miles, 1982, 1989a). If we did so we would recognise that political action around racialised identities ignores class divisions within the Black population and the problems these might cause (Miles, 1984: 221). He maintains that racialised identities do not address the fundamental inequalities endemic in capitalist society because their preoccupation with overcoming 'racism' leaves the basis of capitalist society intact (Miles, 1984: 220). He argues instead that we should reject the political and ideological constructs employed by European capitalists – the categories of Black and white – in favour of the material categories of class groupings (ibid.: 221). Miles suggests that we can never get 'good race relations' because the ideological categories of 'race' mystify more fundamental bases of inequality within capitalist society – it is like chasing a fleeting illusion. For Miles the best political strategy is one that unites all workers, Black and white, in confronting racism, sexism and class inequality.

Though there is considerable merit in this approach – which necessarily locates the problems Black people face in a broader context of inequality and class conflict – others have raised a number of objections (Sivanandan, 1982; Gilroy, 1987a).[4] Miles's critics argue that he continues to reduce racialised inequality to class dynamics alone, and has failed to recognise the distinct racialised nature of all exploitation in capitalist society. In doing so he thus marginalises the significance and consequences of racialised oppression and exploitation which are fundamentally different from class oppression (Sivanandan, 1982: 94). Gilroy adds that Black people have always pursued greater goals than the end of 'racism' (1987a). He argues that Miles pays insufficient attention to the racialised hostility of the white working class, other than to suggest that it is fooled by capitalists; and that Miles cannot conceive of Black political action as a viable way forward (Gilroy, 1987a). I have suggested elsewhere that Miles's approach around this issue reveals several limitations (Small, 1991a). While racialised inequality prevails, racialised identities are a mobilising force to contain and overcome its worst effects; and because it is not only the state and the economically powerful, but also the white working class, that perpetrate and benefit from racialised injustice and inequality.

These are crucial issues but the divergence in the views of Miles and his critics (including myself *on this issue*) necessarily link theoretical analysis with political struggle. The debate is not just about the material bases of inequality, but about the ideological and psychological consequences of such inequality, and the strategies and mechanisms that might be employed to confront and overcome them. I want to identify several major flaws in a strategy based primarily on class alliances, and suggest that within the context of the embraced racialised identities, racialised parity is viable (even within capitalist society). My view is that we should seek this goal, while ever pressing to go beyond it.

Strategies organised around class identities play down racialised hostility, ignore psychological malaise, neglect the role of white working-class hostility towards Black people and fail to make it clear how they will persuade Black people to accept them. Black people continue to face problems which no non-Black people ever face, problems that are inextricably entwined with, but cannot be reduced to economics, class or politics. Racialised hostility impacts on our lives prior to, through, and as a result of, class and economic differences. Racialised attacks, violence and abuse are the worst manifestations of this experience. The racialised ideologies around sexuality and sexual relationships, and sport, described in Chapter 3, are further examples. Moreover, when did a white person get murdered, mutilated or mistreated because of white racism? As people of African descent, our culture, institutions, values and history still remain the most vilified of all racialised groups. Derogatory representations of the most venal kind are pervasive in literature, popular culture, the media and education. Drawing on his analysis of colonialism, Sivanandan offers a summary:

> Admittedly, the economic aspects of colonial exploitation may find analogy in white working-class history. But the cultural and psychological dimensions of black oppression are quite un-

paralleled. For, in their attempt to rationalise and justify to their conscience 'the robbery, enslavement, and continued exploitation of their coloured victims all over the globe', the conquistadors of Europe set up such a mighty edifice of racial and cultural superiority, replete with its own theology of goodness, that the natives were utterly disoriented and dehumanised. . . . If the white workers' lot at the hands of capitalism was alienation, the blacks underwent complete deracination. And it is this factor which makes black oppression qualitatively different from the oppression of the white working class'.

(Sivanandan, 1982: 94)

Many of these problems are perpetrated and reproduced by a substantial section of white working-class people, vast numbers of whom have demonstrated that they can sustain racialised ideologies and discrimination quite independently of the state and the powerful, and in full disregard to the common interests that they share with working-class Black people. Not only are they the most immediate threats to our physical and psychological wellbeing, but they accrue real benefits from their treatment of us, and many are unambivalent in their recognition of this. It is problems like these which we must confront over and above any material problems. A priority for Black people in the United States has always been the need to carve out an autonomous institutional space within which to breathe, recuperate and resist. This has increasingly become the case in England.

There remains another question. How will most Black people be persuaded to adopt a class-based approach, which calls on them to forego Black institutional organisations and groupings in favour of uniting with a white working class that has historically been antagonistic? Though the prospects for such an eventuality are eminently more possible in England than the United States, nevertheless even there it remains extremely unlikely that most Black people will forego racialised identities, ideologies or institutions on the promise of a socialist alliance, certainly not in the context of such endemic structures of racialised inequality. It is also clear that most Black people are committed to the growth of Black businesses and a Black 'middle class'.

In the face of these problems, and given the existing correlations between groups historically defined as Black and all forms of disadvantage, I argue that Black people should reject 'colour-blind' strategies and insist on a strategy that places racialised parity first and foremost, and is organised around racialised identities. By racialised identities I mean building on the strengths of Black organisations, mobilising Black people around common goals, and forming alliances with other racialised groups on the basis of our terms and priorities. Racialised identities offer a number of strengths. Though the idea of 'race' was manipulated in order to oppress and exploit, the dynamics it has generated are currently being embraced with a momentum contrary to its original intent, as a means to organise and mobilise against injustice. We should seek to ensure the adoption of policies that recognise the links between racialised and economic inequality and injustice. A clear initiative in this kind of strategy would be a rigorously applied policy of affirmative action and positive action which are linked to class inequalities.

This approach recognises the fact that many problems facing Black people involve economic obstacles encountered by others and it does not preclude alliances developed around confronting these common problems. But it does insist that until the dispro-portionate disadvantages faced by Black people are recognised and addressed in and of themselves, the possibilities for any alliances between Blacks and non-Blacks will remain remote. The depth of racialised inequalities in the United States, and the inadequacy of colour-blind policies to displace them, provide an example of how significant change can only be achieved via political actions and policies that acknowledge racialised group affiliations. This approach is necessary because the idea that we might attain racial-ised parity without it is unconvincing, and the view that we must await economic equality or the end of capitalist society is insulting and unacceptable.

No amount of insisting by non-Black academics and political activists (or others) on the spuriousness of 'race' as a biological category, or its limitations as an indicator of shared economic, political and social conditions is likely to dissuade us. We must recognise the historical construction of racialised categories, and the contingent racialised identities that derive from them. We must recognise the immense pressures such racialised boundaries and identities have been subjected to, and the likelihood that they will face greater assault in the 1990s. But we must also reject the notion that they are meaningless categories; they must be recognised as political and social categories which are articulated and embraced by people that have faced common racialised barriers. The particular forms which political strategies take, and the shape of policies, will be dictated by the circumstances in which they are developed; strategies must be formulated to recognise the unique configuration of conditions in Los Angeles, Chicago and New York, as well as in London, Liverpool and Leeds.

Of course, this approach is not without its limitations, and they too must be confronted. An indication of these problems is reflected in England in the enduring conflict between the Anti-Racist Alliance (ARA) and Anti-Nazi League (ANL) over strategies to combat racialised attacks and violence. The ARA, whose national secretary is Marc Wadsworth, a key player in the Black sections movement in the 1980s, argue that the most effective tactic is to build Black-led multi-racial organisations in which Black people play a key leading part and establish priorities and agendas. Only in this way will the significance of racialised hostility be conveyed, and the priorities of Black people be taken on board: 'Only black people, it believes can determine the destiny and politics of an anti-racist movement' (Chadhary and Travis, 1993: 21). The ARA link racialised hostility to other systems of injustice but insist that it is a distinctive problem that must be confronted first and foremost (ibid.). The ANL argue that the most effective strategy is one built on a multi-racialised alliance in which Black and non-Black come together on equal terms and play equal roles in confronting bigotry: 'You can only defeat racism by uniting black and white people and tackling the Nazis head-on' (ibid.). They also insist that equal importance be attached to identifying the links between racialised hostility, class hostility and capitalism. There is as much animosity between these two groups as there is between either of them and the British National Party which they oppose.

The possibilities for alliances based on Black-only, or Black-led organisations and initiatives are bound to face many problems, more so in England than in the United States, the latter having a longer history of separate institutions (Landry, 1987). But even there, as responses to the Nation of Islam testify, a fine line must be trodden, and they are confronted if they become too bold. In England, separate Black organisations give rise to fear, condemnation by non-Blacks – especially those indifferent to Black progress; or to frustration and anxiety among those committed to multi-racialised class-based alliances. Yet in light of the racialised hostility which has been so much a part of Black people's experience, cultures and communities of resistance based on alliances between Blacks and non-Blacks are bound to create problems absent from Black-only endeavours. For example, many Black people are exhausted from educating non-Black people out of their ignorance and naivety; others have grown impatient with their indifference or dogma. Black women in particular are reluctant to join forces with non-Black feminist campaigns which have historically been 'racist' and uncritical of racialised stereotypes and myths, especially around sexuality (Carby, 1982; Amos and Parmar, 1984; Amott and Matthaei, 1991).

Undoubtedly this approach will necessarily cement racialised group identities in the foreseeable future. This is unavoidable, and the price that must be paid. It is also likely that promoting racialised parity on its own may simply provide access to resources for some Blacks (and other people of colour) to participate in the exploitation and oppression of others. Policies to achieve parity within capitalist society are bound to make a top-heavy white hierarchy more rainbow-like without necessarily displacing the structural obstacles to resource distribution which inhere in capitalist organisation, nor necessarily challenging other bases of disparity and discrimination, like sexism and homophobia.

If these problems are to be challenged Black people must confront our refusal to openly discuss our own 'dirty washing', to deny and neglect conflicts at the cultural and personal level, to fail to take on board the real variations in occupational position and influence within the community, to gloss over sexism, to bury the issue of drugs, and to regard as taboo ethnic or racialised divisions within our ranks: for example, the animosities expressed popularly by Black men over the presumed economic success of Black women; the arrogance, condescension and contempt which surrounded the Clarence Thomas and Anta Hill affair (Morrison, 1993); the homophobia associated with Buju Banton;[5] the acrimony created by the abandonment of Black children by fathers; the hostilities and accusations around the racialised identities of Black people of mixed origins (Spickard, 1989; Alibhai-Brown and Montague, 1992); and the resentments and accusations over the relative economic and political achievements of African-Caribbeans compared with African-Americans in the United States, and African-Caribbeans and Africans in England. Not only will such issues persist as some Black people continue to make progress, they will increasingly impinge upon questions of sincerity, commitment and betrayal, selfishness and responsibility. To ignore such issues is to leave them festering, in ways that will further antagonise and alienate sections of the Black population from one another.

So while racialised parity must remain a priority it must entail more than just material parity, because a movement concerned only with getting Black people full participation in the mainstream of existing power structures, concerned only with ending the economic disadvantages faced by Blacks, and concerned only with an end to racialised hostility, cannot end isolation, individualism, or exploitation, nor sexism and homophobia. In an economy that offers so little opportunity for social mobility generally, the majority of people born working class (Black and non-Black, male and female) will remain working class even if there is no racialised or gender discrimination. So other kinds of hostility must figure in our strategy. We need to confront divisions within the Black community, address issues of inequality beyond 'racisms', and organise priorities and develop strategies with similar thinking and committed groups and individuals. Those involved in national and local Black organisations, in voluntary groups and agencies, in those organisations concentrating on economics and business, and in the cultural, educational social and recreational groups all have a central role to play.

Much can be achieved within the existing constraints of capitalist society, but it is imperative that we consider broader issues than those taken up by 'mainstreamers' (those trying to develop the 'me-too' isms, and get Blacks into the mainstream of business and politics). In the short run it is imperative that we strive for success within the existing power structures; in the long run, to do it on its own, is disastrous. We must conceptualise goals, policies and practices which go beyond the limits of the so-called 'free market' and which link into struggles which challenge these structures. When I say go beyond I mean by first and foremost confronting such issues as the likely outcomes for different sections of the Black population, for men and women. We should not ignore, neglect, or marginalise major issues and problems (such as white women in the feminist movement have done with Black women). In this light who can demur from Marable's strategy:

We must advance 'reformist' programs within our communities which reinforce Black owned socioeconomic and cultural institutions, advocating the maintenance of needed social service programs that affect the Black working class and the poor. But we must insist uncompromisingly that the social crises confronting Black people reflect a more fundamental contradiction created in part by the crisis of capital accumulation. Self-determination for the Black majority cannot be forged unless our politics, in theory and in practice, also opposes sexual exploitation, imperialism, and monopoly capitalism.

(Marable, 1983: 194)

Similarly, in England, Sivanandan maintains:

Alliances between anti-racist and the working-class struggle are crucial, because the struggle against racism without the struggle against class remains cultural–nationalist. But the class struggle without race struggle, without the struggles of women, of gays, of the Irish, remains economistic.

(Sivanandan, 1990: 76)

The onus here is on clarity in a context in which time and options are limited. Both Marable and Sivanandan call for a set of policy and political actions that transcend racialised concerns, and each calls for broad-based alliances that link together common concerns, common injustices, common strengths. It remains apparent that there are different priorities and different ways of achieving this. Black people and Black organisations have not resolved the difficult balance between aiming for improvement *within* capitalist society, while trying to transcend it. The issue which confronts them is how to ameliorate some of the worst conditions confronting Black people while not restricting ourselves to ameliorative measures alone.

For example, time spent getting Black people into the Houses of Parliament is time lost changing the fundamentals of the political system; time spent building Black businesses is time lost challenging the essential inequality upon which all business is based; time spent developing a large Black 'middle class' is time lost ending the homelessness and unemployment of working-class and never-employed Black people; time spent getting Saturday schools is time lost changing the educational system; time spent putting more Black teachers into schools is time lost fundamentally restructuring the nature of the education system; and time spent promoting racialised integration and harmony is time lost pushing for parity and beyond. Thus we must negotiate in the specific contexts in which we find ourselves, shaped as they are by some of the racialised realities I have outlined in this and earlier chapters. It is most likely that some organisations will continue to take an uncompromising position on this matter, opting entirely for change within capitalist society, others for simply transcending it.

A strategy consistent with racialised identities means that most Blacks and non-Blacks pursue different, though not necessarily separate, priorities in the short term. By this I mean that since most positions of power, authority and decision-making lie with non-Blacks, those that are committed to tackling racialised hostility in all its manifestations and to promoting social justice can best do so by concentrating on challenging the racialised hostility of other non-Blacks, especially in its institutionalised forms. If such individuals insist on 'helping' Black people by focusing on them in their research, decision-taking and so forth, then they can also facilitate the access of Blacks to positions of power so that we may share in the decisions that shape our lives, and actively undertake such decisions ourselves. Most Black people can concentrate on building up organisations and institutions committed to the principles outlined, while most non-Black people can challenge the structures of institutions and organisations which exclude or demean our contributions. Those non-Blacks who are prepared actively to support social justice and fairness – and I am firmly convinced that there are many committed people in this group – should show their cards and facilitate the most conducive action. The time is long overdue for a change in focus.

Of course, this is easier said than done. How can it be done? Instead of preaching to the converted, how do we preach to those who are not yet converted, or who are steadfastly opposed? How do we change the attitudes and actions of those committed exclusively to multi-racialised alliances (particularly those led primarily by non-Black people), as well as those who openly oppose racialised parity? Still yet, how to challenge the opposition of a state apparatus which voices a commitment to equal opportunity while systematically impeding its progress by implementing policies in clear conflict with its spirit and realisation? I believe there are two issues: how to change the views and actions of the powerful and how to mobilise the powerless. Once again, answers to such questions are matters for discussion, debate and negotiation and are unlikely to be resolved in the short term in books such as this; they are more likely to be resolved in the long term in the political and community arena. But a tentative outline can be offered.

First things first: the vast majority of non-Blacks have power – economic, political, educational, institutional – and are not going to give it up without a fight; nor are those Blacks in positions of power and privilege. The objective interests of these groups lie in the maintenance of existing structures of opportunity and reward. But there are many working-class whites and many Blacks with power that are committed to racialised equality. Any strategy designed to confer benefits on a significant section of the Black population must recognise this fact. I have made two sets of assumptions. First, that the evidence reveals that discrimination in various areas remains widespread and significant, though not always direct or easy to identify. The impact of law has more than reached its limits – calls for strengthening of laws go back many years. Any future achievements will be based on a combination of sheer hard work and on how our skills and talents as Black people are harnessed and applied. Second, I assume that success comes via policies and politics developed on several broad fronts, based on a combination of exhortation (moral), and appeal to economic benefits/imperatives (good business) as well as struggle; and that these are sustained by the letter of law (legal).

Any discussion of change must have as a central concern a discussion of power, and of the obstacles that must be confronted in the power struggles to get different items on the agenda. We must mobilise the powerless and challenge the powerful. I am not talking of some magical, mystical notion of power residing in the hands of presidents and prime ministers, governors and directors of multinational companies, and the Royal Family. In the United States, state and municipal office holders, mayors of cities, boards and managers of vast corporations, the professions, education and media – all are holders of power and decision-making with regard to the control and access to resources. In England I mean the power of local authorities, local and national employers, education, social services, health authorities, banking, insurance, the institutions of education, press and the media. These agencies – in conjunction with other national and international agencies – control and influence the nature, quality and duration of Black people's lives in this country. Committed individuals can contain and constrain injustice, promote better opportunities and ensure that the extra obstacles which keep Black people out are removed.

## CONCLUSION

It should be clear from this book that issues of racialised relations are broader than the contours of the two nations in question and more wide-ranging than patterns of migration and settlement. They entail structures and histories longer than many would care to remember or confront, and involve ideologies that are larger and more encompassing than 'racisms'. Therefore the need for clear principles and priorities in order to attain theoretical clarity and to construct effective policies and political action is all the greater.

It is more evident now than it has ever been that the imperatives of industrial society have not demolished racialised or ethnic divisions and identities, as predicted by nineteenth-century social theorists (Omi and Winant, 1986). The twentieth century has given rise to complex and contradictory racialised structures that suggest a perennial if not permanent existence (Bell, 1992). Racialised hostility has been woven into the social fabric of the United States and England in ways which ensure that it will remain entrenched well into the twenty-first century. The reinvigoration of long-established Black organisations and the enthusiasm with which new Black organisations are being established reflect such trends. Communities and cultures based on the strength of racialised identities prevail; from Black Power, the Black Panthers, and the consolidation and expansion of the Nation of Islam, to Afrocentrism in the United States, to the growth of Afro-Centric organisations (such as Kemetic Educational Guidance and the Afro-Centric Reading Group), the Pan-African Congress Movement, the National Black Caucus, the Society of Black Lawyers and a wide range of Black women's groups (like the National Association of Women of African Descent and Osaba Women's Centre) in England, racialised institutions, ideologies and identities abound and proliferate. These reflect only the more prominent elements of a movement which includes the many departments, scholars, activists, courses and a vast literature predicated on the centrality of racialised identities to challenging and escaping the economic, political and psychological tribulations endured by Black people today.

At a time when the eyes of Europe are focused on internal affairs I have taken the opportunity to remind analysts, practitioners and activists of the need to step back and review the larger picture. Critical assessment of the theoretical, conceptual and political frameworks which shape the analyses which we produce and the policies which are proposed, and an analysis of the continued impact of US institutions, ideologies, politics and policies on England, and vice versa, must continue. I have suggested a need to re-evaluate the appropriateness of theories, concepts and policies borrowed from the United States to promote British racialised relations. In England we need to maintain systematic comparisons of the two nations, even though our attention is now turned towards Europe and the European Community. The United States, too, can benefit from such comparisons. We need to unearth and evaluate continuities and discontinuities, disentangle complexities, and establish priorities. Our comparisons should be conceptually clear, theoretically driven, empirically grounded and politically informed if they are to be of any use. These requirements are indispensable components of any thorough research programme, any informed policy formulation and implementation, and any progressive political agenda. Black people in each nation will soon realise that impressions of success are far from real. Those of us who are prepared to take our actions beyond examination and evaluation into the realms of action and implementation need to mobilise around these matters to combat racialised hostility.

The precise ways in which the lessons of comparisons might be extracted, the information disseminated and the benefits formulated and implemented, are matters for discussion and negotiation. These issues are likely to resonate differently with different groups. Those interested primarily in theory may wish to move from a general theory of 'racisms' to a focus on the changing nature of multiple 'racisms', and how contemporary 'racisms' rearticulate present as compared with past influences. Those interested primarily in policy may be concerned more with the particular configuration of forces which perpetuate racialised inequality in different localities and with the policies implemented elsewhere which may be useful in their contexts. Those centrally involved in political activity will want to clarify the strategies they develop to combat it, and consider the possibilities for alliances. All three groups will want to look at how linkages are made (and by whom) in the local, national and international contexts and seek to learn from them. Whatever choices are made, I hope that I have demonstrated the need for an informed and rigorous appreciation of the details of the two contexts.

When the distinguished scholar and political activist Walter

Rodney wrote his classic *The Groundings with my Brothers* (1969), he advocated a constant exchange of views, perspectives and support between everyone in the Black community, not just in one country but throughout the diaspora. Swept away by the political powers of the time – like so many of our spokespersons – his memory lives on, rearticulated and revitalised in our strivings. In this book I have sought to sustain this dialogue. If you have not been persuaded of the importance of these issues, or the efficacy of the strategy proposed, then I shall not be greatly surprised or disappointed. After all, as Rodney himself demonstrated, satisfactory social analysis is usually born more of experience than of theory – just as social and political change is more likely to arise from the two together than from one on its own – and my own studies of political and social change have demonstrated that it is often slow in coming. But if I have made you feel sufficiently uncomfortable to want to pursue comparative analysis further I shall consider that a small step forward and a small contribution to assessing and building on the trials, tribulations and triumphs of Black people across the diaspora. We must extend our horizons and expand our intellects as we express our humanity and affirm our dignity. We must seek knowledge about struggles abroad, learn from others and lend support.

# Notes

## 1 INTRODUCTION

1 There are no 'races' so there can be no 'race relations'. When we analyse relations between Blacks and whites we are studying social relations which have been imbued with 'racial' meaning. The conceptual framework involved is outlined below.
2 The concept of 'racialised' integration is discussed below.
3 The notion of racialised harmony is discussed in the text below and treated in detail in Chapter 5.
4 Several recent striking examples are to be found in the area of higher education. Legislation has been implemented in England to emulate the United States' system, and many are heralding this move as promising major benefits for Black people (Trow, 1988; Smithers and Robinson, 1989). Another area where comparisons are increasingly being made in the press is that of role mentors. A role mentor scheme introduced in London by North London College lecturer Howard Jeffries was reported in the press and on television (Hynes, 1989; *The Guardian*, 24 July 1990; *Hearsay*, Tuesday 21 August 1990). Such views are confirmed by those who would travel abroad, and were certainly part of my own experience in the United States and England. When I began my studies in the United States in 1984, several initial experiences seemed to confirm the American success story. It was at the University of California, Berkeley that I saw for the first time Blacks in large numbers in an institution of higher education. My joy and gratification caused much perplexity to American-born Blacks, familiar with the historically Black colleges across the country, who thought the University of California was the epitome of white institutions. It was also at Berkeley that I was taught for the first time in my life by a Black person. Each time I returned to England friends and associates would constantly inquire as to why Blacks were so successful in the United States, often offering my own success there as evidence of the matter in hand.
5 The notion of 'good race relations' is discussed in the text below and is treated in detail in Chapter 5.

6 I am not using the term 'hostility' in its usual sense of aggressive, explicit action. Rather I use it to refer to attitudes and actions where the intentions and/or outcomes are detrimental to Black people.

7 For example, some groups in England argue that one way forward for Black people is to develop a Black 'middle class' of the sort which has developed in the United States (Cashmore, 1991). This debate is developed in Chapter 4.

8 A more detailed discussion of the comparative literature is provided in Small, 1991a.

9 The outstanding exception to this pattern is the journal *Race and Class* which has been consistently critical of developments in the United States. See, for example, Kushnick, 1981.

10 Examples include the Communities of Resistance Conference in Liverpool in 1990 organised by Black community groups; the Racism and Migration in Europe Conference organised by Warwick University and Birkbeck College in 1991.

11 It is now clear that to talk of 'racism' as if it were a monolithic and unchanging phenomenon with a single identifiable historical origin adds little to our knowledge. It is better to conceptualise multiple 'racisms', manifested in different contexts in unique permutations. While certain continuities are evident, the precise causes, manifestations and consequences of different 'racisms' are matters of empirical enquiry (Banton, 1969; Hall, 1978; Gilroy, 1987; Sivanandan, 1988; Miles, 1989). This is the subject of Chapter 3 where it is suggested that all ideologies are imbued with racialised meanings and that it is better to talk of racialised ideologies than 'racism'.

12 The concept of 'contextualisation' is introduced in the section below to circumvent this problem.

13 I employ the 'racialisation' problematic to escape from this process of mystification. The benefits of this approach are elaborated below.

14 Comparisons of the Brixton riots with 'race riots' in the United States made by Lord Scarman in 1981 were criticised by C.L.R James. Anne Wilson has rejected several of the assumptions made about 'mixed-race' children in England by analysts drawing on studies carried out in the United States (James, cited in Wilson, 1987: 29; Wilson, 1981: 16–20). Michael Banton and, separately, John Rex have described the range of problems that arise when analysts of 'racialised relations' in England borrow uncritically from the United States, though both have argued in favour of the lessons that might be derived from other types of comparisons (Rex, 1970; Banton, 1983; Banton, 1984). Robert Miles has consistently argued in favour of a comparative analysis of 'race' but believes that more useful insights will be forthcoming from comparisons with other European countries (Miles, 1989b: 31; Miles, 1990: 284). One might ask why is it more valid to compare 'racialised relations' in the United States and England rather than in, say, Albania and Afghanistan, or Venezuela and Vietnam? The answer seems to me to be contingent upon the reasons for the comparison, as will become evident in the text below.

15 One of the most publicised books on the recent period of Black

immigration to England started from a premise that is incorrect. Rose *et al.*, comparing the English situation in the 1960s with that in the United States, wrote:

> Great Britain too had owned slaves and had freed them, but her slaves had lived 3000 miles away across the seas. When 100 years after emancipation their descendants came here to seek a living, they came as immigrants and it might therefore be assumed that because they were immigrants they would not be on the conscience of the country in the way that the Negro had for generations been on the conscience of Americans
>
> (Rose *et al.*, 1969: 4)

This was, of course, a flagrant error.

16 Such views were pervasive at all times and became especially prominent after both World Wars. Marks cites the following example from the editorial of a Southern newspaper:

> You niggers are wondering how you are going to be treated after the war. Well I'll tell you. You are going to be treated exactly like you were before the war: this is a white man's country and we expect to rule it.
>
> (Marks, 1989: 98)

That this was not an extremist view is reflected in the fact that the president of the United States at each time sent messages to Black Americans in Europe not to have high hopes about a change of status upon their return (Franklin, 1956).

17 Some analysts may argue that the 'Colour Line' is a class line and that the inequalities are largely or primarily the result of economic and class hostility (Rex and Tomlinson, 1983; Reich, 1981; Taaffe and Mulhearn, 1988). Others may argue that a gender line exists and that gender discrimination is pervasive (Gatlin, 1987). My arguments do not reject the strength of class and gender hostility in keeping Blacks at a disadvantage, though I reject that view that racialised inequality can be explained by class or economic factors alone. My primary goal is to explore the continued role of racialised hostilities in maintaining the 'Colour Line' at every class level, and for both genders.

18 The concept of 'racialised parity' is discussed below.

19 There are numerous comparisons of diverse countries in the literature on racialised relations (Rex, 1973; Wilson, 1976; Banton, 1983).

20 For example, Miles argues decisively:

> Use of the terms 'race' and 'race relations' within everyday discourse usually imply or suggest a belief in the existence of biologically discrete populations, social relations between which are of a different nature when compared with relations between other social groups. It is therefore implied that the very presence of these groups in the same social space gives rise to distinct, and problematic, processes
>
> (Miles, 1988: 429).

21  See the debate between Miles, Ben-Tovim and Gilroy on challenging racialised inequality in contemporary Britain (Miles, 1988). For the United States see Omi and Winant, 1986 and Wilson, W. 1987.

22  It was argued in the *New York Times* that the European Community 'still bows to American political leadership on key world issues' and that at the London summit of the Group of Seven industrialised powers these nations still looked to President Bush 'to set the conditions' over the Soviet aid package (*New York Times*, 1991: E2).

23  As an American author argues, 'Ideas and programs that in the United States flourished and then wilted in the 1960s and 1970s seem to be appearing in another cycle in European investigations' (Suarez-Orozco, 1990: 269). Much can be learned from the relative successes and failures of such programmes.

24  It is not my goal to provide a detailed description and elaboration of the unfolding of 'racialised relations' in each nation, or the debates around them. I presume the reader will have some knowledge of many of these issues, and sources are cited where further relevant information can be obtained in detail.

25  Miles has questioned the narrow focus on certain sections of the state, and the tendency to look only at certain types of 'racists' (Miles, 1989a: 64, 69). However he has yet to develop these issues in his work to the extent that he did with Phizacklea at the start of the 1980s (Phizacklea and Miles, 1980). If there were more linkages between academics and non-academics who study racialised hostility, this might be achieved.

26  Another useful way of proceeding seems to be via an analysis of concrete policies in specific contexts, for example, particular examples of Affirmative Action, Black businesses, ethnic monitoring, higher education and role mentoring.

27  A similar approach was employed by Sanchez-Jankowski in his analysis of Chicano migrants in the contemporary period (Sanchez-Jankowski, 1986).

28  For a discussion of competing paradigms on 'race relations' see Hall, 1978; Fenton, 1980; CCCS, 1982; Miles, 1982; Rex and Mason, 1986; Banton, 1988.

29  For a specification and elaboration of these issues, and examples of texts, see Miles, 1988.

30  As Fenton notes:

> Use of the terms ethnic or racial relations tempts us into the error of thinking that ethnic or racial consciousness is the *defining* characteristic of the relationship that we are studying, when, in fact, 'ethnicity' and 'racial' consciousness are *aspects* of social relations and social structures which are defined more profoundly and more tellingly in other terms – and you can't have a sociology of aspects.
> (Fenton, 1987: 278, 282)

31  It is important to recognise the distinction between 'access to' and 'shares of'. Most whites in the United States take parity to mean 'equal access to' and equal access is usually presumed to exist where there is an absence of racialised discrimination; this in turn is presumed to exist

where there are laws forbidding racialised discrimination. However, most Blacks are less interested in access, and more interested in outcomes. For Blacks then, parity usually means equal shares of resources. It is unlikely that Blacks expect complete equality of outcome, but most would expect a major reduction in existing disparities. Similar racialised attitudes exist around the notion of racialised equality in England. Some of these issues are taken up in Chapter 5.

32 These groups are not always mutually exclusive but I believe that each group involves individuals whose primary concern is first and foremost with theory, policy or achieving broader and more fundamental social change. There are also considerable advantages to taking up these issues with students who might benefit from the reaffirmation of the fundamental principle of social formations (namely that societies are historically determined configurations) and from the obvious cultural introspection which ensues from analysing other countries.

## 2  BLACK PEOPLE IN THE UNITED STATES AND ENGLAND: A PROFILE OF THE 1980s

1 People of mixed Black and white origins are included in the data in this chapter, as many of them face similar problems to other Black people generally.

2 It is not my goal in this chapter to answer the question: is economic and class discrimination more important than racialised hostility in causing and sustaining patterns of racialised inequality? This is a debate taken up in detail elsewhere (Wilson, 1978; Miles, 1988, 1989a).

3 My goal in this chapter is to provide an overview of racialised inequality drawn from official sources. My discussion is not intended to suggest that these are the only facts, or that they remain unchanging. I recognise that such facts are political and contentious (see Bhat, et al., 1988). I draw upon a range of sources and point out some of the limitations as and when they are described.

4 Examples of such texts are provided in Small, 1991a.

5 To talk about 'female-headed' families as if they are intrinsically a problem, with no assessment of families with two parents, and to assume that the 'solution' is to find husbands for lone women with babies is specious. We must recognise that couples continue to face substantial problems (divorce, domestic violence) and confront the fact that female-headed families face additional problems because of the entrenched discrimination against all women, especially Black women, with or without children, in education and the work place (Bryan et al., 1985; Amott and Matthaei, 1991).

6 Census Bureau estimates suggest this number constitutes an under count of nearly 2 million, and thus about 5.7 per cent of African-Americans were missed by the census (O'Hare et al., 1991).

7 With over 97 per cent of African-Americans born in the United States the problems confronting them have little to do with immigration

status in its usual meaning in England, which has to do with immigration controls and family unity. See Miles and Phizacklea, 1984.

8 O'Hare *et al.*, point out that 'The poverty rate is the percentage of families or individuals whose annual income falls below a threshold specified by the Office of Management and Budget. The thresholds vary by family size and composition and are updated for inflation annually. In 1989, the average poverty threshold for a family of four was $12,675' (O'Hare *et al.*, 1991: 31).

9 The language of university appointments in the United States is unlike England and carries different rewards and connotations: a lecturer is usually a temporary position, an instructor is often the same; an assistant-professor on tenure-track leads to a possible tenured position.

10 In the 1980s it was customary in the United States to finish high school at 18 years of age and to 'graduate' with a high school diploma. Anyone finishing prior to 18 years of age is considered a 'high school drop-out'. It was further expected that high school graduates would go on to university and the majority of high school graduates do so (many of them via community college). In England, the custom was for pupils to leave school at 16 years of age (and around 75 per cent of them did so). Those intending to go on to university usually stayed on at school (or a further education college) to the age of 18, to do university entrance exams. At the end of the 1980s higher education in England was restructured to emulate the United States system and increase the proportion of 18-year-olds going on to university.

11 I do not analyse the circumstances of Asians, the largest minority group in England (numbering 1.2 million). In England, 'Asian' refers to anyone from India, Pakistan or Bangladesh and is never used to refer to people from the Far East. Other than Blacks, the remaining ethnic minorities are from South-East Asia, the Mediterranean and elsewhere in the Commonwealth, that is, Britain's former colonies.

12 In this book African-Caribbean is used as synonymous with 'West Indian and Guyanese'.

13 Africans are a small proportion of all Black people in Britain, but it is clear that in many respects they are economically and educationally better off than African-Caribbeans as a whole. For example, there is a larger proportion of Africans in higher education and in the professions (Skellington, *et al.*, 1992). Inclusion of their numbers in the data tends to 'improve' the circumstances of African-Caribbeans.

14 These data have to be interpreted carefully, and cross-checked with other data, because the 1991 Census had a significant undercount, and because the definitions used do not correspond exactly with definitions from other sources.

15 In England the highest proportion of 'Black people of mixed origins' is to be found in Liverpool where they number over 60 per cent of the total Black population (Small, 1991b). In such a context they are for the most part treated by whites in a similar manner to Black people presumed to be of non-mixed origins.

16 A 'family' is defined as 'a married couple on their own' or 'a married couple/lone parent and their never married children, provided these

children have no children of their own within the household' (Haskey, 1989: 8).

17  These counties were Greater Manchester, Merseyside, South Yorkshire, West Yorkshire, Tyne and Wear, and the West Midlands.

18  O levels (Ordinary Level exams of the General Certificate of Education) are a two-year course taken between the ages of 14 and 16 years old. The Certificate of Secondary Education is also a two-year course taken by the same age group. It is a second-rate educational qualification taken by those deemed of insufficient ability to achieve O level standards. Both types of qualification have now been replaced by the General Certificate of Secondary Education (GCSE).

19  A levels (Advanced level of the General Certificate of Education) are two-year courses taken between the ages of 16 and 18 years old. Minimum qualification for entrance to university is 5 O levels and 2 A levels.

20  For example, the median figure for earnings of white women in England was actually £3 lower than for African-Caribbean women (Brown, 1984).

# 3  RACIALISED IDEOLOGIES, CLASS RELATIONS AND THE STATE

1  I am not interested in providing a definition of 'racism' or racialised ideology that is useful for all situations. Others have spent more time on this endeavour, and indicated its strengths and limitations (Banton, 1977; Hall, 1978; Miles, 1982). For me a racialised ideology is a relatively coherent ideology that identifies, specifies and represents Black people (or people of colour) as a distinctive 'other', on grounds of physical appearance or cultural practices, and argues for differential treatment because of presumed inferiority or difference. The issues involved are taken up in the text below.

2  After a response that I wrote to this letter appeared in the same campus magazine, four of five letters offering me strong support were received (see Small, 1989a).

3  The emergence of 'new racisms' is not specific to England and the United States, as others have noted in comments on Europe: 'The new racism today, rather, emphasizes basic and irreconcilable cultural differences' (Suarez-Orozco, 1990: 285. See also, Stavenhagen, 1990).

4  For example, Miles has argued that the multiple meanings now attached to the term 'racism' has led to 'conceptual inflation' and diminishing analytical value (1989a: Chapter 7). He maintains that the term 'racism' should be retained for a particular ideology, especially state sponsored ideologies (Miles, 1989a: 97). This suggestion certainly has much merit, but only within the context of his analytical enterprise – one in which the state as an agent of capitalist rule develops ideologies to sustain that rule. He is concerned with definitions, and implicitly with typologies, of ideologies. My concern is more generally with racialised hostility and the 'Colour Line' whatever its cause. I examine the role diverse and divergent racialised ideologies play in this.

5 I prefer to call this a complex dynamic of racialised attitudes and ideologies because it emphasises the multiple factors involved and the ways in which they relate, loosely or strongly, to each other in specifying racialised 'otherness', and identifying 'the other' for discriminatory treatment. For a treatment of this in a specific context see Small, 1991b.

6 It is common in the literature to refer to these kinds of 'racisms' by the phrase 'relative autonomy of racism' in which 'autonomous' usually means independent of state or economic influences (Genovese, 1968; Centre for Contemporary Cultural Studies, 1982). This is conceptually misleading for two reasons. First, it presumes the primary creator and manipulator of racialised ideologies historically was the state, and that this began with slavery – an untenable position given the widespread representations of 'the other' which precede slavery in the Americas (Miles, 1989a). The state has always played a central role in harnessing and shaping such representations, but there are other aspects to this that are multifaceted in ways bearing no simple correlation to the whims and wishes of the state or capital. Second, 'racism' is not like a disease or smoke – it does not do things on its own. While we must look at the content of such ideologies, our primary concern should be with those groups, institutions and individuals that play key roles in articulating and rearticulating them. Such articulations arise from the interplay of state activities in struggle with other institutions and groups in society. The preeminent problem therefore is to elaborate and explain the unfolding of the intricate interrelationships involved.

7 The 'coat of paint' theory – which suggests analysis of 'racism' must be subordinated to analysis of class – is described by Gilroy, 1990b.

8 For example, see the special edition of the *Review of Radical Political Economics* on 'The Political Economy of Race and Class' (Union for Radical Political Economics, 1985). Omi and Winant provide an early and incisive analysis (Omi and Winant, 1986, 1991). A series of seminars on 'The New Racism' took place at Brown University's *Center for the Study of Race and Ethnicity in America*, in the Fall/Autumn of 1991. A special edition of *The Nation* described 'Race, Rights and the New Orthodoxy' (1991). The playing out of similar kinds of ideologies across the south has also been described, in particular the antics of David Duke (Goldfield, 1990; *Newsweek*, November 1991).

9 The authors point out that some sections of the Far Right have employed new subtleties, as circumstances have required. For example, we may wish to see the activities of David Duke as exemplifying this, though it may be more appropriate to put him closer to the New Right.

10 Collins relates how the 'welfare mother' is labelled a bad mother: 'She is portrayed as being content to sit around and collect welfare, shunning work and passing on her bad values to her offspring'. She also lacks a male authority figure (1991: 77).

11 Another way in which 'racism' has been rearticulated in the United States in the 1980s is grounded in new applications of developments in genetics. The arguments proposed here are based on new technological developments in genetics, are often referred to as sociobiology, and they reaffirm much of the historical 'scientific racism' of this and

previous centuries (Gossett, 1965; Duster, 1990). In its elaborated form this prevails largely in academic circles but does rear its ugly head into politics and popular culture from time to time.

12 Some have added William Julius Wilson to this list though he is clearly not a conservative and has emphatically disavowed any such political orientation (Wilson, W. 1987: viii). However, much of the emphasis of his analysis – disregarding the continuing effects of racialised discrimination, locating the problems within the Black community, emphasising the influence of macro economic and political forces outside state control, and ardently opposing Affirmative Action – lends itself to such an interpretation (Wilson, W. 1978, 1987).

13 A fuller discussion of 'cultural racism' in England would need to take account of the experiences and manipulation of Asians because they are larger in number, offer contrasts to Blacks and because of the Salman Rusdie affair and the Gulf War (See Ball and Solomos, 1990; Sivanandan, 1990).

14 Harris skilfully crafts the subtleties of British double-talk and reveals the mastery of the English language employed by Civil Servants; from prevarication and circumlocution, to sophistry and speciousness.

15 The arguments over the murder offered by many white residents of Howard Beach – of territorial rights – are suggestive of nineteenth century 'racial typologies' in which each 'race' is believed suited to its own 'natural' habitat (Banton, 1977).

16 the varying images of Black women in political and popular portrayals since slavery – including the 'mammy', 'matriarch', 'welfare mother' and 'whore' – have been examined extensively in the United States (Carby, 1987; Collins, 1991).

17 In the literature this is usually called 'interracial sex' (Spickard, 1989; Root, 1992; Alibhai-Brown and Montague, 1992). But using language like this compounds and extends the problematic assumptions of 'race relations', including the notion that there are pure 'races' (see Chapter 1). The issue of racialised marriages, and the children from such relations, is discussed in Chapter 5.

18 Some social scientists see intermarriage as an indicator of movement towards assimilation (Gordon, 1964). In this conceptualisation Black women's views – historically in opposition of such relationships for a variety of reasons – are largely or totally ignored. This issue is discussed in Chapter 5.

19 A plethora of studies in the 1960s identified Blacks as a distinctive 'race' and attributed to them physiological characteristics that enabled them to perform better in certain sports (see Figler, 1981: 238 for a list). Few such studies can be found today.

20 Needless to say, many of the stereotypes and much of the work on Black in sport concerns men not women; the latter remain visible only as an irritant to men's theories. Many of these natural ability theories are applied to men and women generally (Sage, 1990).

21 It makes little theoretical sense, and even less political sense, to pursue this question. It presumes that there is a single racism with a single

cause. Therefore I have as much to say about this question as I would about the origin of the chicken and the egg!

22  Because they can function as part of Black peoples' defence against racialised hostility, and can play a role in facilitating access to resources, some of these ideologies may not be rejected in their entirety. Some beliefs about sporting excellence and sexuality (especially those held about men) are condoned or encouraged (Cashmore, 1982).

## 4  STRATIFICATION AND THE BLACK 'MIDDLE CLASS': TALENTED TENTH OR BLACK BOURGEOISIE?

1  This excludes discussion of Asians, a population which displays greater stratification. See Brown, 1984.

2  The many problems posed by lumping this diverse array of workers and owners together will be discussed later – at present it suffices to say that I am talking about all those not included in the disadvantaged groups that so often command our attention.

3  The 'Black Tax' refers to the idea that successful Blacks should contribute in money or in kind to helping less successful Black people; they should pay a 'tax' that directly benefits the Black poor.

4  Recent discussion of these issues in Britain goes back several decades; there is evidence of similar debates over the last centuries (Parekh, 1974; Walvin, 1973; Ramdin, 1987).

5  It should be noted that Dubois later became estranged from many in Black America's 'Talented Tenth' in the 1930s and beyond, and advocated very different policies (in response to the intransigence of American whites to countenance any dent in racialised segregation) (Rudwick, 1968).

6  Wilson has had the most significant impact on the debate about stratification within the African-American population and it is unnecessary to rehearse the issues here (Wilson, 1978, 1987). Many others have offered theoretical and empirical critiques of his work (Willie, 1978: 10–5; Marable, 1983; Omi and Winant, 1986; Boston, 1988).

7  Given the larger numbers of Asians in Britain, and the higher proportion concentrated among professionals and business owners, this group has attracted more attention than African-Caribbeans (Ward and Jenkins, 1984).

8  The problems of conceptualisation and limited data – as well as the issue of whether occupational categories designed to estimate white men in an overwhelmingly white society are suitable for evaluating the circumstances of economically active Black (men and women) – will be discussed below.

9  Miles has suggested that this is a major aspect of the state strategy to control and contain criticism (see text below).

10  While Sivanandan's view is clear at present, it differs from that which he took in the 1970s. At that time, while noting that a fraction of the 'black bourgeois' would seek to contain 'black revolt', he suggested that Black poor and rich alike still shared a common experience of

racialised oppression that would keep them on the same side 'against their common enemy: the white man, worker and bourgeois alike' (Sivanandan, 1982: 20, 93).

11  I have suggested a preliminary response to this question elsewhere (Small, 1991a).

## 5  RACIALISED INTEGRATION, HARMONY AND PARITY

1  This is to put aside for the moment the idea that government deliberately encourages such confusion in its efforts to manage 'race relations'. I shall return to this idea later in the chapter.

2  White opposition also clearly reflects racialised hostility, and a belief on their part that any gains made by Blacks will leave them worse off.

3  I use 'institutional interest' to mean the interests of Blacks and whites as racialised groups (as reflected in expressed preferences); and the interests of successive governments (as expressed in official policies).

4  As outlined in Chapter 1 (note 31), racialised parity itself has multiple meanings. For white people it invariably means 'equal access to' resources, and this access is presumed to exist when there are laws forbidding discrimination. During the 1980s most whites presumed equal access existed and concluded that inequality continued because Blacks did not make sufficient effort. For Blacks it was more likely to mean 'equal shares of' resources, and while few actually expected a 50 per cent distribution of resources between the racialised groups, they did expect a significant reduction in existing disparities. Most Blacks presumed inequality and unequal access resulted from continued discrimination. These issues are elaborated in the text below.

5  By mystification of 'race relations' I mean that there is a diversity of variables which are drawn upon to assess whether 'race relations' are progressing or regressing, that these variables are not co-terminous, and that the term conflates and confuses them in ways that make any assessment at progress fleeting and ethereal. In particular, it confuses ideas of racialised integration, harmony and parity.

6  Though the language used in each nation is different, nevertheless, common assumptions and goals are evident. In the United States the language usually employed is that of 'integration', an end to 'racial violence' and conflict, and promotion of 'racial parity' (with an emphasis on ending discrimination, achieving equal access rather than outcomes). In England the language employed is that of 'integration', an end to 'racial attacks', promotion of 'racial harmony', and advocacy of 'racial equality' (meant variously as an end to 'racial discrimination', equal access to, and/or equal shares of, resources).

7  For example, in Liverpool, the Black population in 1980 was estimated at no more than 1.5 per cent – 3 per cent of the total population (around 500,000) and even with the majority of them in the Granby-Toxteth ward they add up to no more than 20 per cent of the population at their most dense concentration (Gifford, *et al.*, 1989: 39).

8  This comment was made to the author in a personal discussion in Liverpool during the summer of 1990.

9  The activities of these groups – meetings, conferences, campaigns, newsletters, publications – are not covered in the academic literature on racialised relations, but see Shukra, 1990; Jeffers, 1991, for some examples. Their activities are more likely to be documented in the Black press such as *The Weekly Journal, Caribbean Times* and *The Voice*. For Liverpool see Liverpool Black Caucus, 1986 and Deckon, 1993.

10  Kemetic Educational Guidance, based in Manchester, organise a series of annual conferences and numerous lecture tours, with key contributions made by Molefi Asante, Leonard Jeffries, Malauna Karenga and Jocelyn Maxime, and other exponents of Afrocentric education.

11  In the United States a significant number of Black people opposed affirmative action, though this was due in part to its pejorative image, to the belief that whites were unlikely to support it, and to a more general commitment to individualism.

# 6  CONCLUSION

1  John Taylor, an African-Caribbean, was nominated as Conservative candidate for the town of Cheltenham in 1991, but key members of the local constituency party objected, one of them stating bluntly that they did not 'want a bloody nigger' (Weaver, 1991: 15).

2  I have outlined these issues elsewhere (Small, 1993).

3  As was indicated in Chapter 3, the merits of these analyses and strategies vary greatly. I have suggested that Miles offers one of the better analyses.

4  Miles has responded to such criticisms arguing that his critics exaggerate and/or misrepresent his arguments, and repudiating the idea that he reduces working-class 'racism' to nothing more than ruling-class domination (Miles, 1984, 1988).

5  In 1992 Buju Banton, a popular reggae singer from Jamaica, achieved a number-one hit in the Jamaican music charts and an international success with his record 'Boom bye bye in a Batty-Boy head', calling for the murder of homosexuals.

# References

Action Against Racial Terrorism Group, *Racial Terrorism in Merseyside*, 1986.

Akbar, Na'im, *Chains and Images of Psychological Slavery*, New Mind Productions, Jersey City, 1984.

Alibhai-Brown, Yasmin and Montague, Anne, *The Colour of Love. Mixed Race Relationships*, Virago Press, London, 1992.

Amos, Valerie and Parmar, Pratibha, 'Challenging Imperial Feminisms', *Feminist Review*, No. 17, July 1984, pp. 3–19.

Amott, Teresa L., and Matthaei, Julie A., *Race, Gender and Work. A Multicultural Economic History of Women in the United States*, Southend Press, Boston, MA, 1991.

Anwar, Muhammad, *Race and Politics, Ethnic Minorities and the British Political System*, Tavistock. London and New York, 1988.

Bagley, Christopher, 'Mixed Marriages and Race Relations Today', *Patterns of Prejudice*, Vol. 15, No. 1, 1981.

Ball, Wendy and Solomos, John, *Race and Local Politics*, Macmillan, Basingstoke and London, 1990.

Banks, William M., 'Afro-American Scholars in the University: Roles and Conflicts', *American Behavioural Scientist*, Vol. 27, No. 3, January/February 1984, pp. 325–38.

Banton, Michael P., *The Coloured Quarter*, Cape, London, 1955.

Banton, Michael, 'What Do We Mean by "Racism"?', *New Society*, Vol. 13, 1969.

Banton, Michael P., *The Idea of Race*, Tavistock, London, 1977.

Banton, Michael, *Racial and Ethnic Competition*, Cambridge University Press, Cambridge, 1983.

Banton, Michael P., 'Transatlantic Perspectives on Public Policy Concerning Racial Disadvantage', *New Community*, Vol. 11, No. 3, Spring 1984, pp. 280–87.

Banton, Michael, *Promoting Racial Harmony*, Cambridge University Press, Cambridge, 1985.

Banton, Michael, *Racial Theories*, Cambridge University Press, Cambridge, 1988.

Barker, A. J., *The African Link: British Attitudes to the Negro in the Era of the Atlantic Slave Trade, 1550–1807*, Frank Cass, London, 1978.

Barker, Martin, *The New Racism*, Junction Books, London, 1981.

Barnes, James A., 'Into the Mainstream', *National Journal*, No. 5, 3 February, 1990, pp. 262–6.

Barzung J., *Race: A Study in Modern Superstition*, Methuen, London, 1938.

Bean, Frank D., Verne, Georges and Keely, Charles B., *Opening and Closing the Doors. Evaluating Immigration Reform and Control*, The Rand Corporation, The Urban Institute, 1989.

Bell, Derrick, *Faces at the Bottom of the Well. The Permanence of Racism*, Basic Books, New York, 1992.

Benjamin, Lois, *The Black Elite. Facing the Color Line in the Twilight of the Twentieth Century*, Nelson Hall Publishers, Chicago, 1991.

Benyon, John, (ed.) *Scarman and After. Essays Reflecting on Lord Scarman's Report, the Riots and their Aftermath*, Pergamon Press, Oxford, 1984.

Benyon, John and Solomos, John, *The Roots of Urban Unrest*, Pergamon Press, Oxford, 1987.

Ben-Tovim, Gideon, Gabriel, J., Law, I. and Stedder, K., 'Political Analysis of Race in the 1980s', in C. Husband (ed.) *'Race' in Britain*, Hutchinson, 1982.

Ben-Tovim, Gideon, Gabriel, J., Law, I. and Stedder, K., *The Local Politics of Race*, Macmillan, 1986.

Ben-Tovim, Gideon, 'Race, Politics, and Urban Regeneration: Lessons from Liverpool', in Michael Parkinson, Bernard Foley and Dennis Judd, *Regenerating the Cities: The UK Crisis and the US Experience*, Scott Foresman, Illinois, 1989, pp. 129–41.

Ben-Tovim, Gideon, Gabriel, J., Law, I. and Stedder, K., 'A Political Analysis of Local Struggles for Racial Equality', in Peter Braham, Ali Rattansi and Richard Skellington (eds) *Racism and Antiracism. Inequalities, Opportunities and Policies*, Sage Publications Ltd, London and Newbury Park, California, 1992, pp. 201–17.

Berlin, Ira, *Slaves Without Masters: the Free Negro in the Antebellum South*, Vintage Books, New York, 1974.

Bhat, Ashok, Carr-Hill, Roy, and Ohri, Sushel, *Britain's Black Population. A New Perspective*, Gower, Aldershot, 1988.

Biddis, M., *Images of Race*, Leicester University Press, Leicester, 1979.

Bindman, Geoffrey, 'The Law, Equal Opportunity and Affirmative Action', *New Community*, Vol. 8, No. 3, Winter 1980, pp. 248–60.

Black, Earl and Black, Merle, *Politics and Society in the South*, Harvard University Press, Cambridge, 1987.

*Black Scholar*, 'Special Edition on Anita Hill and Clarence Thomas', July 1992.

Blackett, R. J. M., *Building an Antislavery Wall. Black Americans in the Atlantic Abolitionist Movement, 1830–1860*, Louisiana State University Press, Baton Rouge and London, 1983.

Blackwell, James, *The Black Community. Diversity and Unity* (Second Edition), Harper & Row, New York, 1985.

Blauner, Robert, *Racial Oppression in America*, Harper & Row, New York, 1972.

Bloom, Jack M., *Class, Race & the Civil Rights Movement*, Indiana University Press, Bloomington and Indianapolis, 1987.

Bolt, C., *Victorian Attitudes to Race*, Routledge & Kegan Paul, London, 1971.

Bonnett, Aubrey W. and Watson, G. Llewellyn, *Emerging Perspectives on the Black Diaspora*, University Press of America, New York and London, 1990.

Boston, Thomas, *Race, Class & Conservatism*, Unwin Hyman, London, 1988.

Bovenkerk, Frank, Miles, Robert and Verbunt, Gilles, 'Racism, Migration and the State in Western Europe: A Case for Comparative Analysis', *International Sociology*, Vol. 5, No. 4, December 1990, pp. 475–90.

Breitman, George, (ed.) *Malcolm X Speaks*, Grove Weidenfeld, New York, 1965.

*British Social Attitudes: Cumulative Source Book*, Social and Community Planning Research, London, 1992.

Brown, Colin, 'Ethnic Pluralism in Britain: The Demographic and Legal Background', in Nathan Glazer and Ken Young (eds) *Ethnic Pluralism and Public Policy*, Lexington Books, Toronto, Heinemann Educational Books, London, 1983, pp. 32–54.

Brown, Colin, *Black and White Britain. The Third PSI Survey*, Heinemann Educational Books, London, 1984.

Brown, Colin, '"Same Difference": The Persistence of Racial Disadvantage in the British Employment Market', in Peter Braham, Ali Rattansi and Richard Skellington (eds) *Racism and Antiracism. Inequalities, Opportunities and Policies*, Sage Publications Ltd, London and Newbury Park, California, 1992, pp. 46–63.

Brown, Ronald E., 'Political Action', in James S. Jackson (ed.) *Life in Black America*, Sage Publications, Newbury Park, London, New Delhi, 1991, pp. 254–63.

Brown, Colin and Gay, Pat, *Racial Discrimination: 17 Years After the Act*, Policy Studies Institute, London, 1985.

Brubaker, W. R., (ed.) *Immigration and the Politics of Citizenship in Europe and North America*, University Press of America, Lanham, 1989.

Bruegel, I., 'Sex and Race in the Labour Market', *Feminist Review*, Vol. 32, No. 2, 1989, pp. 49–69.

Bryan, Beverley, Dadze, Stella and Scafe, Suzanne, *The Heart of the Race. Black Women's Lives in Britain*, Virago Press, London, 1985.

Burfoot, Amby, 'White Men Can't Run', *Runners World*, August 1992, pp. 89–95.

Burney, Elizabeth, *Steps to Racial Equality: Positive Action in a Negative Climate*, Runnymede Research Report, The Runnymede Trust, London, 1988.

Calhoun, Donald W., *Sport, Culture, and Personality*, Human Kinetics Publishers, Inc., Champaing, Illinois, 1987.

Carby, Hazel, 'White Woman Listen! Black Feminism and the Boundaries of Sisterhood', in Centre for Contemporary Cultural Studies, *The Empire Strikes Back: Race and Racism in 70s Britain*, Hutchinson, London, 1982, pp. 212–35.

Carby, Hazel, *Reconstructing Womanhood: The Emergence of the Afro-American Woman Novelist*, Oxford University Press, New York, 1987.

Carlson, Margaret, 'Presumed Innocent', *Time*, 22 January, 1990, pp. 10–14.

Carmichael, S. and Hamilton, C., *Black Power: The Politics of Black Liberation in America*, New York, Vintage, 1967.

Cashmore, Ellis, 'Flying business class: Britain's new ethnic elite', *New Community*, Vol. 17, No. 3, April 1991, pp. 347–58.

Cashmore, Ellis, 'Black Entrepreneurs: No More Room at the Top', in

Anthony Giddens, *Human Societies. A Reader*, Polity Press, Cambridge, 1992, pp. 169–72.

Cashmore, Ernest, *Black Sportsmen*, Routledge & Kegan Paul, London, 1982a.

Cashmore, E., 'Black Youth, Sport and Education', *New Community*, Vol. 10, No. 2, Winter 1982b, pp. 213–21.

Cashmore, Ernest and Troyna, Barry, (eds) *Black Youth in Crisis*, Allen & Unwin, London, 1982.

Castles, Stephen, 'Migrations and Minorities in Europe: Perspectives for the 1990s: Twelve Hypotheses', paper presented at Conference on Race and Migration in Europe in the 1990s, University of Warwick and Birkbeck College, University of London, 20–22 September 1991.

Centre for Contemporary Cultural Studies, *The Empire Strikes Back: Race and Racism in 70s Britain*, Hutchinson, London, 1982.

Chadhary, Vivek and Travis, Alan, 'Brothers in Arms Fight for the Streets', *Guardian*, 16–17 October 1993, p. 21.

Christian, Barbara, 'The Race for Theory', *Feminist Studies*, Vol. 14, No. 2, Spring 1988, pp. 67–79.

Claiburne, L. *et al.*, *Race and Law in Britain and the U.S.* (New edition), (Minority Rights Group Report, 22) Minority Rights Group, London, 1979.

Cohen, Robin, *The New Helots: Migrants in the International Division of labour*, Avebury, Farnborough, 1987.

Coleman, David, 'Ethnic Intermarriage in Great Britain', *Population Trends*, Vol. 40, Summer 1985, pp. 4–10.

Collins, Patricia Hill, *Black Feminist Thought. Knowledge, Consciousness, and the Politics of Empowerment*, Routledge, New York and London, 1991.

Collins, Sheila D., *The Rainbow Challenge. The Jackson Campaign and the Future of U.S. Politics*, Monthly Review Press, New York, 1986.

Commission for Racial Equality, *Positive Action in Local Authority Employment*, Seminar Proceedings, Leeds Civic Hall, December 1986, Commission for Racial Equality, London.

Commission for Racial Equality, *Racial Discrimination in Liverpool City Council: Report of a Formal Investigation into the Housing Department*, Commission for Racial Equality, London, 1989.

Connolly, Michelle, Roberts, Kenneth, Ben-Tovim, Gideon and Torkington, Protasia, *Black Youth in Liverpool*, Giordano Bruno Culemborg, The Netherlands, 1992.

Cose, Ellis, 'Rape in the News: Mainly About Whites', *The New York Times*, 5 July 1989, p. 6.

Daniel, W. W., *Racial Discrimination in England*, Penguin, Harmondsworth, 1968.

Davis, Angela, *Women, Race and Class*, The Women's Press, New York, 1984.

Davis, Angela, *Women, Culture, and Politics*, Random House, New York, 1989.

Davis, George and Watson, Glegg, *Black Life in Corporate America. Swimming in the Mainstream*, Anchor Books, New York, 1985.

Debley, Tom, 'Karabel Report Would Dramatically Alter Admissions', *The Berkeleyan*, 21 June–18 July 1989.

Deckon, Shaun, 'Black Politics: Social Change in Liverpool in the

1980s–1990s', unpublished MA thesis, Department of Sociology, University of Liverpool, 1993.

Dimmock, G., 'Racial Hostility in Britain with Particular Reference to the Disturbances in Cardiff and Liverpool in 1919', MA dissertation, University of Sheffield, 1975.

Dubois, W.E.B., *The Souls of Black Folk*, Fawcett World Library, New York, 1961.

Duster, Troy, 'From Structural Analysis to Public Policy', *Contemporary Sociology*, May 1988, pp. 287–90.

Duster, Troy, *Backdoor to Eugenics*, Routledge, New York, 1990.

Dye, Thomas R., *Understanding Public Policy* (7th edition), Prentice Hall, New Jersey, 1992.

Edsall, Thomas B. and Edsall, Mary D., *Chain Reaction. The Impact of Race, Rights, and Taxes on American Politics*, W. W. Norton & Company, New York and London, 1991a.

Edsall, Thomas B. and Edsall, Mary D., 'When the official subject is presidential politics, taxes, welfare, crime, rights, or values . . . the real subject is race', *The Atlantic*, Vol. 267, No. 5, May 1991b, pp. 53–86.

Edwards, G. Franklin (ed.), *E. Franklin Frazier on Race Relations*, University of Chicago Press, Chicago and London, 1968.

Edwards, Paul, 'The Political Economy of Industrial Conflict: Britain and the United States', *Economic and Industrial Democracy*, Vol. 4, 1983, pp. 461–500.

Edwards, Harry, *Sociology of Sport*, Dorsey Press, Homewood, Illinois, 1973.

*Employment Gazette*, July 1989.

*Employment Gazette, Ethnic Origins and the Labour Market. Special Feature*, February 1991, pp. 59–67.

Essed, Philomena, *Everyday Racism. Reports from Women of Two Cultures*, Hunter House Inc, California, 1990.

Estrich, Susan, 'Willie Horton, Racism and Our Campaign', *The Washington Post*, 1–7 May 1989, pp. 9–10.

Farley, Renyolds, *Blacks and Whites. Narrowing the Gap?*, Harvard University Press, Cambridge and London, 1984.

Farley, Renyolds and Allen, Walter R., *The Colour Line and the Quality of Life in America*, Oxford University Press, New York and Oxford, 1989.

Farrell, Walter C., Jr, and Jones, Cloyzelle K., 'Recent Racial Incidents in Higher Education: A Preliminary Perspective', *The Urban Review*, Vol. 20, No. 3, 1988, pp. 211–26.

Federation of Black Housing Associations and Merseyside Area Profile Group., *Race and Public Sector Housing*, Report of a Conference held at Liverpool University, 16 April 1986.

Fenton, Steve, '"Race Relations" in the Sociological Enterprise (A Review Article)', *New Community*, Vol. 8, Nos 1–2, Spring/Summer 1980, pp. 162–8.

Fenton, Steve, 'Ethnicity Beyond Compare', *The British Journal of Sociology*, Vol. 38, No. 2, 1987, pp. 277–82.

Feron, James, 'Yonkers Seeks to End Pact on Housing Ruling', *New York Times*, 3 November 1988, p. B2.

Figler, Stephen K., *Sport and Play in American Life*, Saunders College Publishing, New York, 1981.

Fitzgerald, M., *Black People and Party Politics in Britain*, Runnymede Trust, London, 1987.

Fletcher, M. E., *Report on an Investigation into the Colour Problem in Liverpool and Other Ports*, Association for the Welfare of Half-Caste Children, Liverpool, 1930.

Foot, Paul, *Immigration and Race in British Politics*, Penguin, England, 1965.

Franklin, John Hope, *From Slavery to Freedom*, Alfred A. Knopf, New York, 1956.

Frazier, E. Franklin, *Black Bourgeoisie. The Rise of a New Middle Class*, The Free Press, New York, 1957.

Frazier, Regina Jollivette, 'Is the Black Middle Class Blowing It? NO!' *Ebony*, August 1987, pp. 89–90.

Fredrickson, George M., *The Arrogance of Race. Historical Perspectives on Slavery, Racism, and Social Inequality*, Wesleyan University Press, Connecticut, 1988.

French, Howard W., 'New York Minority Groups Urged to Focus on Economic Concerns', *New York Times*, January 31 Sunday 1988, p. 5.

Frow, Mayerlene and Alibhai-Brown, Yasmin, *Race Through the 90s*, Commission for Racial Equality and BBC Radio 1, London, 1992.

Fryer, Peter, *Staying Power: the History of Black People in Britain*, Pluto Press, London, 1984.

Fusfeld, Daniel R. and Bates, Timothy, *The Political Economy of the Urban Ghetto*, Southern Illinois University Press, Carbondale and Edwardsville, 1984.

Gamble, Andrew, *The Free Economy and the Strong State. The Politics of Thatcherism*, Macmillan, Basingstoke, 1988.

Gatlin, Rochell, *American Women Since 1945*, University Press of Mississippi, Jackson and London, 1987.

Genovese, Eugene D., *In Red and Black: Marxian Explorations in Southern and Afro-American History*, Vintage Books, New York, 1968.

Gibbs, Jewelle-Taylor, 'Biracial Adolescents', in Jewelle-Taylor Gibbs, L. N. Huang, & Associates (eds), *Children of Color: Psychological Interventions with Minority Youth*, Jossey-Bass, San Francisco, 1989, pp. 322–50.

Gifford, Lord, Brown, Wally and Bundey, Ruth, *Loosen The Shackles. First Report of the Liverpool 8 Inquiry into Race Relations in Liverpool*, Karia Press, London, 1989.

Gilbert, Dennis A., *Compendium of American Public Opinion*, Facts on File, New York, 1988.

Gilroy, Paul, *There Ain't No Black In the Union Jack. The Cultural Politics of Race and Nation*, Hutchinson, London, 1987a.

Gilroy, Paul, *Problems in Anti-Racist Strategy*, The Runnymede Trust, London, 1987b.

Gilroy, Paul, 'One Nation Under A Groove: The Cultural Politics of "Race" and Racism in Britain', in David Theo Goldberg, (ed.) *Anatomy of Racism*, University of Minnesota Press, Minneapolis, 1990a, p. 263–82.

Gilroy, Paul, 'The End of Anti-Racism', in Wendy Ball and John Solomos, *Race and Local Politics*, Macmillan, Basingstoke and London, 1990b, pp. 191–209.

Ginsburg, Norman, 'Racism and Housing: Concepts and Reality', in Peter Braham, Ali Rattansi and Richard Skellington, (eds) *Racism and Anti-racism. Inequalities, Opportunities and Policies*, Sage Publications Ltd, London and Newbury Park, California, 1992, pp. 109–32.

Glazer, Nathan, *Affirmative Discrimination: Ethnic Inequality and Public Policy*, Basic Books, Inc., New York, 1975.

Glazer, Nathan, and Young, Ken, (eds) *Ehtnic Pluralism and Public Policy*, Lexington Books, Toronto, Heinemann Educational Books, London, 1983.

Goulbourne, Harry, *Black Politics in Britain*, Avebury, 1990.

Goldfield, David R., *Black, White, and Southern. Race Relations and Southern Culture 1940 to the Present*, Louisiana State University Press, Baton Rouge and London, 1990.

Goldthorpe, John H., 'On the Service Class: Its Formation and Future', in A. Giddens and G. McKenzie (eds), *Social Class and the Division of Labour*, Cambridge University Press, Cambridge, 1982, pp. 162–85.

Gordon, Milton M., *Assimilation in American Life. The Role of Race, Religion, and National Origins*, Oxford University Press, New York, 1964.

Gordon, David M., Edwards, Richard and Reich, Michael, *Segmented Work, Divided Workers: The Historical Transformation of Labor in the United States*, Cambridge University Press, New York, 1982.

Gordon, Paul, 'A Dirty War: the New Right and Local Authority Anti-Racism', in Wendy Ball and John Solomos, *Race and Local Politics*, Macmillan, Basingstoke and London, 1990, pp. 175–90.

Gossett, Thomas, *Race. The History of an Idea in America*, Schocken, New York, 1965.

Graetz, Brian, 'The Class Location of Families: A Refined Classification and Analysis', *Sociology*, Vol. 25, No. 1, February 1991, pp. 101–18.

Graham, Otis Lawrence, 'Shame of the Middle Class', *Essence*, April 1991, p. 116.

Greater London Council, *Racial Harassment in London. Report of a Panel of Inquiry set up by the GLC Police Committee*, 1984.

Green, Madeleine F., (ed.), *Minorities on Campus: A Handbook for Enhancing Diversity*, American Council on Education, 1989.

Green, Marci and Carter, Bob, '"Races" and "Race-Makers": The Politics of Racialization,' *Sage Race Relations Abstracts*, Vol. 13, No. 2, 1988, pp. 4–30.

Greendorfer, Susan L., 'Sociology of Sport and the Issue of Relevance: Implications for Physical Education', pp. 55–66 in Andrew Yiannakis and Susan L. Greendorfer, *Applied Sociology of Sport*, Human Kinetics Books, Champaign, Illinois, 1992.

*The Guardian*, 24 July 1990.

Hacker, Andrew, *Two Nations. Black and White, Separate, Hostile and Unequal*, Charles Scribner's Sons, New York, 1992.

Hall, Stuart, 'Racism and Reaction', *Five Views of Multi-Racial Britain*, Commission for Racial Equality, London, 1978, pp. 23–35.

Hall, Stuart, Crither, C., Jefferson, T., Clarke, J. and Roberts, B., *Policing the Crisis: Mugging, the State and Law and Order*, Macmillan, London, 1978.

Hall, Stuart and Jacques, Martin, (eds) *The Politics of Thatcherism*, Lawrence and Wishart, London, 1983.

Hare, Nathan, 'Is the Black Middle Class Blowing It? Yes!' *Ebony*, August 1987, pp. 85–6.

Hargreaves, John, *Sport, Power and Culture. A Social and Historical Analysis of Popular Sports in Britain*, Polity Press, 1986.

Harris, Clive, 'Configurations of Racism: the Civil Service, 1945–60', *Race and Class*, Vol. 33, No. 1, 1991, pp. 1–30.

Harvey, Bryan C. and McArdle, Alan H., 'Coming and Going. Ten Semester Retention and Attrition Among Students Entering in Fall 1982 and 1983', *Educational Assessment Bulletin*, Vol. 3, No. 1, November 1989.

Haskey, John, 'Families and Households of the Ethnic Minority and White Populations of Great Britain', *Population Trends*, 57, HMSO, London, Autumn 1989.

*Hearsay*, 21 August 1990.

Hesse, Barnor, Rai, Dhanwant K., Bennett, Christine and McGilchrist, Paul, *Beneath the Surface: Racial Harassment*, Avebury, Aldershot, 1991.

Hill, Dave, *'Out of His Skin'. The John Barnes Phenomenon*, Faber and Faber, London and Boston, 1989.

Himmelstein, Jerome L., *To the Right. The Transformation of American Conservatism*, University of California Press, Berkeley, Los Angeles and Oxford, 1990.

Hiro, Dilip, *Black British, White British*, Eyre and Spottiswoode, London, 1971.

Home Office, *Racial Attacks, Report of a Home Office Study*, Home Office, London, 1981.

Home Office, *Racial Attacks and Harassment*, HMSO, 1989.

hooks, bell, *Yearning. Race, Gender, and Cultural Politics*, South End Press, Boston, MA, 1990.

Hoose, Phillip M., *Necessities. Racial Barriers in American Sports*, Random House, New York, 1989.

Hoover, Kenneth R., 'The Rise of Conservative Capitalism: Ideological Tensions within the Reagan and Thatcher Governments', *Society for Comparative Study of Society and History*, 1987.

Hoover, Kenneth and Plant, Raymond, *Conservative Capitalism in Britain and the United States. A Critical Appraisal*, Routledge, London and New York, 1989.

Howe, Darcus, 'Darcus Howe on Black Sections in the Labour Party', *Race Today Publications*, 1985.

Hynes, Claire, 'Taking a Leaf out of America's Cop Book' *The Voice*, 23 May 1989, p. 15.

Institute for Research in History, *Ethnic and Immigration Groups: The United States, Canada, and England*, Haworth Press, New York, 1983.

Institute for the Study of Social Change, 'The Diversity Project. An Interim Report to the Chancellor', unpublished report, University of California, Berkeley, 1990.

Institute for the Study of Social Change, *Diversity Project. Final Report*, University of California, Berkeley, November 1991.

Jackson, Peter, (ed.) *Race and Racism. Essays in Social Geography*, Allen & Unwin, London, 1987.

Jacobs, Brian D., *Black Politics and Urban Crisis in Britain*, Cambridge University Press, Cambridge, 1986.

Jeffers, Syd, 'Black Sections in the Labour Party: The End of Ethnicity and "Godfather" Politics?' in Pnina Werbner and Muhammad Anwar, *Black and Ethnic Leaderships in Britain: The Cultural Dimensions of Political Action*, Routledge, London, 1991, pp. 63–83.

Jenkins, Richard and Solomos, John (eds), *Racism and Equal Opportunity Policy in the 1980s*, Cambridge University Press, Cambridge, 1987.

*Jet*, January, 1992.

Jewson, Nick and Mason, David, 'The Theory and Practice of Equal Opportunities Policies. Liberal and Radical Approaches', in Peter Braham, Ali Rattansi and Richard Skellington, *Racism and Antiracism. Inequalities, Opportunities and Policies*, Sage Publications, London, 1992, pp. 218–34.

Johnson, Oscar, 'How Far Have We Come?', in *Sports Illustrated*, 'The Black Athlete Revisited', Vol. 75, No. 6, 5 August 1991, pp. 38–41.

Jones, Jacqueline, *Labor of Love, Labor of Sorrow. Black Women, Work and the Family, From Slavery to the Present*, Vintage Books, New York, 1986.

Jones, Trevor, *Britain's Ethnic Minorities*, Policy Studies Institute, London, 1993.

Jordan, Winthrop D., *White Over Black: American Attitudes towards the Negro, 1550–1812*, University of North Carolina Press, Chapel Hill, 1968.

Joshi, S, and Carter, B., 'The Role of Labour in the Creation of a Racist Britain', *Race and Class*, Vol. 25, No. 3, 1984, pp. 53–70.

Jowell, R., Witherspoon, S. and Brooks, L. (eds), *British Social Attitudes. The 1986 Report*, Gower, Aldershot, 1987.

Jowell, R., Witherspoon, S, and Brooks, L., *British Social Attitudes. The 4th Report*, Gower, Aldershot, 1987.

Katznelson, Ira, *Black Men White Cities. Race, Politics, and Migration in the United States 1900–30 and Britain 1948–68*, Oxford University Press, London and New York, 1973.

Kerckhoff, Alan, Campbell, Richard T. and Winfeld-Laird, Idee, 'Social Mobility in Great Britain and the United States', *American Journal of Sociology*, Vol. 91, No. 2, 1985, pp. 281–308.

Killian, Lewis M., 'School Busing in Britain: Policies and Perceptions', in Ralph H. Turner and Lewis Killian, *Collective Behavior*, 1987a.

Killian, Lewis M., 'Two Decades of Anti-Discrimination Laws in U.S. and Britain: Policies and Results', *New Community*, Vol. 14 No. 1/2, Autumn 1987b.

Kilson, Martin, 'Politics of Race and Urban Crisis: The American Case', in John Benyon and John Solomos, *The Roots of Urban Unrest*, Pergamon Press, Oxford, 1987, pp. 51–61.

Krieger, Joel, *Reagan, Thatcher and the Politics of Decline*, Oxford University Press, New York, 1986.

Kushnick, Louis, 'Racism and Class Consciousness in Modern Capitalism', in B. Bowser and R. Hunt, *The Impact of Racism on White Americans*, Beverley Hills, 1981, pp. 191–216.

*Labour Force Survey, 1985*, Office of Population Census and Surveys, HMSO, 1987.

*Labour Force Survey, 1987*, Office of Population Census and Surveys, HMSO, 1989.

*Labour Force Survey, 1988–1989*, Office of Population Census and Surveys, HMSO, 1991.

*Labour Force Survey, 1990–1991*, Office of Population Census and Surveys, HMSO, 1992.

Landry, Bart, *The New Black Middle Class*, University of California Press, Berkeley, Los Angeles, London, 1987.

Larew, John, 'Who's the Read Affirmative Action Profiteer?' *The Washington Monthly*, June 1991, pp. 10–14.

Law, Ian and Henfry, June, *A History of Race and in Racism Liverpool, 1660–1950*, Merseyside Community Relations Council, 1981.

Lawrence, E., 'Just Plain Common Sense: the "Roots" of Racism', in Centre for Contemporary Cultural Studies, *The Empire Strikes Back: Race and Racism in 70s Britian*, Hutchinson, London, 1982, pp. 47–94.

Layton-Henry, Zig, *The Politics of Race in Britain*, Allen & Unwin, London, 1984.

Layton-Henry, Zig and Rich, Paul, *Race, Government and Politics in Britain*, Macmillan, London, 1986.

Lester, A. and Bindman, G., *Race and Law*, Penguin Books, Harmondsworth, 1972.

Lester, Julius (ed.) *The Seventh Son. The Thought and Writings of W.E.B. Dubois*, Vols 1 and 2, Vintage Books, New York, 1971.

Levine, Art, 'America's Youthful Bigots', *U.S. News & World Report*, 7 May 1990, pp. 59–60.

Lieberson, Stanley, *A Piece of the Pie. Blacks and White Immigrants since 1800*, University of California Press, Berkeley, 1980.

Lieberson, Stanley and Waters, Mary C., 'Ethnic Groups in Flux: The Changing Ethnic Responses of American Whites', *The Annals of the American Academy of Political and Social Science*, Vol. 487, September 1986, pp. 79–91.

Lieberson, Stanley and Waters, Mary C., *From Many Strands: Ethnic and Racial Groups in Contemporary America*, Russell Sage Foundation, New York, 1988.

Little, Kenneth, *Negroes in Britain*, Routledge & Kegan Paul, International Library of Sociology and Social Reconstruction, London, 1948.

Liverpool Black Caucus, *The Racial Politics of Militant in Liverpool*, Merseyside Area Profile Group and Runnymede Trust, Liverpool, 1986.

Lloyd, Cathie and Waters, Hazel, 'France: One Culture, One Nation?' *Race and Class*, Vol. 32, No. 3, January–March 1991, pp. 49–65.

Lorimer, Douglas A., *Colour, Class and the Victorians: English Attitudes to the Negro in the Mid-nineteenth Century*, Leicester University Press, Leicester, 1978.

Lourde, Audre, *Need: A Chorale for Black Woman Voices*, Freedom Organizing Series, No. 6, Kitchen Table, Women of Colour Press, 1990.

Loury, Glen C., 'A New American Dilemma', *The New Republic*, December 1984, pp. 14–18.

Lustgarten, Laurence, *Legal Control of Racial Discrimination*, Macmillan, London, 1980.

McCruddon, Christopher, Smith, David J., and Brown, Colin, *Racial Justice at Work*, Policy Studies Institute, London, 1991.

McIntosh, Neil and Smith, David J., *The Extent of Racial Discrimination*, PEP Broadsheet N. 547, Political and Economic Planning, London, 1974.

Mama, Amina, 'Black Women, the Economic Crisis and the British State', *Feminist Review*, No. 17, July 1984, pp. 22–34.

Mama, Amina, *The Hidden Struggle: Statutory and Voluntary Sector Responses to Violence against Black Women in the Home*, Race and Housing Research Unit/Runneymede Trust, London, 1989.

Mama, Amina, 'Black Women and the British State: Race, Class and Gender Analysis for the 1990s', in Peter Braham, Ali Rattansi and Richard Skellington, (eds), *Racism and Antiracism. Inequalities, Opportunities and Policies*, Sage Publications Ltd, London and Newbury Park, California, 1992, pp. 79–101.

Marable, Manning, *How Capitalism Underdeveloped Black America*, Southend Press, Boston, MA, 1983.

Marable, Manning, *Black American Politics. From the Washington Marches to Jesse Jackson*, Verso, London, 1985.

Marable, Manning, *The Crisis of Color and Democracy. Essays on Race, Class and Power*, Common Courage Press, Maine, 1992.

Marcus, Frances Frank, 'Louisian Still Trying to Mix Races at Its Colleges', *New York Times*, 27 December 1988, p. B5.

Marger, Martin N., *Race and Ethnic Relations. American and Global Perspectives*, Wadsworth Publishing Company, Belmont, CA, 1991.

Marks, Carlole, *Farewell–We're Good and Gone. The Great Black Migration*, Indiana University Press, Bloomington and Indianapolis, 1989.

Martin-Jenkins, Christopher, 'Lifestyle may explain poor Test Record', *Daily Telegraph*, 3 June 1991, p. 21.

Martinez, Elizabeth, 'Willie Horton's Gonna Get Your Alma Mater', *Z Magazine*, July/August 1991, pp. 126–30.

Marwick, Arthur, *Class in the Twentieth Century*, St. Martin's Press, London, 1980.

Mason, Tony, *Sport in Britain*, Faber and Faber, London and Boston, 1988.

May, Rob, and Cohen, Rob, 'The Interaction between Race and Colonialism: a Case Study of the Liverpool Race Riots of 1919', *Race and Class*, Vol. 16, No. 2, 1974, pp. 111–26.

Meier, August, *Negro Thought in America, 1880–1915*, Ann Arbor Paperbacks, University of Michigan Press, 1963.

Miles, Robert, *Racism and Migrant Labour*, Routledge & Kegan Paul, London, 1982.

Miles, Robert, 'Marxism Versus the "Sociology of Race Relations"?', *Ethnic and Racial Studies*, Vol. 7, No. 2, 1984, pp. 217–23.

Miles, Robert, 'Racism, Marxism, and British Politics. A Review Article', *Economy and Society*, Vol. 17, No. 3, August 1988, pp. 428–60.

Miles, Robert, *Racism*, Routledge, London and New York, 1989a.

Miles, Robert, 'Migration Discourse in Post-1945 British Politics,' *Migration*, June 1989b, pp. 29–55.

Miles, Robert and Phizacklea, Annie, *White Man's Country: Racism in British Politics*, Pluto Press, London, 1984.

Miles, Robert, 'Whatever Happened to the Sociology of Migration?' (Review Article), *Work, Employment & Society*, Vol. 4, No. 2, 1990, pp. 281–98.

Mirza, Heidi, *Young, Female and Black*, Routledge, London and New York, 1992.

Modood, Tariq, '"Black", Racial Equality and Asian Identity', *New Community*, Vol. 14, No. 3, 1988, pp. 397–404.

Moore, Robert, *Racism and Black Resistance in Britain*, Pluto Press, London, 1975.

Moore, Robert, 'Ethnic Divisions and Class in Western Europe', in Richard Scase, (ed.), *Industrial Societies. Crisis and Division in Western Capitalism and State Socialism*, Unwin Hyman, London, 1989, pp. 146–67.

Moore, Robert, and Wallace, Tina, *Slamming the Door. The Administration of Immigration Control*, Martin Robertson & Company Ltd., London, 1975.

Morris, Aldon, *The Origins of the Civil Rights Movement. Black Communities Organizing for Change*, The Free Press, New York, 1984.

Morrison, Toni, (ed.) *Race-ing Justice, En-Gendering Power. Essays on Anita Hill, Clarence Thomas and the Construction of Social Reality*, Chatto & Windus, London, 1993.

Murray, Charles, *Losing Ground. American Social Policy, 1950–1980*, Basic Books, Inc. Publishers, New York, 1984.

Myrdal, Gunnar, *An American Dilemma: The Negro Problem and Modern Democracy*, Harper, New York, 1944.

*The Nation*, special edition on 'Race, Rights and the New Orthodoxy', Adolph Reed Jr. and Julian Bond (eds), 1991.

*New York Times*, 1991, p. E2.

*New York Times*, 1991, p. 4.1.

*Newsweek*, 'Black and White in America. A Special Report', March 7 1988, pp. 18–43.

*Newsweek*, 18 November 1991.

Njeri, Itabari, 'A Sense of Identity', *Los Angeles Times*, 5 June 1988, p. 7.

O'Hare, William P., Pollard, Kelvin M., Monn, Taynia L., and Kent, Mary M., 'African Americans in the 1990s', *Population Bulletin*, Vol. 46, No. 1, July 1991.

Omi, Michael, 'In Living Color: Race and American Culture', in Ian Angus and Sut Jhally (eds) *Cultural Politics in Contemporary America*, Routledge, New York and London, 1989, pp. 111–22.

Omi, Michael, and Winant, Howard, *Racial Formation in the United States. From the 1960s to the 1980s*, Routledge & Kegan Paul, London and New York, 1986.

Omi, Michael, and Winant, Howard, 'Contesting the Meaning of Race in the Post-Civil Rights Period', paper presented to the Eighty-sixth Annual Meeting of the American Sociological Association, Cincinnati, Ohio, 23–27 August 1991.

Ouseley, Herman, 'Local Authority Race Initiatives', in M. Boddy and C. Fudge (eds), *Local Socialism?* Macmillan, London, 1984, pp. 133–59.

Ouseley, Herman, Silverstone, Daniel and Prashar, Usha, *The System*, Runnymede Trust and South London Equal Rights Consultancy, London, 1981.

Owen, David, 'Ethnic Minorities in Great Britain: Population Totals for Counties, Regions and Local Authority Areas', *Centre for Research in Ethnic Relations*, University of Warwick, Coventry, November 1992.

Parekh, Bikhu, *Colour, Culture and Consciousness. Immigrant Intellectuals in Britain*, George Allen & Unwin, London, 1974.

Parekh, Bikhu, 'Preface', in John W. Shaw, Peter G. Nordlie and Richard M. Shapiro, *Strategies for Improving Race Relations. The Anglo-American Experience*, Manchester University Press, Manchester, 1987.

Phizacklea, Annie, 'Entrepreneurship, Ethnicity and Gender', in Sallie, Westwood and Parminder Bhachu (eds), *Enterprising Women. Ethnicity, Economy, & Gender Relations*, Routledge, London, 1988, pp. 20–33.

Phizacklea, Annie and Miles, Robert, *Labour and Racism*, Routledge & Kegan Paul, London, 1980.

Phizacklea, Annie and Miles, Robert, 'The British Trade Union Movement and Racism', pp. 30–45 in Peter Braham, Rattanis Ali and Richard Skellington (eds), *Racism and Antiracism*, Sage and Open University, London, Newbury Park and New Delhi, 1992.

Piliawsky, Monte, 'Racial Politics in the 1988 Presidential Election', *Black Scholar*, January/February 1989, pp. 30–37.

Pinkney, A., *The Myth of Black Progress*, Cambridge University Press, New York, 1984.

Pitts, David, 'To Be Young, British and Black', *Black Enterprise*, December 1989, pp. 86–98.

Platt, Steve, 'Black and Blue', *New Society*, 3 October 1986, pp. 9–13.

Pohlmann, Marcus D., *Black Politics in Conservative America*, Longman, New York and London, 1990.

*Population Trends*, 57, HMSO, London, 1985.

*Population Trends, 61*, HMSO, London, 1990.

Priscoll, Bob, 'Ron is White Out of Order', *Daily Star*, 13 September 1991, p. 8.

Pryce, Ken, *Endless Pressure*, Penguin, Harmondsworth, 1979.

Ramdin, Ron, *The Making of the Black Working Class in Britain*, Gower, Aldershot, 1987.

Redkey, Edwin S., *Black Exodus. Black Nationalist and Back-to-Africa Movements, 1890–1910*, Yale University Press, New Haven, 1969.

Reeves, Frank, *British Racial Discourse. A Study of British Political Discourse about Race and Race-Related Matters*, Cambridge University Press, Cambridge, 1983.

Reich, Michael, *Racial Inequality*, Princeton University Press, Princeton, New Jersey, 1981.

Reid, Aldoph Jr. and Bond, Julian, 'The Assault on Equality. Race, Rights and the New Orthodoxy', *The Nation*, 9 December 1991.

Rex, John, *Race Relations in Sociological Theory*, Weidenfeld & Nicolson, London, 1970.

Rex, John, *The Ghetto and the Underclass. Essays on Race and Social Policy*, Gower, Aldershot, 1988.

Rex, John, and Mason, David, *Theories of Race and Ethnic Relations*, Cambridge University Press, 1986.

Rex, John and Tomlinson, Sally, *Colonial Immigrants in a British City: A Class Analysis*, Routledge & Kegan Paul, London, 1979.

Rex, John and Tomlinson, Sally, *Colonial Immigrants in a British City*, Routledge & Kegan Paul, London, 1983.

Reyburn, Ross, 'Left Standing at the Starting Gate of Life', *The Birmingham Post*, 7 June Thursday 1990, p. 9.

Rich, Paul, 'Philanthropic Racism in Britain: The Liverpool University Settlement, the Anti-Slavery Society and The Issue of "Half-caste" Children, 1919–51', *Immigrants and Minorities*, Vol. 3, No. 1, March 1984a.

Rich, Paul, *Race and Empire in British Politics*, Cambridge University Press, Cambridge, 1986.

Richmond, Anthony, *Colour Prejudice in Britain – a Study of West Indian Workers in Liverpool*, Routledge & Kegan Paul, London, 1954.

Richmond, Anthony H., 'Britain', in UNESCO, *Research on Racial Relations*, 1966, pp. 181–209.

Roberts, Kenneth, *Youth and Leisure*, George, Allen & Unwin, London, 1983.

Rodney, Walter, *The Groundings With My Brothers*, Bogle L'Ouverture, London, 1969.

Root, Maria P., (ed.), *Racially Mixed People in America*, Sage Publications, Newbury Park, 1992.

Rose, Steven, 'Scientific Racism and Ideology: The IQ Racket from Galton to Jensen', in Hilary Rose and Steven Rose, *The Political Economy of Science*, Macmillan, London and Basingstoke, 1976, pp. 112–41.

Rose, E. J. B. *et al.*, *Colour and Citizenship, A Report on British Race Relations*, Oxford University Press, London, New York and Toronto, 1969.

Rudwick, Elliott M., *W.E.B. DuBois. Propagandist of the Negro Protest*, University of Pennsylvania Press, Philadelphia, 1968.

Russell, Jennifer M., 'Nothing To Be Ashamed Of', *Essence*, August 1991, p. 140.

Sage, George H., *Power and Ideology in American Sport*, Human Kinetics Books, Champaign, Illinois, 1990.

Sanchez-Jankowski, Martin, *City Bound. Urban Life and Political Attitudes among Chicano Youth*, University of New Mexico Press, Albuquerque, 1986a.

*San Fransisco Examiner*, October 1990.

*San Francisco Tribune*, Thursday, 12 January 1989, p. A4.

Satzewich, Vic, 'The Canadian State and the Racialization of Caribbean Migrant Farm Labour, 1947–1966', *Ethnic and Racial Studies*, Vol. 11, No. 3, July 1988, pp. 282–304.

Satzewich, Vic, 'Racisms: The Reactions to Chinese Migrants in Canada at the turn of the Century', *International Sociology*, Vol. 4, No. 3, September 1989, pp. 311–27.

Savage, Mike, 'Making Sense of Middle-Class Politics: A Secondary Analysis of the 1987 British General Election Survey', *The Sociological Review*, Vol. 39, No. 1, February 1991, pp. 26–54.

Sawyerr, Ade, 'Black-controlled Business in Britain: Particular Problems and Suggested Solution', *New Community* Vol. 11, Nos. 1–2, Autumn/Winter 1983, pp. 55–62.

Scarman, Lord, *The Scarman Report: The Brixton Disorders;, 10–12 April, 1981*, Pelican, Harmondsworth, 1982.

Schaefer, Richard T., *Racial and Ethnic Groups*, (4th ed.), Scott Foresman, Glenview, IL and London, 1990.

Schuman, Howard, Steeh, Charlotte and Bobl, Lawrence, *Racial Attitudes in America: Trends and Interpretations*, Harvard University Press, Cambridge, 1985.

Shao, Maria, 'Is Balkanized Berkeley a window on the Future?', *Business Week*, 14 May 1990, pp. 61–3.

Shaw, John W., Nordlie, Peter G., and Shapiro, Richard M., *Strategies for Improving Race Relations. The Anglo–American Experience*, Manchester University Press, Manchester, 1987.

Shukra, Kalbir, 'Black Sections in the Labour Party', in Harry Goulbourne (ed), *Black Politics in Britain*, Avebury, Aldershot, 1990, pp. 165–89.

Shyllon, Folarin, *Black People in Britain, 1553–1833*, Oxford University Press, London, 1977.

Sivanandan, A., 'Race, Class and the State: The Black Experience', *Race and Class*, Vol. 17, No. 4, Spring 1976, pp. 347–68.

Sivanandan, A., *A Different Hunger*, Pluto Press, London, 1982.

Sivanandan, A., 'The New Racism', *New Statesman and Society*, 4 November 1988.

Sivanandan, A., *Communities of Resistance. Writings on Black Struggles for Socialism*, Verso, London and New York, 1990.

Skellington, Richard, Morris, Paulette and Gordon, Paul, *'Race' in Britain Today*, Sage Publications, London, 1992.

Skocpol, Theda, and Somers, Margret, 'The Uses of Comparative History in Macro-social Inquiry', *Society for the Comparative Study of Society and History*, 1980, pp.173–97.

Small, Stephen, 'Black Youth in England: Ethnic Identity in a White Society', *Policy Studies*, Vol. 4, Part 1, July 1983a.

Small, Stephen, *Police and People in London. II A Group of Young Black People*, Policy Studies Institute, London, November 1983b.

Small, Stephen, *Racism Within Trade Unions, Report of A Survey*, Anti-Racist Trade Union Working Group, Greater London Council, London, 1984.

Small, Stephen, 'Sociologist has Unique View of Race Relations', *The Alumnus*, Vol. 19, No. 6, October–November 1988, pp. 8–10.

Small, Stephen, 'Sociologist finds letter writer's views "pernicious, detrimental" to effort toward equal opportunity', *The Alumnus*, Vol. 20, No. 3, April–May 1989a, p. 2.

Small, Stephen, 'Racial Differentiation in the Slave Era: A Comparative Analysis of People of "Mixed-Race" in Jamaica and Georgia', unpublished PhD dissertation, University of California, Berkeley, 1989b.

Small, Stephen, 'The Black Experience in Britain. The Historical Dimension', *The Daily Collegian*, Tuesday 21 February 1989c, p. 16.

Small, Stephen, 'Racialized Groups in the Slave Era: People of "Mixed-Race" in Jamaica and Georgia', paper presented at the Twelfth World Congress of Sociology, Madrid, 9–13 July 1990a.

Small, Stephen, *Research on the Training, Education and Enterprise Needs of Liverpool 8*, unpublished report submitted to Merseyside Training and Enterprise Council, August 1990b.

Small, Stephen, 'Attaining Racial Parity in the United States and England; We Got to Go Where the Greener Grass Grows!', *Sage Race Relations Abstracts*, Vol. 16, No. 3, May 1991a, pp. 3–55.

Small, Stephen, 'Racialised Relations in Liverpool: A Contemporary Anomaly', *New Community*, Vol. 11, No. 4, 1991b, pp. 511–37.

Small, Stephen, 'Unravelling Racialised Relations in the United States of America and the United States of Europe', in Wrench, John and Solomos, John (eds), *Racism and Migration in Europe*, Berg Publishers Inc, Oxford and New York, 1993.

Smith, David J., *Racial Disadvantage in Britain*, Political and Economic Planning, London, 1976.

Smith, David J., *Racial Disadvantage in Britain*, Penguin Books, 1977.

Smith, David J., *Police and People in London I. A Survey of Londoners*, Policy Studies Institute, London, 1983.

Smith, David J. and Gray, Gerald, *Police and People in London IV. The Police in Action*, Policy Studies Institute, London, 1983.

Smith, J. Owens, Rice, Mitchell F. and Jones Jnr, Woodrow, *Blacks and American Government: Politics, Policy and Social Change*, Kendall/Hunt, Iowa, 1987.

Smith, Susan. J., *The Politics of 'Race' and Residence*, T. J. Press Ltd., Great Britain, 1989.

Smithers, Alan and Robinson, Pamela, *Increasing Participation in Higher Education*, BP Educational Service, 1989.

*Social Trends 22*, Central Statistical Office, 1992.

Solomos, John, *Black Youth, Racism and the State. The Politics of Ideology and Policy*, Cambridge University Press, Cambridge, 1988.

Solomos, John., *Race and Racism in Contemporary Britain*, Macmillan Education, Basingstoke and London, 1989.

Solomos, John, 'Political Language and Racial Discourse', *European Journal of Intercultural Studies*, Vol. 2, No. 1, 1991a, pp. 21–33.

Solomos, John, 'Contemporary Forms of Racial Ideology in British Society', *Sage Race Relations Abstracts*, Vol. 16, No. 1, February 1991b, pp. 1–15.

Sowell, Thomas, *Race and Economics*, David McKay Company, Inc, New York, 1975.

Sowell, Thomas, *The Economics and Politics of Race. An International Perspective*, Quill, New York, 1983.

Sowell, Thomas, *Preferential Policies. An International Perspective*, William Morrow and Company, Inc., New York, 1990.

Spickard, Paul, *Mixed Blood. Intermarriage and Ethnic Identity in Twentieth-Century America*, University of Wisconsin Press, Madison, 1989.

Stavenhagen, Rodolfo, *The Ethnic Question. Conflicts, Development, and Human Rights*, United Nations University Press, Tokyo, 1990.

Steele, Shelby, *The Content of Our Character: A New Vision of Race in America*, St. Martin's Press, New York, 1990.

Steinberg, Stephen, *The Ethnic Myth. Race, Ethnicity and Class in America*, Beacon Press, Boston, 1981.

Student Affairs Research and Evaluation Office, *Racism Survey*, University of Massachusetts, Amherst, September, 1987.

Suarez-Orozco, Marcelo, 'Migration and Education: United States–Europe

Comparisons', in George A. De Vos and Marcelo Suarez-Orozco, *The Self In Culture*, Sage Publications Inc, Newbury Park, London, New Delhi, 1990, pp. 265–87.

Suro, Roberto, 'When Minorities Start Becoming Majorities', *New York Times*, 23 June 1991, p. 5.

Taaffe, P. and Mulhearn, T., *Liverpool. A City that Dared to Fight*, Fortress, London, 1988.

Takaki, Ronald T., *Iron Cages. Race and Culture in 19th-Century America*, University of Washington Press, Seattle, 1982.

Taylor, Peter J., 'Britain's Changing Role in the World-Economy', in John Mohan (ed.) *The Political Geography of Contemporary Britain*, Macmillan Education, Basingstoke and London, 1989, pp. 18–34.

Third Community Action Programme concerning the Economic and Social Integration of the Economically and Socially Less Privileged Groups in Society, Liverpool City Council, Liverpool Council of Social Service, Merseyside Community Relations Council, Merseyside Region Churches Ecumenical Assembly, Merseyside Task Force, 5 October 1989.

Thompson, Keith, *Under Siege. Racial Violence in Britain Today*, Penguin Books, London, 1988.

Trow, Martin, 'Comparative perspectives on Higher Education Policy in the UK and the US', *Oxford Review of Education*, Vol. 14, No. 1, 1988, pp. 81–96.

T'Shaka, Oba, *The Art of Leadership. Volume 1*, Pan Afrikan Publications, Richmond, California, 1990.

Union for Radical Political Economics, 'The Political Economy of Race and Class', Special Edition of *Review of Radical Political Economics*, Vol. 17, No. 3, Fall 1985.

Vanneman, Reeve, 'U.S. and British Perceptions of Class', *American Journal of Sociology*, Vol. 85, No. 4, 1980, pp. 769–90.

*Voice*, 1990.

*Voice*, 5 February 1991.

*Voice*, 22 January 1991.

*Voice*, 26 March 1991.

*Voice*, 11 June 1991.

*Voice*, 26 November 1991.

*Voice*, 6 October 1992.

*Voice* 27 October 1992.

Walker, Martin, *The National Front*, Fontana Paperbacks, 1977.

Wallace, Michelle, *Black Macho and the Myth of the Superwoman*, Verso, London and New York, 1978.

Walton, Anthony, 'Willie Horton and Me,' *New York Time Magazine*, 20 August 1989, pp. 10–13.

Walvin, James, *The Black Presence: A Documentary History of the Negro in England*, Orbach and Chambers, London, 1971.

Walvin, James, *Black and White: The Negro and English Society 1555–1945*, Allen Lane, London, 1973.

Walvin, James, *Football and the Decline of Britain*, Macmillan, Basingstoke, 1986.

Ward, Robin, 'Caribbean Business Enterprise in Britain', in M. Cross and Han Entzinger, *Lost Illusions. Caribbean Minorities in Britain and the Netherlands*, Routledge, London, 1988, pp. 204–20.

Ward, Robin and Jenkins, Richard (eds), *Ethnic Communities in Business. Strategies for Survival*, Cambridge University Press, Cambridge, 1984.

Waters, Mary C., *Ethnic Options. Choosing Identities in America*, University of California Press, Berkeley and Los Angeles, 1990.

Weaver, Maurice, 'Is It Politics, Or Is It Race?' *The Daily Telegraph*, Tuesday, 8 January 1991, p. 15.

*Weekly Journal*, 3 June 1991, p. 3

Wellman, David, 'The New Political Linguistics of Race', *Socialist Review*, Vol. 16, Nos. 87–8, May–August 1986, pp.43–61.

Wellman, David T., *Portraits of White Racism*, second edition, Cambridge University Press, Cambridge, 1993.

White, Jack E., 'Bush's Most Valuable Player', *Time*, 14 November 1988, p. 20.

Wilkerson, Isabel, 'Two Decades of Decline Chronicled by Kerner Follow-Up Report', *New York Times*, 1 March 1988, p. 12.

Williams, Eric, *Capitalism and Slavery*, Andre Deutsch, London, 1944.

Williams, Patricia J., *The Alchemy of Race and Rights. Diary of a Law Professor*, Harvard University Press, Cambridge and London, 1991.

Williams, Richard, *Hierachical Structures and Social Value. The Creation of Black and Irish Identities in the United States*, Cambridge University Press, Cambridge, 1990.

Willie, Charles, 'The Inclining Significance of Race', *Society*, 15, July/August, 1978, pp. 10–15.

Wilson, Anne, 'Mixed Race Children; An Exploratory Study of Racial Categorisation and Identity', *New Community*, Vol. 9, No. 1, Spring–Summer 1981, pp. 36–43.

Wilson, Anne, *Mixed Race Children*, Allen & Unwin, London, Boston, Sydney Wellington, 1987.

Wilson, William Julius, *Power, Racism and Privilege: Race Relations in Theoretical and Sociohistorical Perspectives*, Free Press, New York, 1976.

Wilson, William Julius, *The Declining Significance of Race: Blacks and Changing American Institutions*, Chicago, University of Chicago Press, 1978.

Wilson, William Julius, *The Truly Disadvantaged*, University of Chicago Press, 1987.

Wilson, William Julius, (ed.) 'The Ghetto Underclass: Social Science Perspectives', *Special Edition of The Annals of the American Academy of Political and Social Science*, Sage Publications, Newbury Park, January, 1989.

Woodward, C. Vann, *The Strange Career of Jim Crow*, Oxford University Press, New York, 1966.

Wrench, John, 'New Vocationalism, Old Racism and the Careers Service', *New Community*, Vol. 16, No. 3, 1990, pp. 425–40.

Wrench, John and Solomos, John, *Racism and Migration in Europe*, Berg Publishers, Oxford and New York, 1993.

Wright, James D., 'How Long, Oh Lord, How Long?' *Contemporary Sociology*, Vol. 17, No. 5, 1988, pp. 584–6.

Yinger, Milton, 'Intersecting Strands in the Theorisation of Race and Ethnic Relations', in John Rex and David Mason (eds) *Theories of Race and Ethnic Relations*, Cambridge University Press, Cambridge, 1986.

Young, Ken and Connelly, Naomi, *Policy and Practice in the Multi-Racial City*, Policy Studies Institute, London, 1981.

# Index